FOR THE LOVE OF FLYING:

THE STORY OF LAURENTIAN AIR SERVICES

Laurentian's Grumman Goose, CF-BXR, preparing for take-off on one of the many beautiful lakes in the Ottawa region. (PG)

FOR THE LOVE OF FLYING

THE STORY OF LAURENTIAN AIR SERVICES

Danielle Metcalfe-Chenail

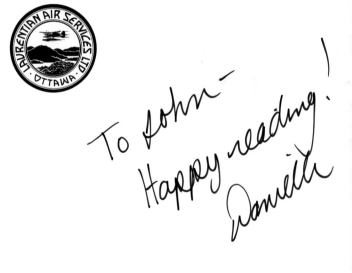

To John —
Happy reading!
Danielle

ROBIN BRASS STUDIO

For my grandfather, André (Andy) Chenail,
who spent a lifetime slipping the surly bonds of earth.

Published 2009 by Robin Brass Studio Inc.
Reprinted 2010
www.rbstudiobooks.com

ISBN-13: 978-1-896941-57-8
ISBN-10: 1-896941-57-5

Printed and bound in Canada by Marquis Imprimeur Inc., Cap-Saint-Ignace, Quebec

Library and Archives Canada Cataloguing in Publication

Metcalfe-Chenail, Danielle

    For the love of flying : the story of Laurentian Air Services / Danielle Metcalfe-Chenail.

Includes bibliographical references and index.
ISBN 978-1-896941-57-8

    1. Laurentian Air Services – History. I. Title.

HE9815.L38M48 2009   387.706'571   C2009-901075-5

CONTENTS

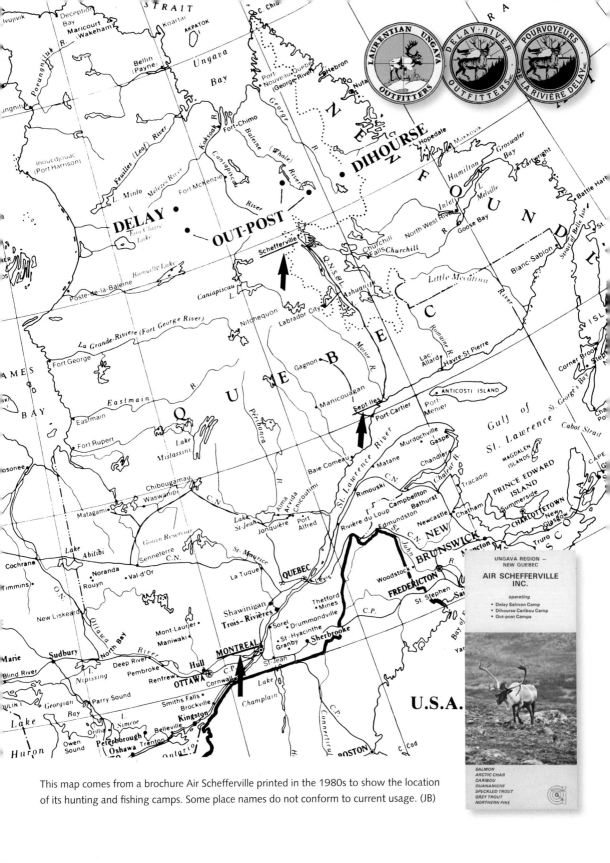

This map comes from a brochure Air Schefferville printed in the 1980s to show the location of its hunting and fishing camps. Some place names do not conform to current usage. (JB)

PREFACE

"My father loved his work more than anyone I know: Life does not get any better than that."[1] Dick Pickering wrote this statement about his late father, Doug, who worked at Laurentian Air Services for over 35 years – first in the cockpit and then in the office. This sentiment appears to be the consensus among Laurentian's pilots and staff, even when the conditions were rough, the hours long and the pay meagre. When Barnet Maclaren founded the company in 1936, he certainly was not looking to make a fortune flying hunters into Ottawa's back country. Flying was something he truly enjoyed, and he was willing to sacrifice dollars for dreams. Gerry Taillefer, who worked for Laurentian in a number of capacities over the years, once told a reporter: "Hell, it doesn't pay at all. Not in money, I mean. It pays a great deal in personal satisfaction, though."[2]

Although the job could be demanding, when I spoke with former pilots, engine shop workers, and company presidents, I was always struck by their pride and enjoyment when recalling the years they spent with Laurentian. They genuinely embraced the challenges and revelled in the freedom of making their own paths through the skies of Canada's northern territories, setting down in the sub-arctic tundra's open spaces or on tiny, unnamed lakes.

There was one person in particular with whom I passed many enjoyable hours talking, and who really sparked this project: John Bogie. He spent much of his early years entranced by his uncle Barnet's flying, and joined the company on a part-time basis during his summers off from school. Before long, he was a full-time pilot and then became Laurentian's president for over 30 years.

I first met John during the summer of 2007, when his cousin – my father-in-law, John Kenny – introduced us. We spent the afternoon chatting on the dock, in the shade cast by a DHC-2 Beaver (C-FFZM, c/n 869), and I soon realized why my father-in-law wanted to record his 81-year-old cousin's memories: not only are his stories amusing and full of adventure, they are an important part of Canada's aviation history.

What began as a family history project quickly expanded into plans for a book when John Bogie showed me boxes of documents, photos, film reels and publications relating to the company that he had collected over the years. Having recently completed grad school and begun work as a writer, I was looking for a new project. I could not believe my good fortune, and could not have felt more honoured, when John entrusted me with his original records and the setting down of his company's history.

While I had never heard of John Bogie, Barnet Maclaren or Laurentian Air Services before the summer of 2007, there were certainly many people who had. Since beginning this book I cannot count the number of times I have been told that it is long overdue – that Barnet and John, and the company they created, were pioneers in Canadian aviation and their stories need to be told. After wading through John's boxes, spending long hours at various libraries and archives, and interviewing former employees, I could not agree more. The history of these two men, their company and the dozens of employees who made it such a success, has enthralled me. I hope I have done it justice.

Going into this project, I am ashamed to say, I could not tell the difference between a Beaver and an Otter. Luckily I had a willing spirit and a wonderfully capable network on which to draw. The Canadian Aviation Historical Society has been central to my education in the field and has connected me with top researchers and writers, as well as those who have helped make aviation history. In particular, I am indebted to the National and Ottawa chapter president, Tim Dubé, the Montreal chapter president Dick Pickering (and his lively wife, Jane), Paddy Gardiner, Terry Judge, Bill Peppler, Jack "Thumper" Thorpe, Hugh Halliday, George Fuller, Ian Macdonald, Clark Seaborn, Bill Wheeler, Bob Baglow and Rod Digney. I would also like to thank the general membership for making me feel so welcome at meetings and conferences and for being so supportive of this project.

Aviation enthusiast and webmaster of the wonderful <www.dhc-2.com> site, Neil Aird, took me under his wing (so to speak), and was very generous with his time, humour and knowledge. I have also relied heavily on Fred Hotson and Larry Milberry's excellent works of aviation history, and their well-timed words of encouragement. Larry also provided invaluable last-minute assistance with photos and captions.

I spent many days doing research at Library and Archives Canada and am very grateful to the knowledgeable staff there. I would like to thank Odile Girard, Dan German and Dan Summers, all of whom were particularly helpful. The library at the Canada Aviation Museum was also indispensable and its library technician, Ian Leslie, knows the collection backwards and forwards. While drafting the second half of the manuscript in my new home town of Green River, Wyoming, I inevitably discovered I needed to refer to some materials in Ottawa. Thank goodness for my 12th hour research assistant, Aaron Boyes, who squeezed a few hours in at the microfilm machines. A big thanks also to my talented friend Luke Weaver, who created the maps for this book.

The following people shared their homes, memories and photos with me, and their generosity made this project possible: Keith and June Baker, Iain Bogie, Penny Bogie, Betty

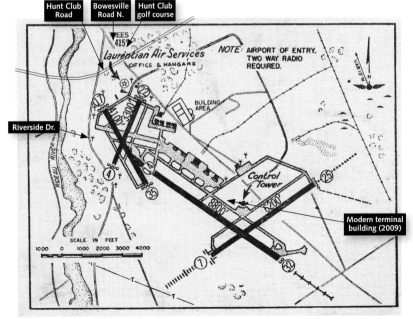

This map of Ottawa Airport, enlarged from a 1950s-era Laurentian business card, is interesting to compare with the aerial photograph on page 12. We have added Hunt Club Road and some annotations. The Hunt Club golf course, then as now, lay on both sides of Bowesville Road. (DP)

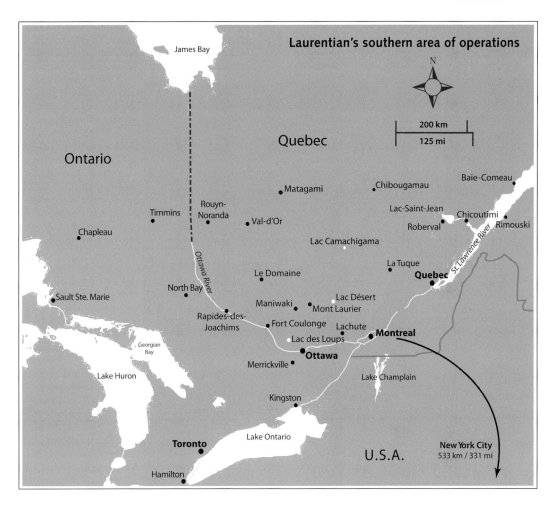

Laurentian's southern area of operations

Campbell, Tim Cole, Albert Diamond, Peter Gendron, John Gill, Peter (Lou) and Bev Goodwin, Jack Hume, Richard Hume, Wendell Hume, Babe Kenny, Eddy Lord, Brad Mackie, Rudy Mauro, Colin McOuat, Bill Peppler, Jules Pilon, Kevin Psutka, David Saunders, Web Stayman, Carmen VanDette and Jean-Guy Whiteduck.

This book would not exist were it not for my wonderful in-laws, John and Dawn Kenny, who appreciated the value of this history and believed in my ability to bring it to life; my amazing parents, Mary Metcalfe and Jacques Chenail, who continually cheered me on and were always on call to read drafts and answer questions; and my husband, Doug, who supports my "writing habit" in so many ways.

Last but certainly not least, I want to thank Robin Brass, who skilfully (and patiently) guided me through the editing and publishing process, turning my manuscript into the book you now hold in your hands.

I love hearing from readers and if you have any comments, questions or would like to share photos or stories from your time at Laurentian, please visit www.laurentianstory.com to get in touch. You will also find aviation links, photos and more Laurentian material posted there.

Danielle Metcalfe-Chenail
Green River, Wyoming

Picture credits

Many people have kindly shared their collections of photographs and other items. They are acknowledged in the picture captions as follows:

Keith Baker (KB)

Iain Bogie (IP)

John Bogie (JB)

Betty Booth (BB)

Tim Cole (TC)

Paddy Gardiner (PG)

John Gill (JG)

Peter (Lou) Goodwin (LG)

Jack Hume (JH)

Wendell Hume (WH)

Dick Pickering (DP)

Jules Pilon (JP)

A NEW COMPANY
FOR A NEW AGE

I n its August 1936 issue, *Canadian Aviation* announced to its readers that "the Capital City of Canada, heretofore sadly lagging in that direction, will have at its disposal a well-organized commercial air service."[1] The magazine was reporting on the formation of Laurentian Air Services by two Ottawa aviation enthusiasts, A. Barnet Maclaren and Walter N. Deisher. Within three short years the two founders would pioneer commercial aviation in the nation's capital, own the only airport in town and be at the forefront of the growing field of air tourism.

"I guess you could say I was a bush pilot."

Barnet and Walter were among the first in the region to take to the skies and see the potential in commercial aviation.[2] In 1919, Walter and his business partner at Reo Sales Ltd., E.J. Draper, bought a Curtiss JN-4, G-CADC, the first privately owned airplane in Ottawa. They hired Lieutenant G. Mercier, a former RFC-RAF pilot, to take people for rides, charging $15 per flight.[3] By 1921 Walter had obtained a licence for a commercial aerodrome at Hunt Club Field, the future site for the Uplands and Ottawa airport.[4] He was also elected the first president of the newly formed Ottawa Flying Club (OFC) – albeit briefly – in 1929.

Barnet was equally keen. John Bogie, his nephew and future owner of Laurentian, still recalls his uncle's early love of flying:

In the First World War Barnet served in the military overseas. He wanted to learn how to fly but he went in at 17 and they said he was too young. When he returned to Canada, he learned how to fly. He had a two-seater open cockpit biplane. Barnet came down to Lake Placid – where my parents had a summer home at Saranac Lake – with Roy Maclaren, his cousin. I remember as a kid him coming and landing at his father's farm in the hayfield up in Buckingham and, boy, the airplane bouncing and everything! Nowadays when you look back at it you wouldn't dare try to do something like that. I guess he wanted to come and show his father the airplane.

By the 1930s Barnet had also joined the OFC, having earned his private and commercial pilot's licences. It was there he met Walter. Both men kept private airplanes at the OFC hangar at Uplands airfield.

Barnet and Walter were not the only people involved in forming Laurentian. Barnet's father, Alexander Maclaren, and his cousin, Gordon Maclaren, were also on the board of directors. Alex Maclaren, who was 76 years old when his son went into business, was still heavily involved in Maclaren Power and Paper Company, which he and his four brothers had founded in 1895 under the name James Maclaren Company Ltd. Barnet could have easily stayed in the family business. But Alex felt it was important to learn the trade from the bottom up, which meant that

The Ottawa Flying Club's hangar at Uplands in the late 1930s. Eastern Canada's oldest flying club, the OFC managed the airfield for almost a decade and attracted local aviation enthusiasts like Walter Deisher and Barnet Maclaren. The aircraft to the left is likely an Aeronca KC Scout, as the club owned one (CF-BIO). To the right is an Avro Avian, an aircraft often used by flying clubs at the time. Several sources suggest Laurentian operated an Avro Avian when it first started, but it is possible Maclaren and Deisher were simply seen flying the OFC's aircraft, such as CF-CBJ and CF-CBB, which it operated in 1936. (JB)

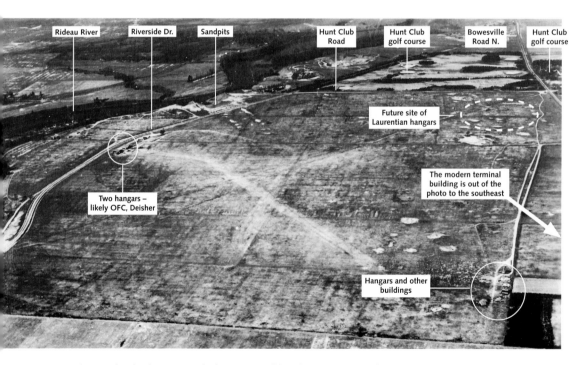

An aerial view of Uplands sometime before it was sold to the Department of Transport in 1938 and the latter began major improvements. Most notably, there are no paved runways yet. The DOT accomplished that feat by hiring the Dibblee Construction Co. to build Dibcol hard-surfaced runways, which required about 110 men working continuously on two 8-hour shifts a day for a month. The Laurentian hangars and DOT buildings were constructed on the northern part of the field near Hunt Club Road. At the time, the airfield was six miles south of Ottawa's city limits; now it is the site of the Macdonald-Cartier International Airport (mostly out of this frame to the southeast) and suburban sprawl has surrounded it. Compare this view with the map on page 8. (JB)

in 1936 Barnet was doing grunt work under the direction of his brother-in-law, Bob Kenny, who was general manager and president of the company.[5] As Barnet's nephew, John, remembers, he was not thrilled with the arrangement:

Barnet's brother-in-law was pretty rough on him at the Maclaren Company. Bob was a very demanding man. Barnet was flying at the time and he and Walter Deisher got thinking about a company to service different lumber companies. That's how they got started.

After all, there were several companies in the region using aircraft for backwoods operations, timber cruising and forest fire prevention. Laurentide Pulp and Paper Company, for example, created Laurentide Air Services and Price Brothers, another large timber company, also used airplanes at the time.[6]

Walter and the three Maclarens were joining a growing group of pilots and businessmen getting involved in commercial aviation in Canada. While the Great Depression in the 1930s put a squeeze on expansion for several years, by 1935 the situation seemed to be improving. Flying clubs across Canada, for example, reported a combined increase in flying time of 31 per cent over the previous year.[7] The OFC announced it had issued its highest number of pilots' licences since the onset of the Depression and membership had more than doubled.[8]

The editors of *Canadian Aviation* reflected the general optimism. In January 1936 they noted that "Today, looking back over the vista of the last few years, it seems as though our most difficult period is behind us and that from now on aviation in Canada is headed for truly great developments."[9] To capitalize on this momentum they called for "clearcut action by those in positions of higher authority."[10]

Those in authority by the mid-1930s obliged, returning to the project of developing the nation's airways. In October 1935 William Lyon

A. Barnet Maclaren, Laurentian's co-founder and president, fuelling up one of the company's Waco biplanes in the late 1930s at Uplands. (JB)

Mackenzie King's Liberals returned to power. By November 1936 civil aviation was transferred from the Department of Defence to the newly created Department of Transport (DOT).[11] C.D. Howe – perhaps better known for his work as "Minister of Everything" during the Second World War – was appointed the first Minister of Transport. Many in Canada's aviation community saw this as the beginning of a "new era." The writers at *Canadian Aviation*, for example, reported that "Almost overnight the situation has changed from one of stagnation to one of feverish preparation for expansion" and they largely attributed this change to the "vigorous leadership evidenced by the Minister."[12]

As his biographers have noted, Howe was an entrepreneur who brought "business experience, intelligence, energy and toughness" to the task of building a national air transport system.[13] In the December 1936 issue of *Canadian Aviation* the editor wrote that "The highlight in the air picture during recent weeks was extensive personal examination of U.S. air lines by the Minister of Transport …. he wisely decided to go out and

Two views of Laurentian co-founder Walter Deisher and the company's first aircraft, a DH.80A Puss Moth, at Uplands in 1936. Deisher bought the first privately-owned aircraft in Ottawa, a Curtiss JN-4, in 1919, and was elected the Ottawa Flying Club's first president in 1929. (JB)

see for himself what it was all about."[14] While Howe's pet project was to reinstate the abandoned Trans-Canada Airway scheme, his enthusiasm encouraged the expansion of aviation generally. He was able to generate positive publicity for air travel through his words but it was his actions that spoke loudest: "Mr. Howe," the *Canadian Aviation* editor remarked, "has shown impressively that he believes in air transportation, by using it."

Barnet and Walter created Laurentian during these years of expanding interest in aviation. After incorporating on June 19, 1936, the two set about advertising their charter services. The company began with Walter's de Havilland Puss Moth, CF-AVB, on wheels. One of the highest-performance private aircraft of the early 1930s, the Puss Moth could carry two passengers in staggered seating. Barnet's Standard Cabin Waco YKS-6, CF-AYP, however, could comfortably seat four people. In July he sold it to the company,

doubling its fleet. As Barnet later told a reporter, the float-equipped Waco was soon in "considerable demand, especially for fishing parties pursuing the sport in the lake areas north of Ottawa."[15]

I was the first pilot and flew short trips all around the country north of Ottawa. One of the first of these was to take fishermen up to 31-Mile-Lake. I guess you could say that I was a bush pilot. Initially, we depended to a large extent on sportsmen to keep our airplanes profitably employed.

To advertise its services, Laurentian printed a brochure that summer with pictures of its brand-new Waco floatplane as well as the Puss Moth. On August 10, 1936, the secretary-treasurer of the Gatineau Fish and Game Club sent out the brochure along with a letter about Laurentian assuring members that "The personnel of the company are well known to the Club as being reliable people" and that "this service has

Laurentian bought this four-seater Standard Cabin Waco YKS-6 in July 1936 and it became popular among fishermen looking for remote spots in the Ottawa region. (PG)

LAURENTIAN AIR SERVICES
LIMITED

HEAD OFFICE
239 Queen Street + Ottawa
Phone Queen 50

++

AIRPORT
Phone Carling 2476

1936 brochure printed by Laurentian. (JB)

already been used by Mr. Sherwood, the [Club's] President."[16] That month, Barnet and Walter hired George L. Beveridge away from the OFC to work as their air engineer.[17]

Laurentian also worked for the timber companies Barnet and Walter initially intended to target. The E.B. Eddy Company, for instance, became one of their best customers in the early days.[18] Mining exploration, which would later make up a large part of their contracts, had not yet blossomed in the region according to Barnet:

At that time I can recall little interest among the mining people. Although, in 1936, I do remember flying two men and their equipment up to a lake in the Gatineau. After landing, on the "nice lake" the two "prospectors" had requested, they spent three days doing little more than lounging around. I think what they really wanted was a holiday![19]

In October 1936, Laurentian reported to *Canadian Aviation* that its business had seen "increasing activity" over the season and things were going well.[20] In the company's first five months of operations, it had logged 291 flying hours and had carried 512 passengers and 42 tons of freight over a total of 31,310 miles.[21]

"A first-class airport for the Capital of the Dominion"

Laurentian kept its aircraft, when on floats, at the Ottawa New Edinburgh Canoe Club on the Ottawa River at Rockcliffe and by June 1937 had a private seaplane base there with a fuelling station.[22] Laurentian also leased space at Uplands from the OFC. The company's choice of land-base location should not be surprising: not only did it allow Walter and Barnet to maintain ties with their flying club, but Uplands was the only real airfield in the Ottawa-Hull area.

Initially Laurentian's business headquarters were at Deisher's Reo Sales office at 239 Queen Street in downtown Ottawa.[23] By the summer of 1936, though, Laurentian had built a hangar and office at Uplands, prompting the editors of *Canadian Aviation* to comment that "Uplands is actually beginning to look like an airport."[24] That spring, the OFC had begun trying to improve Uplands under pressure from the DOT, which was threatening to revoke its airfield licence. In May of 1936, following Transport specifications, work was underway to construct two runways 1,800 feet in length.[25] Up to that point, Uplands had invited nothing but censure from those concerned with aviation in the nation's capital. In February 1936, *Canadian Aviation* reported that "The aerodrome at Uplands is about the most unsatisfactory place one could imagine, except for teaching rough surface landings. Then, too, the civic fathers of this capital city of Ottawa

continue to be delightfully indifferent to any sense of responsibility for airport facilities."[26]

While municipal authorities were certainly dragging their feet regarding local aviation, commentators at the time recognized it was largely due to an absence of a cohesive federal policy on aviation in Canada. R.B. Bennett's Conservatives had abandoned their fledgling air program during the early days of the Depression. Defending this move in the House of Commons on March 22, 1937, Bennett said: "We discontinued it … because with the crop failure in western Canada, and with 300,000 of a population receiving some form of relief, there was very little gratification in seeing an aeroplane passing by, day after day, when the unfortunate owner of the soil could hardly see the aeroplane because his crop had gone up in dust."[27] Nevertheless, in October 1932, Bennett's government instituted a make-work scheme for unemployed men to build 50 airports and landing fields across the country. These airports, however, were mostly built in northwestern Ontario and southern British Columbia – nothing was built in Ottawa.[28]

By 1936, the general stagnation of the Depression had led to a sorry state for the nation's airports. As one writer lamented, "Airport facilities are so far below standard as to cause a feeling bordering on dismay."[29] This was certainly the case for Uplands. The controversy there over airport development, however, far from originating during the Depression, actually dated back

Constructing Laurentian's new hangar at Uplands in the fall of 1938. The job would not be completed until the following year. Until then, Laurentian used Walter Deisher's hangar, where the OFC also shared space while its hangar was being moved from the east side of the field to the west side. (PG)

to the 1920s. After Charles Lindbergh landed at Uplands in his *Spirit of St. Louis* on July 2, 1927, there was public pressure for the Department of National Defence (DND)to improve the newly christened Lindbergh Field. They refused, saying it was the municipality's responsibility since the Royal Canadian Air Force (RCAF) already had an airfield at Rockcliffe. The City of Ottawa was likewise uninterested. One year after Lindbergh's visit, the OFC – which had already begun leasing the site from Ottawa Uplands Ltd. for $300 a year – stepped in, receiving an airport licence.

The OFC, a not-for-profit organization, did not have the funds to undertake major improvements. While it made do with rough surfaces and short airstrips, it did build a hangar, a club house and office, and provided refuelling services to visiting aircraft through Imperial Oil. In November 1935, however, an official at the newly-created Civil Aviation Branch of the Department of Transport contacted the OFC and notified the club that it was "concerned about the condition of the airport" and "recommended that the licence be suspended until the 'surface and dimensions of the field have been improved.'"[30]

This seemingly sudden interest can be attributed to C.D. Howe's growing determination to create a trans-continental air service in Canada. For this to happen, appropriate municipal airports were essential.[31] Initially, the DOT asked the OFC to spend $3,000 on improvements to the field.[32] But the OFC did not have the funds to undertake even these modest changes.

By the spring of 1937, when it was clear that the OFC would have to relinquish its airport licence, Laurentian stepped in to undertake the required improvements to Uplands.[33] It is not clear from the records, but several sources suggest that Ottawa Uplands Ltd. may have also been considering turning Uplands into a housing development; Laurentian would then have had to find a new site for its land-based operations. According to a letter Barnet wrote in February 1938, he "went to considerable trouble and expense in making a survey of other possible sites surrounding Ottawa and endeavouring to obtain option agreements on same" but did not find any promising ones.[34] It was therefore very important to Laurentian that it rescue the only airfield in Ottawa.

Barnet wrote a letter to G.W. McNaughton of Ottawa Uplands Ltd. on April 13, 1937, in which he outlined the policy quandary surrounding the development of Uplands: the City of Ottawa might one day want to turn the site into a municipal airport, but at the time it was not prepared to make the investment. While the city held this position, the federal government could not step in, since its policy was to develop public airports only with municipal co-operation. Bar-

The Department of Transport and Laurentian both began building their hangars during the fall of 1938 but did not complete them until the following year. Here the two are seen mid-construction. (JB)

Laurentian's Standard Cabin Waco, CF-AYP, in the late 1930s. Engineer George Beveridge is standing next to it and on the far left is president Barnet Maclaren beside his brother-in-law, Robert Bogie. (JB)

net's frustration with the status quo is evident in the letter. He was willing to make the improvements, but without the guarantee of a long-term lease, undertaking any development of the Uplands site did not make business sense.[35] In the end, McNaughton agreed to the proposal to grant Laurentian a 10-year lease "with the proviso that in the event of the City of Ottawa or the Government deciding to develop the airport, that L.A.S. would relinquish their lease upon being suitably reimbursed for expenditures already made on development program."[36]

Two weeks later, on April 26, 1937, J.A. Wilson, Controller of Civil Aviation for the Department of Transport, sent a letter to the OFC regarding Uplands. The site "must either be improved immediately or abandoned," he said, adding that the "nature of the soil "makes it difficult to hold a decent surface and therefore makes maintenance costs high" and that it might be necessary to put in hard-surfaced runways to be included in the "Trans-Canada scheme." Wilson estimated that these improvements would run to about $150,000 – much higher than the original $3,000 investment Transport had requested of the OFC.[37]

This jump in cost reflected the development of faster and heavier aircraft. As *Canadian Aviation* noted in its March 1937 issue, in 1929 aircraft had a "maximum cruising speed of approximately 120 mph and were of the single-engined type." This meant that when the federal government created standards for airfields, the minimum was set at 1,800 feet, and this was the standard the OFC initially expected to meet when it was told it would have to build new runways. By 1936, though, with the introduction of multi-engine aircraft, cruising speeds had increased to 200 mph and takeoff and landing speeds had also increased. This meant that runways had to be at least 3,000 feet long at sea level. Furthermore, the article noted that "modern high-speed aircraft require smoother surfaces than types previously in use."[38] Since the DOT intended to land its Lockheed 12s and Douglas DC-3s at Uplands and other airports along the Trans-Canada Airway, the new airstrips would have to accommodate these types of airplanes.

This higher development cost understandably shocked Barnet. Nevertheless, on May 18, 1937, he responded to Wilson's letter, saying that Laurentian planned to proceed with the improvements immediately and enclosed a copy of its lease for Uplands.[39] Two months later, with immense development costs looming, he wrote a letter to C.D. Howe himself explaining the situation:

As the only commercial flying service operating with their base at Ottawa, we are vitally interested in the future of aviation in this district and in the securing of a first class airport for the Capital of the Dominion. We believe that the development of an airport should be primarily a municipal project, but as the City of Ottawa have refused to help in the undertaking, and as the Ottawa Flying Club, the previous lessees of Uplands Airport, were in no position to carry out any development, in order to protect our interests and to assure ourselves of a base for our operations, we have secured a lease on the Uplands Airport for [a] period of ten years from last May.

Laurentian's base at Domaine d'Estérel. Barnet Maclaren, Laurentian's founder and president, smokes his pipe in the foreground. Behind him are a group of sportsmen and Laurentian's Waco, CF-AYP. (JB)

At the time, our intention was to carry out sufficient development to retain the licence for the airport for our own needs for light and medium aircraft, entailing a moderate investment only. It now appears that a more pretentious plan of development is needed to meet the requirements of aviation in this district, and we are prepared to go ahead and carry out the required development provided we can be assured of a sound investment. To this end we would request the Department of Transport to grant us a proportion of the cost of

such development. If such an arrangement can be negotiated, and we can secure sufficient revenue from other contracts for the use of the airport, we will undertake to carry out the development of the airport on approved lines.[40]

Two days later Barnet received a favourable reply from Howe's office, requesting definite numbers after Laurentian had surveyed the site.[41]

In September 1937, Laurentian was no longer satisfied with the prospect of being a tenant at Uplands, and began negotiations with Ottawa Uplands Ltd. to purchase the site. Ottawa Uplands Ltd. balked at the company's initial offer of $12,000 and president J.P. Crerar countered first with $150,000 and then with $80,000 since "Uplands fields [was] dry and level [and] would have low improvement costs."[42] Crerar, it would appear, was unaware of J.A. Wilson's earlier estimate for the high costs of construction and maintenance on the site. Barnet replied that $25,000 was their best offer and that they had one week to make a decision.[43] As Barnet wrote in his records, they "completed the purchase of the property on Oct. 30th 1937."

At year's end Uplands was still not the airport Howe had envisioned for his adopted country's capital. *Canadian Aviation* perhaps summed up the state of Uplands the most succinctly: "sod, sandy, natural drainage, marked level area near centre of field, remainder very rough…. Day facilities only. Property of Laurentian Air Services. Extensive improvements planned for 1938. Est. cost of improvements: $125,000."[44] Who would pay for the improvements and what the result of the negotiations would be was still anyone's guess.

In mid-February 1938, J.A. Wilson told Barnet at a meeting that the DOT wanted to buy their land to build an airport. This put Barnet in an "embarrassing position," as he wrote to C.D. Howe on February 12, 1938. In this letter, he outlined the sequence of events leading to Laurentian's purchase of Uplands. Laurentian, he noted, had repeatedly approached both the city and the federal government about Uplands and both assured him they were not at all interested in purchasing the land. Furthermore, "It may be pointed out that the Directors of Uplands Limited were all our personal friends and we appealed to them to let us have the field at a figure we could finance…. On the strength of our statements to them and because of our personal friendship they agreed to sell us the airport at a very low figure and this purchase was completed as of November 1st, 1937." Ottawa Uplands Ltd. had in fact agreed to sell the land to Laurentian for the same price it had paid in 1911: $25,000.[45] This was undoubtedly a much lower price than the DOT would have paid.

In a letter from Barnet to Walter Deisher on March 2, 1938, he recounts the settling of affairs:

I had a good talk with the Colonel [V.I. Smart] yesterday before Messrs. [J.A.] Wilson and [Lieut. Commander C.P.] Edwards popped in, when I more or less shut up. Provided Uplands [Ottawa Uplands Ltd.] are appeased I have definitely concluded that selling is the surest and best way out of the present situation, and told the Colonel so. I mentioned $75,000, whereupon he looked at me and laughed. He said that was out of the question, I had to admit that between ourselves I felt that was too much for the property, and told him I was no horse trader, but wanted to make a

fair price and above all else protect ourselves for future operations. I pointed out that what we paid for the property had nothing to do with the price now, that we looked on it from a view of the cost of ultimate development, that we did not buy it as farm land, and there was no doubt that this site could be developed for much less than any other site around Ottawa. He agreed to this, and when Wilson and Edwards came in stressed this argument to them. He told me to put down all our out of pocket expenses, plus our time, and that he would have no hesitation in recommending this figure to the Minister plus a reasonable profit.[46]

By March 7 Walter and Barnet had come up with a total figure of $45,425.85. This included the $25,000 they had paid Ottawa Uplands Ltd. for the land, as well as various taxes, licensing fees, surveying costs, engineering and legal services, and the hours they had spent in the process. On March 15, 1938, Colonel V.I. Smart countered with an offer of $37,500, which was what Laurentian finally sold it for two months later. In the end, Laurentian kept 1.54 acres for its hangars, received a 21-year lease for $1 per year (with the right of renewal for another 21 years) and the right to land its aircraft free of charge on the field.[47]

Once the federal government owned Uplands, it did not take long for Howe and the Department of Transport to take matters in hand. The July 1938 issue of *Canadian Aviation* noted that the federal government had earmarked approximately one million dollars for airport development that summer. At Uplands, it reported, "An improvement program is under way, including [the] building and hard-surfacing of two runways (200 by 3,000 feet). Ultimately a third runway will be built and all will be extended to 4,500 feet."[48] The official opening of the airport took place on August 20, 1938, with Howe and his wife in attendance. Approximately 5,000 spectators flocked to the site and 50 civil,

Each fall, Laurentian would fly hunters to remote locations in southern Quebec for the moose hunt. Here a group of satisfied customers display their prize next to Laurentian's Standard Cabin Waco, CF-AYP, in the late 1930s. (JB)

commercial and military aircraft lined the new runway nearest the official platform. The Canadian Broadcasting Corporation covered the event in detail for listeners across the country.[49] The capital of the Dominion finally had her airport.

"Our new customer, the air tourist, is here."
During the two-year period of prolonged negotiations and uncertainty surrounding its land base at Uplands, Laurentian remained open for business. *Canadian Aviation* published a review of commercial aviation companies in Canada in its March 1937 issue, writing that Laurentian "is a new company doing general charter work out of Ottawa and specializing in hunting and fishing trips throughout the Laurentian country north and east of the Capital City."[50] Combined

with previous marketing – such as Laurentian's own brochures – this press helped to spread the word about Laurentian.

It seems, though, that there were still those who were not aware of Laurentian's existence.[51] On May 25, 1937, Barnet wrote a letter to Lieutenant Commander C.P. Edwards, Chief of Air Services at the Department of Transport:

I wish to bring to your attention that on Friday, May 7th a Royal Canadian Airforce [sic] seaplane took a party of fishermen from the Air Station at Rockcliffe to the Echo Beach Fishing Club on Echo Lake. One member of this party had written in to us previously to arrange for us to fly him in. Again, about the middle of last week, two gentlemen, one a member of Parliament, were flown into Lac Désert in an RCAF seaplane, from the Rockcliffe

Air Station. As a commercial air service we object strenuously to such practice, and would point out that we are unable to compete with the RCAF if such is allowed to continue.[52]

Barnet's letter touched off a short burst of internal correspondence between the departments of Transport and National Defence. R.K. Smith from the office of the Deputy Minister of Transport wrote a mild rebuke to Edwards at DND: "In past years, no adequate air service has been available in the Ottawa district but there are now modern aircraft, both on wheels and floats, here catering for business in this district. As this may not have been brought to the attention of your Department, I deem it advisable to inform you of the altered circumstances."[53] The stiff reply from Acting Deputy Minister H.W. Brown at DND came on June 3:

I beg to state that this Department does not consider that any transportation which has been authorized in the Ottawa district this year, has interfered with the legitimate business of commercial air operating companies. Only occasional instances have occurred wherein other than Service personnel have been transported in RCAF aircraft, and in these cases, the flights were considered to be in the best interests of the Government, and were duly authorized by the Minister. You are assured that it is the policy of this Department to ensure that flying carried out by this Department should be in the National interest.[54]

Even with competition from the RCAF, Laurentian did well in 1937. In July the company bought a four-seater Custom Cabin Waco ZQC6-7 floatplane, CF-BDO, to meet the increased demand from businessmen, fishermen and the timber companies.[55] Often compared to luxury automobiles at the time, Custom Wacos were known for their plush interiors and reliability. As engineer George Beveridge recalled, CF-BDO "really put us in business – on land and water. One of the first jobs was a sports event in Rideau Lake country. We flew joy rides. Four passengers for a half hour at four dollars a head."[56]

By the end of the year Laurentian had logged 413 flying hours, had doubled the number of passengers carried the previous year and contin-

The General 102-A Aristocrat Laurentian chartered from Fleet Aircraft during the summer of 1938 for $4/hour. CF-ALG came to Canada in February 1930 and had several owners in the Maritimes before being sold back to Fleet in August 1937. The identity of the man is unknown. (JB)

Laurentian's hangar in the late 1930s: in the back left is Laurentian's Puss Moth, CF-AVB, and back right is the company's Standard Cabin Waco, CF-AYP. The airplane in front is a D.H. 60 Moth, and it is likely CF-AVF, a DH.60M Moth registered to the Winnipeg Flying Club before being traded to the RCAF for CF-CFR, another aircraft of the same type. (JB)

ued to haul large amounts of freight.[57] During the summer, it also took over the OFC's Imperial Oil contract, providing modern refuelling services at Uplands as well as at its Rockcliffe seaplane base.[58]

Laurentian continued to grow. In the summer of 1938, Barnet hired William H. (Bill) Irvine, a pilot and air engineer, and chartered a General 102-A Aristocrat, CF-ALG, from Fleet Aircraft to handle additional business.[59] As an article in the June 1938 issue of *Canadian Aviation* noted, Laurentian had begun offering charter services not only from Ottawa but also from a new base at Sainte-Marguerite-Domaine d'Estérel in Quebec. Laurentian had found a niche market, providing "air taxi service" for mostly American hunters and fishermen "arriving in Montreal or Ottawa and bound for one of the many sportsmen's resorts or fish and game areas within a 200-mile radius of Ottawa."

The article reported, for example, that pilots Barnet and Bill flew George Earle, the governor of Pennsylvania, and his party of ten from Montreal to Baskatong, in the company's two Wacos, visiting several "choice fishing spots." Canadian businessmen and sportsmen were also "taking the sky routes to favourite fishing areas" as photos from the time of Barnet with Bob Bowman, director of special events broadcasts for the CBC, attest.[60]

After getting the company solidly off the ground, so to speak, Walter Deisher sold his shares in Laurentian. On September 15, 1937, the company held a board meeting at which Laurentian bought Walter's hangar at Uplands and his Puss Moth for 400 shares in the company. Walter was by no means retiring from aviation. After a stint at Fleet Aircraft Ltd. in Fort Erie, Ontario, he went on to hold senior executive positions with A.V. Roe.

Two Custom Cabin Wacos at Fleet Aircraft's dock on the Niagara River at Fort Erie, Ontario circa 1938. Laurentian bought the Custom Waco ZQC6-7, CF-BDO, at left in July 1937, flying sportsmen to remote fishing and hunting spots during float season and outfitting it with skis to fly downhill skiing enthusiasts to the Laurentian hills in winter. Here it is pictured with another Custom Waco, CF-BJS, which first came to Canada with Fleet Aircraft in May 1938 as a demo airplane before being sold to Peace River Airways in Alberta. (PG)

By 1939, *Canadian Aviation* had coined a term for what companies like Laurentian – as well as individuals – were engaging in: air tourism. As the magazine noted in August 1939, people could now be "free from the dust and traffic hazards of highway travel." Air travel was becoming more affordable: "flying costs have come down in such a sensational manner that, in any one of three or four light aeroplane types on the market, two people can fly from Montreal to Vancouver and back at an operation cost of about twenty-seven dollars apiece."[61]

While most of Laurentian's air tourists were interested in flying to remote fishing, hunting or vacationing spots, some also saw the potential for getting a closer look at visiting dignitaries. In April 1939, for instance, the company had a number of customers charter its services to "wit-ness the celebrations" accompanying the visit of the King and Queen of England.[62]

As Laurentian started to focus more on passenger travel (and less on freight), it tried to make the hangar facilities at Uplands more comfortable for its customers.[63] In the summer of 1939, for example, the company applied to build an extension to its hangar so that a Mr. Percy Burgess could run a lunch counter.[64] A water supply system was also installed, as the hangar had formerly been without water or sewage facilities.[65] In September 1939, though, war was declared with Germany. Just when it seemed Laurentian had finally reached firmer footing, Canada entered the Second World War, and the company's – and indeed the world's – future once again appeared uncertain.

WARNER BROS.
AND THE WAR EFFORT

2

Laurentian had only been in existence for three years when Canada joined Britain in declaring war against the Axis powers. Up to then Laurentian pilots had mostly flown sportsmen and vacationers to idyllic lake retreats north of Ottawa. The dark days of war led Barnet Maclaren to completely redirect Laurentian's operations. This was partially due to necessity: as the war continued, the federal government increasingly restricted non-essential flying as well as the use of aviation fuel and oil. But mostly it was Barnet's principles and his patriotism that drove Laurentian's expansion into new areas. To assure Allied victory, wrote *Canadian Aviation*'s editor in the September 1939 issue, the country had to put "all necessary machinery in motion as efficiently and expeditiously as possible."[1] Barnet heeded these words, putting Laurentian's resources to work wherever they were required. When the RCAF needed pilots to test and ferry hundreds of military aircraft around the country, Laurentian's pilots were in the cockpit. When thousands of RCAF engines needed overhauling, George Beveridge and his team worked around the clock to get the job done. Laurentian's contribution to the war effort also went beyond planes and parts; it also became involved in the making of Warner Bros.' air epic *Captains of the Clouds,* to boost morale and market the British Commonwealth Air Training Plan.

"If it weren't for Barnet Maclaren, Cessna wouldn't be here today."

Shortly after the war began Barnet had his first chance to help the Allied cause. In late 1939, an American by the name of Dwane Wallace came to Canada, trying to sell his aircraft to the Canadian government. Decades later he sat beside Barnet's nephew, John Bogie, at an Air Transport Association (ATA) meeting. Glancing at the Laurentian Air Services name tag on Bogie's chest, he asked, "John – how's Barnet Maclaren?" John remembers looking at him and saying, "'How the heck would you know Barnet Maclaren?' and Wallace replied, 'If it weren't for Barnet Maclaren, Cessna wouldn't be here today.'"

Dwane Wallace, nephew to Clyde Cessna, was in fact the owner of Cessna Corporation. The Depression had hit the company hard, and Cessna had closed his manufacturing plant temporarily in the early 1930s, reopening it in 1934. With a degree in aeronautical engineering Wallace was hired as manager of his uncle's struggling plant, working without pay for the first year.[2]

As Wallace told John at that ATA meeting, in 1939 he flew into Ottawa hoping to convince the Canadian government to order some of his new twin-engine light transport aircraft. He ended up at Laurentian, the only refuelling facility in the area, and met Barnet. They became friendly and he confided his reason for coming to Ottawa. As Wallace later recounted to John:

More than 800 Cessna Cranes were used by the RCAF for twin-engine pilot training under the British Commonwealth Air Training Plan. Cessna Crane FJ201 was on strength from 1942 to 1948. (Photo by Howard Anderson. CANAV Books Collection)

Barnet gave Cessna enough money to buy materials and engines for two prototypes for the RCAF to try out. Dwane had employees and he was flying in air races to make enough money to keep going. They had an airplane that he'd designed and built and he had, I think, six or eight employees and their shop. But he was flat broke and nobody'd loan him any money – the banks wouldn't look at him down in Kansas. It was about $25,000 that Barnet gave him, which was a lot of money in those days.

Barnet's financing allowed Dwane Wallace to buy four Jacobs L-4MB engines, but, as John recalls, his support did not end there: "Barnet lined him up with C.D. Howe and all the right people." Howe was a crucial contact. During the war, he was appointed Minister of the Department of Munitions and Supply and became "near-absolute ruler of the whole industrial economy of Canada."[3] Howe and the Canadian government finalized contracts to order the aircraft Wallace had designed, a military trainer later dubbed the Cessna T-50 Crane in Canada, or Bobcat as it was known in the United States. Initially the Canadian order was only for 140 units, but this was enough to get American banks to agree to finance the company. Cessna was now on solid ground financially and Wallace could afford to repay Barnet's loan. Being a fair businessman, he told John Bogie that he'd asked

"How much interest do I owe you, Barnet?" and Barnet replied, "I don't want any interest. I don't want to make any money on the war effort."

This little-known episode in aviation history gave the Cessna Corporation the orders it needed to stay afloat, and the Crane, a "robust and reliable airplane," provided Canada with a much-needed training aircraft. While the Canadian government may have only purchased 140 initially as a substitute for Canadian-built Avro Ansons, a total of 820 Cranes saw service with the RCAF and it became "one of the most important aircraft" used by the British Commonwealth Air Training Plan (BCATP).[4]

A pilot with much to recommend him

When the war began, Laurentian had a fleet of three aircraft – a Puss Moth and two Cabin Wacos[5] – and Barnet had hired Bill Irvine and Art Hollingsworth as pilot managers for Laurentian's recently acquired leases at Mont-Laurier and Sainte-Marguerite in Quebec.[6] He had also hired Jack Charleson in 1938 to fly the mail run down to Rimouski on the lower St. Lawrence in the Wacos.[7] Laurentian's president had good instincts when it came to choosing airmen: these pilots went on to have long careers in Canadian aviation. Bill Irvine became the Department of Transport Regional Director at Vancouver and Art Hollingsworth became a senior Trans-Canada Air Lines captain.[8] In 1945, Jack Charle-

Barnet Maclaren hard at work in his office in 1943. (JB)

Laurentian pilot Doug Pickering (right) with former Laurentian pilot Jack Charleson in front of a Grumman Goblin, one of the aircraft types they ferried to various RCAF stations during the war. The Goblin was manufactured by Canadian Car and Foundry in Fort William, Ontario, and was a two-seat naval biplane fighter the RCAF originally considered unsuitable. Once the war began, however, and the RCAF had a difficult time mustering sufficient aircraft, it became more attractive. (DP)

son was the first Canadian to get his helicopter pilot's licence and by 1961 he was vice-president of Okanagan Helicopters.[9]

It is commonly said in the aviation community that there are two types of pilots – old ones and bold ones. Jack Charleson, it would seem, fit into the latter category, though he went on to have a long career. William (Bill) Wheeler of the Canadian Aviation Historical Society (CAHS), described him as "probably the most colourful guy to fly with Laurentian." Apparently he already had a reputation before he joined the company. As Robert Rennart writes in his book *A City Takes Flight*, in January of 1935 Jack and a friend, Yvan LeMoine, flew their Avro Avian, CF-AIE, from Ottawa to Kingston, Jamaica. They immediately "angered a local groundskeeper by landing on a Polo Field. After two months in Jamaica, local

officials became suspicious that Charleson and LeMoine were up to no good and they were asked to leave the country. The pair returned to Ottawa, their plane full of Jamaican rum."[10] John Bogie also recalls Jack being a bit of a risk taker:

Jack flew off with his fiancée from Uplands field and they got married somewhere down in the States. I don't know if his father-in-law ever spoke to him again. I remember he got into trouble because he flew under the Victoria Bridge here on the Ottawa River. He was kind of a wild fellow but he was a good pilot.

By the time Canada declared war, Charleson was no longer working for Laurentian, having moved on to the Aviation Division of the Department of Transport.[11] His work with the Ferry Command, though, still brought him regularly into contact with pilots at Laurentian doing similar work. As he recalled in a talk to the CAHS in 1985, however, unlike Laurentian's pilots he did not feel he was paid enough for his work:

Future Laurentian pilot and Barnet Maclaren's nephew, John Bogie, climbing out of the prototype Curtiss-Wright Model 25 Jeep at the Massena Airport in New York State in 1942. The 16-year-old roomed near the airport that summer while he took lessons at the Captain Duke Dufort Flying School. When it was time for his solo, he flew cross-country to the Ottawa Airport. "There were Harvards landing every 17 seconds on touch and go's when I arrived and I had no radio," he remembers. "But they knew I was coming so the RCAF gave me the green light to land." (JB)

I was with Ferry Command and was moving some Grummans around for Canadian Car with Leigh Capreol and Barnet Maclaren, who flew the other aircraft. When we delivered them we were given cheques as payment for our services. I was immediately approached by a man from Munitions and Supply, who asked if I worked for the government. When I replied that I did he directed me to return the cheque. "You can't receive two pay cheques from the Crown," he told me. Capreol and Maclaren were both allowed to pocket theirs – and they were both far more affluent than I was.[12]

By the 1940s Laurentian was mainly focused on testing and ferrying RCAF aircraft, although it still flew regular fire patrols in the area.[13] Normally Barnet would have coordinated these different activities, but by 1939 he was being pulled in several directions. As John Bogie remembers, Barnet's father, Alex, and his uncle, Albert, died within a year of each other.[14] With two of the Maclaren Power and Paper Company's founders dead, Barnet was busier than ever at the company and, as John says, "he needed an experienced pilot to run the operation" during the hectic war years.

Enter Douglas S. Pickering, or Doug, as everyone knew him. He began working for Laurentian on July 31, 1940, and had much to recommend him: the 33-year-old pilot had been flying for over a decade, collecting numerous trophies at the Hamilton Aero Club and participating in the Maritime Goodwill Tour, flying 2,800 miles from Toronto to the Maritimes and back in 1933.[15] In addition to having private and commercial pilot's licences, he also had an air engineer's certificate. And he had worked for Starratt Airways and Transportation Ltd., flying 3,000 hours on 12 different aircraft during his three years of service for the company. Dick Pickering, Doug's son, thinks his father may have seen that Starratt's fortunes were changing, as Doug left shortly before the company was sold to the Canadian Pacific Railway.

Starratt's loss was certainly Laurentian's gain: Doug brought his skill and experience to bear on his work as chief pilot. He did a lot of ferrying work for the RCAF and often came into contact with Jack Charleson. As Doug recalled, in October 1940 they "ferried a number of Grumman Goblins built at the Canadian Car and Foundry

Doug Pickering prepares to test fly a Hawker Hurricane at the Canadian Car and Foundry Co.'s Fort William plant. The CCFC built 1,451 Hurricanes under licence. Shipped to Britain beginning in the summer of 1940, they saw service with RAF and RCAF squadrons in all theatres of operations, as well as with Canadian Home Defence squadrons from 1942. (DP)

at Fort William to various RCAF stations."[16] In March 1941 Doug was in charge of ferrying a Northrop Delta IA (No. 668) from Vickers to No. 12 Bomber and Reconnaissance Squadron, Patricia Bay, B.C. Ferrying the Delta IA, Doug remembered, began as a challenge but luckily ended well:

Naturally many of these aircraft were unfamiliar to the ferry pilots.… I never did get any first hand information on the aircraft [Delta]. This meant I had to familiarize myself with the aircraft and do my own check-out. Several takeoffs and landings convinced me that the Delta was quite a normal aircraft to handle.

Checking with the forecaster the next morning, I was advised a major storm was moving in from the East and if I did not get away within the hour there would be a delay of two or three days. Fine snow had started to fall by the time I was ready for take-off; however, after several miles on my way, flew into crystal clear sky conditions through

A Northrop Delta IA like the one Doug Pickering ferried from Vickers to No. 12 Bomber and Reconnaissance Squadron at Patricia Bay, B.C., in March 1941. Very few Deltas were made as a change in American regulations in 1933 prohibiting single-engine aircraft from carrying passengers at night or over rough terrain made the type largely obsolete. Two years later, the RCAF began using it as a photographic survey aircraft. When war broke out, the aircraft were diverted to coastal patrol work on floats. Salt-water corrosion forced the Deltas back to land after two months and they were withdrawn from operations late in 1941. (DP)

to Kapuskasing and Winnipeg, with a strong tail wind. Similar conditions prevailed next day, and the flight across the Prairies to Lethbridge and over the Rockies to Patricia Bay was completed with a total flying time of twelve hours and forty minutes from Ottawa in two easy days. The sixty-five degree temperature, with the tulips and daffodils in bloom at Patricia Bay, further added to an enjoyable experience.

In addition to ferrying RCAF aircraft around the country, Doug and the pilots at Laurentian test-flew Avro Tudors, Fairey Battles, Westland Lysanders, Hawker Hurricanes, Avro Ansons and even an RCMP Noorduyn Norseman, CF-MPF, in the first years of the war.[17] For the most part these test flights were routine, but every once in a while Doug noted in his logbook such problems as "oil tank blew up" or "Automatic boost control froze (no throttle)."[18] Even so, after ferrying and testing hundreds of aircraft in often challenging conditions, Doug remained accident free.[19]

While ferrying, test flying and forest fire patrolling made up the bulk of Laurentian's flying hours during the war, the company also supported the war effort in other ways. On the night of March 29, 1941, for example, Doug flew Laurentian's Custom Waco, CF-BDO, on a 30-minute flight over downtown Ottawa to publicize the Canadian War Services Fund.[20] Laurentian was actually brought in at the last minute for this show because the three aircraft scheduled to take part were grounded that morning due to Ottawa's changeable March weather. That night, Doug pretended to be a German bomber while a "broad, 800,000,000 candle-power beam knifed through a darkened sky" to "shoot" him down. As the *Ottawa Citizen* later reported, "The demonstration, which gave onlookers some idea of the grim game of death being played nightly over England, was given a realistic touch as fire sirens wailed in the distance as city firefighters responded to two alarms in other parts of the city during the display."[21]

These war-related flights became the basis of Laurentian's flying business. Since flying deemed non-essential was strictly curtailed by the Civil Aviation and Oil Controller's offices, Laurentian had to make special applications to them for exceptional situations. A few days after Doug's night flight over Ottawa, for example, Laurentian had to ask to be allowed to take a *Toronto Star* photographer up to take photos of the CPR railway accident near Inkerman, Ontario, the "worst railway disaster in years," according to the *Ottawa Citizen*.[22]

While the federal government permitted this flight, on at least one occasion Laurentian had to turn away a wealthy client due to increasing oil and fuel rationing. During the summer of 1944, for instance, Laurentian applied to W.H. Rea, Oil Controller at the Department of Munitions and Supply, for a special allowance to fly Mr. T.V. Hartnett and his wife, "an invalid," to Lac Désert in the Laurentians.[23] Hartnett was president of Brown and Williamson Tobacco Corp. in Louisville, Kentucky, but the Oil Controller's office was not to be trifled with: two years earlier

On June 1, 1941, Laurentian pilot Doug Pickering (at left) married his sweetheart, Dorothy. Laurentian engineer George Beveridge, pictured here with his wife, was best man (DP).

it had issued an order "stopping the use of aircraft for pleasure and other non-essential purposes" in order to conserve oil for the war effort.[24] Furthermore, they were particularly wary of "certain individuals, who in other days, have used the airplane as a means of transportation to and from summer cottages and such. They are of the opinion that a slackening of restrictions would be abused by such unthinking people."[25] It is not surprising, then, that Rea's reply to Laurentian's request was curt: "if Mrs. Hartnett's condition does not permit her to travel by other means, then possibly she should choose a more accessible location."[26]

Before the oil rationing came into full effect, Laurentian pilots did manage to sneak in a few pleasure cruises. One instance in particular stands out: on June 1, 1941, Doug Pickering flew his new wife, Dorothy, on a honeymoon in one of Laurentian's Wacos.[27] It is not clear if he secured government approval for the flight, but his colleagues at Laurentian certainly supported him: chief engineer George Beveridge even stood up as his best man at the happy event.

"His engine shop was first class."

The fact that George was in Doug's wedding party speaks volumes about Doug's character. According to Tim Cole, who was chief pilot for Laurentian in the late 1960s and early 1970s, George "hated young pilots" because of their supposed recklessness. He was British and had started as an air engineer in England. Tim remembers: "He always wore a white shirt and tie, and his engine shop was first class. I had a lot of faith in his engines."

George Beveridge had been with Laurentian since 1936, after having worked for Ontario Air Services and the Ottawa Flying Club.[28] He began as chief air engineer, maintaining Laurentian's engines on the ground and often riding along with the pilots in case anything happened during a flight. He continued to do this during the war.[29] Some of George's – and Laurentian's – most important contributions to the war effort happened on the ground, though. As Doug later wrote, the company built an engine overhaul shop and test house in late 1940:

The engines were overhauled for the Air Training Schools. It soon became apparent added facilities were required and a large addition was built, incorporating a second test house, receiving and shipping, stores and office facilities. George L. Beveridge, as Chief Engineer, and a large staff operated on a twenty-four hours a day, seven days a week basis and were responsible for overhauling, testing and delivering over 5,000 aircraft engines for the Air Training Schools in addition to carrying

out much experimental work on various makes of engines for the RCAF.[30]

The addition Doug mentioned was completed in early 1942. As an article in *The Salesmotor* noted, this extension meant that Laurentian had "two complete installations, serving two separate test rooms so that work can be done in both areas simultaneously."[31] According to this article, the equipment in the test facilities was developed by Barnet and George along with representatives of Imperial Oil's Ontario Division Engineering Department. This equipment "was designed to permit Intava Aviation Gasolines of correct specifications to reach the carburetor of aircraft engines on test under conditions simulating actual flying." Laurentian was on the cutting edge of engine overhauling and testing.

Laurentian's "large modern aircraft engine maintenance plant" and good track record made it an easy choice when the Department of Munitions and Supply needed a company to do maintenance on engines for the RCAF in 1943. On July 1 of that year, the company signed a contract with the department that would last until "the termination of the war in which His Majesty is currently engaged."[32] The company was mainly to overhaul and repair Jacobs and Ranger engines for the RCAF, but the federal government had their people work on other engines and airplanes as needed.[33] This tireless work led the writer for *The Salesmotor* to proclaim that Laurentian's engine shop contributed "in a large degree to the success of the Commonwealth Air Training Plan in Canada."[34]

The Department of Transport hangar (left) and the Laurentian hangar (right) circa 1940. In front of the DOT hangar are a Trans-Canada Air Lines Lockheed 14H2 Super Electra, CF-TCE, a visiting U.S. civil Lockheed 10A Electra, NC14947, and an RCAF Fairchild 71B, possibly no. 629. At the Laurentian hangar are an RCAF Blackburn Shark and an Armstrong Whitworth Atlas. (JB)

Captains of the Clouds: Canada's first air epic

Laurentian's contribution to Canada's war effort was not confined to the physical work of overhauling RCAF engines and ferrying and testing military aircraft. The company was hired by Warner Bros. in 1941 to help make a film that would rouse support for the Allied cause and especially the British Commonwealth Air Training Plan.

In the October/November issue of *Canadian Aviation*, the editor wrote:

Oct. 10, 1939, will perhaps stand out for all time as the most important date in the history of aviation in Canada. On that day the Governments of Great Britain, Australia, New Zealand and Canada jointly announced an Empire air training scheme to be centred in Canada. Under the scheme, thousands of young men from Britain and the Dominions will come to this country for advanced training in air force duties.[35]

He went on to assert that Lord Riverdale, head of the British Air Mission, estimated that "between 20,000 and 25,000 men, including pilots, gunners and wireless operators, will be turned out about every six months when the programme gets in full swing." Two years later *Canadian Aviation* reported "an American newspaperman" as stating that the BCATP was "the Canadian effort most likely to exert a decisive influence on the course of the war."[36]

The BCATP, though, was suffering from, in the words of historian Rudy Mauro, "a serious image problem" by the fall of 1940. This in turn meant that it faced "a critical shortage of trained pilots for its bombing and gunnery schools."[37] To bolster its public image, the head of the newly formed RCAF Directorate of Public Relations, Joseph W. G. Clark, along with First World War flying ace Billy Bishop and senior bureaucrats at the Department of National Defence for Air, "hit upon the idea of a full length feature motion picture to illustrate the work of the RCAF before mass audiences in Canada as well as abroad." While the National Film Board of Canada had been created two years earlier for just this kind of wartime "morale boosting," Clark had higher ambitions. He went straight to Hollywood and on January 28, 1941, signed a deal to make *Captains of the Clouds.*

Production was set to begin a few months later on July 16, 1941, so preparations had to be made quickly.[38] Producer Hal B. Wallis worked with Canadian Department of National Defence officials to scout suitable filming sites.[39] They decided that the bush flying sequences in the first half of the movie would be filmed near North Bay, Ontario, and the RCAF scenes in the second half would take place at Uplands, the actual site of No. 2 Service Flying Training School.[40] Warner Bros. quickly put together a cast of some of its biggest stars: James Cagney, Hollywood's highest paid actor at the time, was chosen to play the lead character, Brian MacLean, and his bush flying competitors-turned-buddies were to be played by Dennis Morgan, Alan Hale, George Tobias and Reginald Gardiner. Brenda Marshall was cast as the female lead.

For a movie that was slated to be Canada's first air epic, however, having suitable aircraft was perhaps even more important than which Hollywood actors appeared. This is where Laurentian came into the picture – literally. When Joseph Clark went looking for aircraft for the bush flying sequences, J.A. Wilson, Controller of Civil Aviation, provided him with "a list of 17 Waco, Norseman, Fairchild and other types of bush aircraft currently equipped with floats, and available for lease from such firms as Austin Airways, Dominion Skyways and Laurentian Air Services."[41] In the end, Laurentian signed a contract with Warner Bros. two days before production was set to begin, agreeing to lease it the Custom Waco, CF-BDO.[42]

On July 16, 1941, Doug Pickering flew the Waco to the seaplane base at Trout Lake near

Some of the cast and crew of Canada's first air epic, *Captains of the Clouds*, pose for a photo while shooting in North Bay, Ontario. In the middle of the front row are actors Dennis Morgan and James Cagney. Laurentian pilot Doug Pickering is second from right in the back row. (DP)

North Bay, Ontario, where he and the airplane would remain for the duration of filming.[43] Aside from ferrying CF-BDO, Doug's job was to "check out the Hollywood stuntmen" who would be performing the bush flying sequences. In 1992 Doug told Rudy Mauro that he was "surprised to learn that none of the pilots had experience on the types of aircraft hired for the picture. Even more disconcerting was his discovery that they had no float experience."[44] Mauro wrote that Doug, in keeping with his laid-back nature, did not "appear to have had any reservations about turning his well-kept Waco over to the stuntmen." From the sounds of it, however, perhaps Doug should have been a little more concerned as the stuntmen performed "manoeuvres not usually associated with bush flying" and several airplanes were damaged during filming, "one badly enough to require the flying in of a replacement from Toronto."[45]

In *Captains of the Clouds*, the Laurentian Waco belongs to Alan Hale's character, Tiny Murphy, and appears in the opening scene. Warner Bros. had it and the other leased aircraft

"repainted in bright colors for the benefit of the Technicolor cameras"[46] and it was given the fake registration of CF-GHV. As Mauro discovered during the course of his research, Warner Bros. used water paint to transform the leased planes and had to repaint them after the frequent rainstorms that summer.[47]

When Rudy and Doug spoke in 1992, Doug told him that among his "most vivid recollections of the filming of *Clouds* at North Bay and Temagami, were the countless retakes of the same scenes, the long waits between filming sessions, for sufficient light or for the weather

The *Captains of the Clouds* playbill featured an RCAF Lockheed Hudson bomber.

to clear, and the comic relief provided on the set by Michael Curtiz, the Hungarian-born director." He also "recalled 'hoisting' his share of Old Vienna lager" at the Empire Hotel in North Bay where the pilots roomed, as well as at Whitehouse Lodge, "the small inn on Trout Lake … which served as operations headquarters for Warner Brothers."[48]

Rudy had his own recollections of the filming of *Captains of the Clouds*. He was 16 years old when Warner Bros. descended on North Bay in July 1941. His grandfather would drive him over to Trout Lake to watch the bush flying sequences, and when the movie premiered in North Bay in March 1942, he and everyone else in town went to see it. He remembers thinking it was "a fantastic movie – a tremendous morale booster. It blew us all away. Not long after I joined the Air Force, along with other young men."

A month before, the RCAF had transported copies of *Captains of the Clouds* to cities around the world so that it premiered simultaneously in New York, London, Ottawa, Cairo, Melbourne, Toronto, Winnipeg and Vancouver.[49] Air Marshal W.A. Bishop – otherwise known as World War I flying ace "Billy" Bishop – attended the New York opening, along with 200 RCAF cadets and other officials.[50] The film did well at the box office, becoming Cagney's second highest grossing film.[51] More importantly for the RCAF and Laurentian, it succeeded in showing Canadians and their Allies the importance of the British Commonwealth Air Training Plan. As the *New York Times* movie reviewer, Bosley Crowther, wrote of the film in February 1942, "the scenes of RCAF training are impressive and dignified, a sequence showing the presentation of wings to graduates by Air Marshal Bishop is moving, … and a shot of bombers taking off for England in the hour before dawn is pulse-quickening."[52] These scenes stirred the hearts and minds of audiences, prompting some – like Rudy Mauro – to join up, and others to keep faith that the Allied forces would win the war.

By 1945, Laurentian had firmly established its reputation. The company had expanded physically: it had gone from having two pilots to five and had constructed a large, state-of-the-art engine overhauling and testing facility at Uplands. It had also branched into new areas and tackled new challenges to support Canada's war effort by ferrying and testing RCAF aircraft and participating in the making of *Captains of the Clouds*. In the midst of all this activity, though, Laurentian was already thinking ahead to postwar planning for Canadian aviation, and was poised to once again be on the cutting edge.

Laurentian's Standard Cabin Waco, CF-AYP, with George Beveridge standing on it (left) and the company's Custom Cabin Waco, CF-BDO, at a beach near Mont Laurier, Quebec. (JB)

A GROWING FLEET AND
A GOING CONCERN

On November 15, 1943, the Air Industries and Transport Association of Canada (AITAC) held its annual meeting at the prestigious Royal York Hotel in downtown Toronto. In the midst of war, this organization had convened to discuss what should happen once hostilities inevitably ceased. In attendance that day were representatives from the federal government, aircraft manufacturers and commercial aviation companies who all shared a common goal: to learn from the mistakes of the First World War and avoid a post-war crash in the aviation industry.

Three men in the audience that day were particularly interested in the peacetime picture for commercial operators. Barnet Maclaren, Doug Pickering and J.P. McIntyre of Laurentian Air Services sat at a table with representatives from Fleet, Noorduyn and the Civil Aviation Board, listening closely to the speeches to figure out how to ensure Laurentian's success in the coming years.[1] Even though the war would not end until 1945, Laurentian's directors already had their eye on a time when they would be able to resume civilian flying operations.

When the war was finally over, Laurentian was one of the first companies to be awarded an operating licence by the new Air Transport Board. And while the company did not abandon its wartime engine overhaul services, the post-war years were a time when Laurentian returned to flying activities in a big way, especially in air tourism and forest fire prevention. To accommodate its expanding operations, Laurentian pioneered the commercial use of the Grumman G-21 Goose and the newly-designed

Post-war holiday: Laurentian's Custom Cabin Waco CF-BDO, likely at Domaine d'Estérel, a luxury hotel complex built by Baron Louis Empain of Belgium in the 1930s about 50 miles north of Montreal. The hotel regularly used Laurentian's services in the early post-war years. (JB)

The cover of the brochure Laurentian had printed in 1939. The Second World War interrupted the company's plans to bring American skiers to Quebec's Laurentian mountains, but it was able to resume this service quickly once peace was declared. (JB)

de Havilland Canada DHC-2 Beaver. When the decade came to a close, these new aircraft proved to be a wise investment and contributed to the company's growng success.

Returning to the skies

Within a month of the end of the war in Europe, Laurentian was once again flying commercially out of Ottawa. In June 1945, it received an operating certificate for its land base at Uplands as well as its seaplane base at the New Edinburgh Canoe Club on the Ottawa River.[2] By September, the company also had a licence to operate a charter air service from those bases. According to *Canadian Aviation*'s editor, the board "was proceeding cautiously" and did not grant a licence for non-scheduled service until August 1, 1945.[3] This made Laurentian one of the first aviation firms to receive Air Transport Board approval for non-scheduled services following the war.

From its main bases in Ottawa, Laurentian sought to resume its passenger services to the beautiful country north of Ottawa and Montreal. Before the war, Laurentian had founded a sub-base at Sainte-Marguerite-du-Lac-Masson, Quebec with the intention of providing year-round non-scheduled flights for urbanites seeking fresh air and relaxation. The company even printed a brochure in 1939 to attract an American clientele featuring two young men enjoying the newly popularized sport of downhill skiing with a Waco flying overhead. "Breakfast in New York! In the afternoon ski in the Laurentians!" the cover announced to potential customers. Inside, readers learned that they could depart Newark Airport in New Jersey at 8:30 a.m. aboard a Canadian Colonial Airways aircraft headed for Saint-Hubert airport near Montreal. There they would be met by a Laurentian Air Services airplane that would bring them into the "heart of the skiing country" by noon. If a day-trip was all the skiers had in mind, they could be back at Newark by dinnertime. If they desired a longer stay, there were several well-appointed "luxurious resorts" in the area, including Domaine d'Estérel and Pointe-Bleu Hotel.[4] Although the war had prevented Laurentian from building up this air tourism business, it received a second chance in November 1945, when the Air Transport Board granted the company a new licence to operate out of Ste-Marguerite-du-lac-Masson.[5]

In the years before the war, Laurentian had also flown tourists and sportsmen between

In the post-war years, Laurentian resumed flying skiers, many of them Americans, to the Laurentian mountains in southern Quebec. This group of skiers was flown directly to a ski hill aboard Laurentian's two ski-equipped Cabin Wacos, CF-AYP and CF-BDO. All they had to do was strap on their skis, grab their poles, and they could enjoy the great outdoors for an afternoon. Here they are pictured in front of CF-BDO with pilot Buster Brown. (JR)

Laurentian was the first Canadian company to use the Grumman G-21A commercially. While this amphibious aircraft was designed initially in 1937 to ferry wealthy Long Island residents to New York City, it was widely used later as a communications and patrol aircraft by the U.S. Navy, the RCAF and the RAF, which named it the "Goose." Laurentian converted its ex-RCAF Goose, CF-BXR, back to a "flying yacht" for wealthy passengers with much success. (PG)

Ottawa and Gray Rocks Inn, in lovely Saint-Jovite, Quebec.[6] Once the war ended, the company sought to reinstate this route, and on December 18, 1945, Barnet submitted an application to the Air Transport Board. In his cover letter he wrote: "Since we commenced operations in 1936 we have been serving this district both summer and winter, from Ottawa.... The traffic has increased consistently each year and we confidently expect that it will continue to do so in the future.... This centre has become extremely popular and, from our past experience and knowledge of this district, we believe that there is a need for such a service between Ottawa and Saint-Jovite, as a centre for the Laurentians."[7] The Air Transport Board agreed with Barnet's assessment and granted a licence March 8, 1946, in time for Laurentian to prepare for what it hoped would be a busy summer season.[8]

War birds: Laurentian's Grumman Goose and Cessna Crane

During the war, Barnet and the staff at Laurentian had already begun to anticipate increased passenger traffic. While Laurentian's two Wacos were still solid, reliable aircraft — on skis, floats or wheels — the company decided that it needed additional airplanes, ones that would appeal to a more sophisticated clientele. After the war, hundreds of surplus aircraft were being sold by the federal government's War Assets Corporation and Barnet saw an opportunity to acquire new machines.

The first addition came in March 1945, when Laurentian bought a Grumman Goose, CF-BXR, for $35,000.[9] According to Dick Pickering, 'BXR was built in 1938 for Lehman Bros. in the United States. During the war the U.S. Navy acquired it, later transferring it "to the RCAF for Eastern coastal patrol."[10] It was a deluxe twin-engine amphibious flying boat seating eight passengers that became the "Queen" of Laurentian's fleet. 'BXR also became the first commercially operated Goose in Canada.[11]

Later that year, Laurentian purchased another war surplus aircraft, one that perhaps had some personal meaning for Barnet: the Cessna T-50 Crane, the very model he had helped Dwane Wallace finance and sell to the RCAF a few years earlier. The Crane was a popular war-surplus aircraft and several bush operators had begun converting them for charter work as they were excellent for executive transport.[12] Barnet

Part-time Laurentian pilot John Bogie exits the company's Cessna T-50 Crane, CF-DAC, circa 1947. The Crane, or Bobcat as it was known in the U.S., was a popular war-surplus aircraft and several bush operators snatched them up. (PG)

purchased CF-DAC for his growing fleet, and by January 1946 Laurentian had a licence to use this five-passenger airplane in its commercial operations. As John Bogie recalls, the company began using it alongside its Wacos to ferry downhill skiers between Montreal and Saint Jovite at a cost of $25 per passenger, round trip.[13]

Buying the new Beaver

Laurentian's new Grumman Goose and Cessna Crane were excellent aircraft, but they were not ideal for all aspects of the company's bush op-

erations. None of the other war-surplus aircraft measured up either, as R.F. Corless Jr. argued in a March 1945 article for *Canadian Aviation*: their main drawback was "their performance on floats – pathetic."[14] What bush fliers really needed, he declared, was "a truly useful aircraft" that performed well on floats, could "carry a fair load, have a high ceiling, a good range [and] a good rate of climb [to] be able to get on and off small lakes and streams." Corless also noted that it would have to be a fairly small airplane with a high wing and a payload of about 600 lb with full tanks and equipment to be economical. Since it would be competing with dog teams, boats, cars, and trains, it did not need a cruising speed much above 90 mph. Above all, the airplane had to be equipped for Canadian winters and have the minimum number of "gadgets."

Within two years, Corless would have his perfect "northern work horse." De Havilland Canada (DHC) general manager Phil Garratt was also contemplating "a new Canadian bushplane" immediately after the war, as Fred W. Hotson notes in his history of the company.[15] By September 1946, DHC had authorized "preliminary engineering studies" for what would soon be christened the DHC-2 Beaver, after one of Canada's most recognizable and hard-working animals. Two months later, DHC sent a detailed questionnaire to a list of 80 hand-picked bush pilots and operators. As *Canadian Aviation* noted in April 1947, the respondents overwhelmingly ranked short take-off as their number one concern, with payload, economy, range and cruise following in that order. Interestingly, not far down the list was having "the necessary insulation, ash trays, etc., to make smoking by passengers permissible."[16] Doug Pickering, who was now Laurentian's operations manager as well as a pilot, was one of those asked to complete the questionnaire. As his son, Dick, remembers, one thing his father was adamant about was that the design of the rear cargo door allowed an operator to roll a gas drum in sideways. John Bogie also remembers George Beveridge backed Pratt & Whitney's R-985 engines over the Gipsy Queen 50 engines, which he did not think could withstand Canada's cold winters – among other

To Seabee or not to Seabee?

In the post-war years Laurentian expanded its fleet to include several new airplane models, including the new DHC-2 Beaver, the Grumman Goose and the Cessna T-50 Crane. Each of these aircraft types had its pros and cons, but they were all relatively easily integrated into Laurentian's operations.

One aircraft, however, was not as promising as they hoped. During the summer of 1948 unofficial dock boy Peter Fleming witnessed Doug Pickering come in with a Republic Seabee. As Peter recalls, this particular aircraft "looked like it would be the ideal aircraft to take fishermen out to lakes to do some fishing since the front canopy opened up such that you could stand at the front and cast." As Peter looked on from the dock, Doug, who was a talented and experienced float pilot, "made several abortive take-off attempts, and was only able to get it airborne again after Bus Brown roughed up the water by taxiing back and forth with the Waco across the take-off run."

Unsurprisingly, there is no evidence that Laurentian ever bought a Seabee. --

problems. Barnet Maclaren, John notes, had had enough of 45-minute refuelling sessions with the Wacos and recommended a belly tank that could be easily filled while the aircraft was on floats – and did not require using a hand pail.

DHC took these concerns to heart in designing the Beaver, and in June 1947, it approved the limited production of 15 Beavers. These airplanes, as Fred Hotson notes, "had a functional, rugged look with a square-sided fuselage and sturdy undercarriage legs. The strut-braced wing was of constant chord with large-span, slotted flaps. It had two doors up front and two large removable doors in the cargo/passenger area. There was accommodation for six and the pilot: three on a hammock seat across the back, two on single seats and one beside the pilot."[17] Dick Septer noted in an article celebrating the Beaver's 50th anniversary that this aircraft type had a 450 h.p. engine for a speedy take-off, was entirely made of metal (critical for Canada's winters), had "an average cruise speed of 110 mph," and a range of about 400 miles. It also carried a good payload, was still fairly economical to maintain, and was able to haul external loads like canoes.[18]

This was precisely the sort of aircraft Laurentian was looking for to expand its bush operations in the post-war years. On August 16, 1947, when DHC's chief test pilot, Russ Bannock, took the prototype Beaver, CF-FHB-X, on its first flight, a group of Laurentian employees was there to witness it. On that humid afternoon at DHC's Downsview plant near Toronto, Doug Pickering, George Beveridge and Barnet's nephew, John Bogie, watched as Bannock took the Beaver up for two flights.[19] They were impressed with what they saw, and quickly ordered one complete with wheels, skis and floats for about $30,000.[20]

On May 21, 1948, Beaver no. 6, CF-GIB, was delivered to Laurentian. The company had now pioneered the commercial use of both the Grumman Goose *and* the DHC-2 Beaver by using them in their bush operations.[21] These

Laurentian's second DHC-2 Beaver, CF-FHR, being launched onto the Ottawa River circa 1950. Laurentian acquired this aircraft in 1949 and would purchase five more by 1953, becoming Canada's leading commercial operator of this rugged bushplane at the time. (JB)

two aircraft served different but complementary roles in the 1940s. As an early short take-off and landing (STOL) type aircraft, the Beaver could get in and out of small lakes and rivers, even when they were "lined with trees and exposed to winds that blew in the wrong direction."[22] In fact, when Ronald Keith, *Canadian Aviation's* editor, did a ride-along in the Beaver in 1948, he reported that "under these conditions we found the Beaver to be next-of-kin to the helicopter."[23] These qualities made the Beaver ideal for Laurentian's firefighting operations. As operations manager Doug Pickering wrote to the Air Transport Board, the company was still flying for the E.B. Eddy Company, Gillies Brothers and the Ottawa River Forest Protective Association, "servicing fire towers," cruising timber limits, and transporting men, supplies and equipment into threatened areas north of Ottawa.[24] Laurentian found the Beaver so useful for this work that it agreed to be included in a DHC advertisement in *Canadian Aviation's* April 1949 issue:

Our Beaver has flown 347 hours during the past summer, and a good deal of this time has been spent on forest fire suppression work. Many days 20 and 25 flights were made, and one particular day, no less than 35 flights. The Beaver is easy to handle, load and unload, and otherwise it would

have been impossible to make 35 flights in a single day from points where no extensive base facilities exist, and into lakes and rivers where no docks were available. The pilot claims that the Beaver is the only aeroplane in the world which could have carried out this work.[25]

Laurentian's actions backed up this praise: on May 18, 1949, it took delivery of its second Beaver, CF-FHR (no. 46), and immediately put it to work.

The Beaver was an excellent aircraft for fire suppression, but in the early years, as the *Canadian Flight* editor remarked in its July/ August 1961 issue, it "was not too popular" with passengers "because of the noise emanating from the short exhaust stacks."[26] Laurentian's Grumman Goose, CF-BXR, however, was ideal for transporting wealthy clients to and from their country retreats. Many felt safer because it had two engines, although, as Tim Cole, a pilot who worked for Laurentian during the 1960s, points out, this feeling of security was largely an illusion. According to him, the two engines were really to help the Goose get into the air – not necessarily to keep it there if one of them failed! Nevertheless, 'BXR continued to be the aircraft of choice for these wealthy passengers and by 1961 Laurentian had amassed an impressive list

Jack Fleming refuelling Laurentian's Canuck CF-DQY at the company's dock on the Ottawa River in 1948, and at right, Betty Booth, who came to Laurentian to be checked out on floats, with unexpected consequences. (BB)

of clients. A *Canadian Flight* edition celebrating Laurentian's 25th anniversary mentioned just a few of the movie stars, corporate executives, and politicians who had taken a flight in 'BXR:

Miles Tramnel of NBC; W. Irving, past chairman of the Board of United States Steel; Tom Watson, chairman of IBM; Harley Earl, a former design Vice-President of General Motors; and movie stars Franchot Tone, Joan Crawford, and Hume Cronyn. Premier Duplessis of Quebec, the Chandlers of Scripps-Howard Newspapers, the Governors of the Hudson's Bay Company, and many others added their names to Laurentian's impressive passenger list.

Some of these individuals were regular customers, as John Bogie recalls. John, Barnet's nephew, had begun flying with Doug Pickering in 'BXR during his summers off from university starting in 1947. One of his favourite regulars during those summer seasons was Mrs. Berger. As John recalls,

Her husband had died during the war. Prior to the war they owned their own airplane – a Lockheed or something – and they had a big camp up 31 Mile Lake, just north of Ottawa, they used

to call Bergerville. They owned Kaywoodie Pipes and she had Milkmaid Cosmetics and Duragloss nail polish – that was their big income. Heck of a nice lady! She used to come out once a week to the Château Laurier in Ottawa to have her hair done– we'd fly her out. She spent practically the whole summer up there at Bergerville. She lived in the Waldorf Astoria Hotel in New York City, and had her chauffeur up there with her as well, of course, but she didn't want to drive down – she wanted to fly.

During those 200-mile round trips to her hairdresser, Mrs. Berger got to know John quite well and decided that the young pilot and her niece from Texas, "a nice, red-headed girl," would make a good couple.

Laurentian's Fleet Canuck: Love, beer and the occasional float check

While John and Mrs. Berger's niece did not end up together, in the summer of 1948 another of Laurentian's young pilots met the girl of his dreams in the cockpit of the company's newly-acquired Fleet Canuck, CF-DQY. That summer, Jack Fleming was flying for Laurentian to pay for his studies at Ottawa's Carleton University.

Fleming had joined the RCAF during the war and had received his commercial pilot's licence afterwards. On April 25, 1948, Laurentian's Buster Brown cleared Fleming on the Canuck and the latter spent the summer mostly checking out pilots for float operation in CF-DQY from Laurentian's floatplane base on the Ottawa River.

On August 8, 1948, Betty Booth arrived to get her float certification. The year before she had received her pilot's licence at a flying club in Vancouver, where she had attended the University of British Columbia, earning degrees in maths and physics. She had recently moved to Ottawa for a job in the physics division of the Canada Research Council (as the National Research Council of Canada was called at the time) and had asked around to find the best place to get checked out on floats. Everyone told her to go to Laurentian.

She wasn't looking for love when she went down to the floatplane base that day, but Betty and Jack hit it off immediately. Chatting in her Ottawa backyard in June of 2008, Betty recalled that summer 60 years earlier: "I remember Jack borrowed Paul Saunders' car to take me on a date to Hog's Back one time, and another time he flew me up to 31-Mile-Lake where all the cottages and fishing lodges were. We ended up getting married and later bought a Cessna 195 that Laurentian serviced for us … but he did all the flying! Don't marry a commercial pilot if you want to get your share of the flying!"

Jack Fleming's little brother, Peter, was 15 years old the summer of 1948 and spent a lot of time hanging around the Laurentian docks when Jack was working. He clearly remembers some of Laurentian's younger employees used the Fleet Canuck for other important errands as well:

It was the habit of the fellows down at the dock to take the outboard motor boat (used to move aircraft or access planes at anchor) to run over to the Quebec side to get a beer supply when it wasn't available in Ottawa.

Some of Laurentian's employees in the post-war years. From left: Pilot Paul Saunders, office manager J.P. McIntyre, pilot and operations manager Doug Pickering, Greenway (first name unknown), pilot Buster Brown and engineer George Beveridge. (DP)

Part-time Laurentian pilot John Bogie with his Beechraft Model 35 Bonanza, NC3412V, circa 1947 in New York State, where he was living at the time. (JB)

*It came to pass that one day when the need
arose the outboard motor wasn't working. An
engineer's inspection of DQY found a "missing"
bolt on the engine or prop. The "repair" of which
necessitated a test of the aircraft's serviceability …
all duly entered into the aircraft log.*

*The "serviceability test" was to taxi DQY
across the river and back, incidentally picking up
beer while on the Quebec side!"*

Flying for Laurentian in the summer of '48
was not just about wooing women and making
beer runs, though: those were just perks. As Jack
wrote in his logbook, in addition to checking
out pilots on floats he also made 62 flights north
of Ottawa to deliver passengers to the hunting
and fishing lodges in the Laurentians. Betty
remembers him telling her "about taking Franchot Tone, the movie actor, up there. He also
flew Ed Dodd, the man who created the comic
strip "Mark Trail," and Mr. Dodd gave him one
of the original drawings for the strip. He found
out that summer that a bush pilot's job was 90
percent stevedoring and 10 percent flying!"

Roughing it in comfort

Jack flew to many of the popular lakeside fishing
retreats north of Ottawa. These private fishing
and hunting clubs began appearing during the
late 1800s, and were created by wealthy sportsmen, often American, who came north to fish
Eastern Canada's salmon rivers.[27] As D. Leo
Dolan, chief of the federal Tourist Bureau in
Ottawa told *Canadian Aviation*'s editor in August 1945, this kind of sportsman did not want
to "rough it": "You have to provide him with
comfort, clean linen and good food."[28] Many of
the clubs went beyond Dolan's basic suggestions.
The Seigniory Club in Montebello, Quebec, for
instance, was established by American businessman, Harold M. Saddlemire, in 1930 on 65,000
acres of beautiful land comprising 70 lakes full
of fish and wooded areas where game could

be found.[29] The "club house" was the famed
Château Montebello, a huge log palace, but
members could also use "the network of trails"
fanning out from the château and spend the
night at more remote camps.[30]

Initially the Seigniory Club had 160 members, but by its peak in the mid-20th century,
more than 1,300 men had memberships. One
of these members in the 1940s was Laurentian's
president, Barnet Maclaren. As Dick Pickering
notes, this was a great source of clients for
Laurentian, which would fly American members
up to the club.[31] "One day," Dick recalls, "Dad
had the Goose there and was picking people up.
As he was waiting for passengers, water started
filling the hull of the plane. He had to cancel
the flight, and managed to get the plane off the
water and back to Uplands. It turned out the
maintenance guy had forgotten to put the drain
plug back in the hull!"

On a more successful flight, Doug Pickering
transported a wealthy group of passengers to the
Echo Beach Fishing Club, north of Buckingham,
Quebec. That day, he flew long-time members
Robert A. Laidlaw of Ontario's Long Point Company Club and Henry Borden, president of Bras-
can and Norwich Union Insurance (who was
also a director of IBM and Bell Canada).[32] Two
other well-connected men were aboard as well:
Charles L. Gundy, president of Wood Gundy
and Canron Ltd., and Dr. Hurst Barwa.[33] This
passenger list seems to fit with what John Bogie
remembers of the Echo Beach Club; according
to him, all the "famous Toronto businessmen
were members!"[34]

As Sylvain Gingras notes in his history
of hunting and fishing in Quebec, "When
well-heeled American executives went to their
Quebec fishing clubs, it was to escape to their
favourite corner of paradise and leave the stress
and strain of business far behind them."[35] During the day they would go out on the water with
their guides, hopefully bringing in a good day's

(Left) At Lac Désert, fishermen pose with Barnet Maclaren and Waco CF-BDO in 1947. (JB)

(Right) Another group of fishermen at Lac Désert in 1947. From left: guide Art Boisvert, unknown, Robert Bogie, unknown. (JB)

(Above) Doug Pickering at the Echo Beach Fishing Club, an exclusive retreat north of Buckingham, Quebec. With him are: Robert A. Laidlaw, Henry Borden, Charles L. Gundy and Dr. Hurst Barwa. The aircraft is likely the Goose. (Echo Beach Fishing Club Fonds, Library and Archives Canada e008443948)

(Above) Doug Pickering about to tie-up CF-BDO. (DP)

(Left) The Grumman Goose again with Barnet Maclaren, Mrs. Berger and Tom Watson Jr., president of IBM in 1952. (JB)

Sir Patrick Ashley-Cooper, Governor of the Hudson's Bay Company, and his wife before their departure from Montreal on July 28, 1949, for a 19-day tour of HBC posts in Quebec and Labrador in Laurentian's Grumman Goose. (DP)

From left: G. J. Lane, divisional manager, Quebec North Shore Paper Company; Sir Patrick Ashley-Cooper; L.J. Poitras, manager of the HBC store in Baie Comeau. (DP)

The Governor does a spot of fishing. Operations manager and pilot Doug Pickering, with H.I. Witney and Sir Patrick Ashley-Cooper at Lake Nipishish in Labrador. (DP)

catch or even a record-breaking fish. In the evenings, they could join a game of bridge, or simply sit around chatting while they smoked the best cigars and drank the best liquors.[36] During these fishing and hunting excursions and evening gatherings, businessmen could make new contacts, build relationships or learn valuable information. These clubs were also a way that executives could "reward steady customers."[37] For Laurentian, they were a great source of passengers throughout the post-war years.

On official HBC business

For 19 days during the summer of 1949, the wealthy sportsmen would have to do without Laurentian's Goose or its chief pilot, Doug Pickering. On July 28 Doug was charged with flying the Governor of the Hudson's Bay Company (HBC), Sir Patrick Ashley-Cooper, his wife and Mr. George Watson of the St. Lawrence Section of the HBC. The Governor and his wife had come over from England to visit the company's posts along the Gulf of St. Lawrence and Doug flew his passengers to 13 different posts in Quebec and Labrador, as well as the Grenfell Mission at Harrington Harbour. They also stopped at several industrial, power and mining developments in Quebec.

As the HBC's official magazine for its fur traders, the *Moccasin Telegraph*, reported: "A large part of the flight was over particularly rugged terrain and radio signals were frequently out. The flight, however, was capably handled by Mr. D. Pickering, Operations Manager of Laurentian Air Services, who personally piloted the aircraft. The trip terminated at Montreal on 16th August having been completed without undue incident."[38] What the HBC's magazine failed to mention was that Doug had also flown the Governor to Lake Nipishish and, looking very much a Canadian bushman in his plaid shirt, the Governor braved the bugs and caught some nice-looking fish.

A difference of opinion

With an experienced pilot like Doug Pickering in the cockpit, Laurentian's Grumman Goose did an admirable job getting in and out of tight bodies of water. So much so, that in December 1946 Doug entered into correspondence with A.T. Cowley, Director of Air Services, contesting a Department of Transport circular that restricted pilots from landing on Hydroplane Lake when carrying passengers.

Doug stated he had "never hesitated using this lake." A.T. Cowley, however, replied that one of the department's inspectors had made "a number of approaches to this lake" in a Beechcraft D17S, CF-DTF. He did not attempt to land, though, after considering the lake: "It is 1½ miles in its longest dimension, [and] high hills rise from the water's edge and surround the lake. These hills are estimated, and checked with the altimeter at 200 feet above the surface of the water. In my opinion it is not safe for seaplane or skiplane operations."[39]

Doug Pickering on Laurentian's Goose. In this view the bow hatch, essential when mooring at buoys, can be seen. (JB)

The aftermath when Fleet Canuck CF-DQG crashed into Laurentian's hangar. In the photo at left, part of the Canuck's wing lies in the foreground while the remainder of the aircraft rests against the wall behind. Laurentian's Grumman Goose sustained serious damage, including the dislodged and mangled left float clearly visible in both photos. (PG)

"The most I could do was hang on."

While the 19-day Governor's tour in the Goose had gone smoothly, a month later the "Queen of the Fleet" got into a major scrape.[40] Interestingly enough, it occurred when the Goose was where she should have been safest: Laurentian's hangar at Uplands. At about 11 a.m. on September 10, 1949, David Gordon Frosst arrived at Uplands from Cartierville, Quebec, in a two-seat Fleet Model 80 Canuck, CF-DQG. Frosst, a student pilot, was on a "solo cross-country from Cartierville to Kingston, Ont." according to the accident report. As Frosst wrote in his statement:

Prior to making my report at 1207 hours, I had been motioned to a tie-down position adjacent to the tarmac in front of the Laurentian Air Services hangar. Having completed my flight plan, I went to my ship with the intention of taxiing over to Atlas Aviation Limited on the other side of the field. At the time there were no mechanics to help me in sight and consequently I employed an emergency procedure for starting the ship on my own. I set the brakes, made sure the switches were "OFF", and primed the engine, standing on the right side of the machine. Then, reaching in through the door, I set the throttle and reached past it to turn the switches "ON". While doing this I must have knocked the

throttle ahead with my arm for when I swung the propeller the engine caught hold with considerable power.

I clutched the wing strut and made a dive for the door, but I was too late. The most I could do was hang on to the door and the wing strut. As long as I held on the ship continued to race around the grass in circles and I realized that, at least in this case, the plane couldn't do any damage. At length, however, before any help was available, I lost my grip and was thrown to the ground.

The plane then shot downwind, weathercocked, and headed for the open hangar. It entered the hangar at a good speed and hit a Grumman Goose Aircraft doing considerable damage. As soon as I got to the damaged plane, which was almost immediately, I turned the switches off.

As Frosst noted, the Goose sustained heavy damage in the crash. According to M.M. Fleming, a DOT inspector for Air Regulations, the Goose was missing its left wing and wing tip float as well as the right elevator. In addition, the "right front side hull station 16 forward and inside formers" were also shorn off and the nose piece was "badly damaged."[41]

What Frosst did not mention was that the Canuck also narrowly missed a Trans-Canada Air Lines DC-3 that was loading, caused superficial hull damage to another airplane in Laurentian's hangar – a Republic RC-3 Seabee,

CF-DKH, which belonged to pioneering woman aviator Margaret Carson – and dented a "Buick car bearing New York Licence Plates 7X17.79."[42] Laurentian's Cessna Crane, apparently, was spared. Total damage, according to an *Ottawa Citizen* article, was estimated at $4,000.[43]

After an investigation, Inspector Fleming concluded that "A combination of inexperience and poor aircraft maintenance" were the likely causes for the accident.[44] David Frosst himself, in a letter to the Department of Transport on October 2, 1949, admitted, "I realize now that my search for assistance was too brief, for as soon as I was in trouble a lot of attendants did show up."[45] Laurentian had to replace the Goose's wing and Hart Pickering remembers his father flying 'BXR to the Grumman plant in the United States for further repairs. The Queen was out of commission for several months – luckily by then it was the slow season for hunting and fishing.[46]

Tim Dubé uncovered the following story behind this photograph: On March 9, 1948, Custom Waco CF-BDO had taken off from Lac des Ecores near Mont Laurier, Quebec. At about 1300 hours, when the aircraft was near the end of its landing run on Carp Lake, the left ski struck a hidden boulder. The impact caused the left oleo leg to break off at the upper fitting, in turn allowing the aircraft to drop on to the left lower wing and nose, fracturing both lower wing spars and bending a blade of the propeller. The pilot, G.A. "Bus" Brown, and the three passengers were uninjured. The aircraft was repaired temporarily and ferried back to Ottawa March 18, 1948, by Doug Pickering. (PG)

Laurentian's Custom Cabin Waco, CF-BDO, taxiing on the Niagara River near Fort Erie, Ontario, and in flight over a snowy landscape in the post-war years. After operating 'BDO for 14 years, the company sold it in 1951 to Eldon B. McEachern, operating as Northland Lumber Company at Campbell's Bay, Quebec. The aircraft retained the registration CF-BDO until sold to Blount Sea Food Company, Warren, Rhode Island, in May 1953, when it was assigned the U.S. Registration N1130V. Although the Certificate of Airworthiness has been revoked, the Waco may still exist. (PG)

A FAVOURABLE TIME
FOR FLYING

Laurentian had done well in the early post-war years and at the beginning of the 1950s was poised for an exciting and profitable decade. Canadians were revelling in prosperity after lean times, and there was a general sense of optimism in the country. Increasing numbers of people on both sides of the border were engaging in air tourism and using Laurentian's flying services to reach popular fishing and hunting clubs in the Ottawa region.

While Ottawa was still the centre of Laurentian's charter operations, in 1952 the company decided to open a new seaplane base in Maniwaki, Quebec, to provide flying services to the growing numbers of sportsmen. This new base also helped Laurentian serve the local lumber companies better. To meet the demand, however, Laurentian required additional aircraft. After its success with its first two DHC-2 Beavers, it decided to acquire several more of that type, especially now that DHC had added passenger-friendly modifications such as a cabin heater and improved exhaust system.[1] This was important as the company was expanding its executive flying services and these discerning customers wanted to travel in comfort.

By 1953, some of Laurentian's pilots had left southern Ontario and Quebec to fly further afield. A few years earlier, Newfoundland had joined Confederation and this newest province's premier, the indefatigable Joey Smallwood, was busy extolling its natural riches both at home and overseas. What was then known only as Newfoundland – but actually included the lands and people of Labrador – had few roads or maps. Exploring this territory's economic potential efficiently required knowledgeable pilots and hardy bushplanes. During the 1950s, Laurentian was equal to this task and more.

Moving to Maniwaki

By the end of the 1940s, Laurentian had built up a solid business flying out of its bases in Ottawa and Sainte-Marguerite-du-Lac-Masson. Sportsmen were eager to get up to the fishing and hunting clubs north of Ottawa and there were large timber limits that needed constant aerial spotting. It seemed that one Quebec community was at the centre of all this flying activity: Maniwaki or Kitigan Zibi, as the local Anishnabeg call it. Jean-Guy Whiteduck grew up in Maniwaki and later worked as a pilot for Laurentian for several years before becoming chief of the community's band council. He remembers the company doing a lot of flying there when he was young: "Laurentian was based out of the lake at the community – Lac des Oblats – back in the 1940s. In 1950 they brought the Beaver and they were giving rides to passengers. I was five years old and I really, really wanted to go flying but my parents couldn't afford it." Nevertheless, the seeds had been sown for a future Laurentian pilot.

By May 1952, Laurentian had built up enough business out of Maniwaki that it decided

Three of Laurentian's Beavers at Maniwaki circa 1950. The company was one of the largest commercial operators of this type of aircraft by the early 1950s, with seven in its possession in 1953: CF-GIB, 'FHR, 'DJI, 'GCW, 'EYN, 'EYT and 'EYU. (JB)

to apply for a seaplane base at Lac des Oblats. As the company wrote in its application to the Air Transport Board, one of the main reasons it wanted a base there was that "Maniwaki is the main centre of a large lumbering operation." The application went on to list all the lumber companies in the area for which Laurentian had provided services: Canadian International Paper Co., E.B. Eddy Company, James Maclaren Co., Gillies Bros., as well as the Lower Ottawa River Forest Protective Association. In 1951, Laurentian reported to the board, it had logged 250 flying hours out of Maniwaki for these companies and it anticipated an average of 300 hours yearly in the foreseeable future. In addition, the company noted that it planned to tap into the summer tourist market there, as many tourists took the train to Maniwaki, which was a railway terminus, and from there chartered flights to fly-in fishing and hunting resorts.[2] In July 1952, Laurentian received approval for its Maniwaki base and started working from existing buildings until a new dock as well as storage and maintenance structures could be constructed.[3]

To accommodate the increased business at Maniwaki and its other bases, Laurentian acquired new aircraft and let go its outdated Wacos. In September of that year, the fleet for Maniwaki consisted of a Cessna 170A (CF-FPQ), the Goose (CF-BXR) and three Beavers (CF-FHR, 'GIB and 'GCW). These airplanes could not stay in Maniwaki full-time, though: to comply with Department of Transport regulations, Laurentian had to rotate the aircraft flown from Maniwaki frequently with those at Uplands to ensure all had regular access to proper maintenance facilities.[4]

Laurentian went through some personnel changes in the early 1950s. Doug Pickering was still general manager and chief pilot and Paul Saunders, who had joined Laurentian after flying Lancaster bombers for the RCAF during the Second World War, was still flying for the company. John Bogie, Barnet's nephew, had graduated from university and was now working for the company full time as a pilot, as was Douglas Fahlgren.[5]

Expanding into executive flying

By the time Laurentian opened its base at Maniwaki, de Havilland Canada had made the necessary modifications to the DHC-2 Beaver to make it more passenger-friendly. These upgrades explain why Laurentian continued to buy the aircraft even though the company was trying to expand its executive flying services. While many of Laurentian's wealthy clients still preferred the Grumman Goose because of its size, its two engines and the fact that it was amphibious, customers increasingly warmed to the Beavers. On August 4, 1951, for example, Doug Pickering flew W.A. Davidson and Joseph Messenger, the Singer Manufacturing Company's president and vice president, respectively. Once they had completed their inspection tour of Canadian operations, Doug picked them up at Montebello and flew them home to Basin Harbor on Lake Champlain, Vermont, in Laurentian's Beaver CF-FHR.[6]

John Bogie also flew a corporate bigwig in a Beaver in the early 1950s, although he did not realize who his passenger was immediately. According to John,

All these people had cottages on 31 Mile Lake and we flew them all. We often flew this Ottawa real estate agent – of Sherwood Real Estate – up to his cottage in the Beaver in the 1950s and one day we get a call from him that he was going to meet me at the seaplane base in Ottawa. So I'm there waiting and the agent comes with this fellow in a brown shirt and pants – like a working suit.

I said, "Have you ever flown up through here?"
He replied, "No, I never have."
I said, "OK, you sit up beside me here."

The real estate guy says, "Go up to Bergerville" because Mrs. Berger had died and the place was up for sale. And so we landed there and he got talking with this fellow. And he said, "Mr. Weston do you want to see the Earle's place" which was also up for sale – it was an island, Earle's Island.

And so we came back down to 31 Mile Lake to where the agent's cottage was and he had it set up for lunch and that's when I realized it was Garfield Weston – of Weston bread and biscuits!

But all the way up I was showing him this and that, pointing things out to him, and he really appreciated it. And I told him I'd gotten married that spring and he congratulated me. Two weeks later, a huge box of Weston cookies arrived at the house!

Later he moved to England and whenever I went there – his office was up on the top floor of Fortnum & Mason, the famous department store in London – I would call him and he'd say, "John, come on up!" and I'd go up and visit with him, and he'd be asking about Doug Pickering and all the fellows.

Paul Saunders became a pilot for Laurentian in 1946 after flying Lancaster bombers with the RCAF during the war, where he earned a Distinguished Flying Cross. Here he is pictured in Ottawa with a Bellanca 31-55 Senior Skyrocket, one of 20 that were made and the last series of bushplanes Bellanca produced. (Courtesy Dave Saunders)

John Bogie with one of Laurentian's early DHC-2 Beavers on skis, likely CF-GIB as it lacks the small, circular window that many call the porthole, added by DHC sometime after the 40th Beaver, circa 1949. (JB)

"We're having a hell of a time, aren't we kid?"

Like Weston in his working clothes, other millionaires did not necessarily look or act the part. One passenger in particular stands out in John's memory: Harry Falconer McLean. As John notes, "Harry McLean was a great Canadian character" who had a reputation as an eccentric. McLean worked his way up in the construction business during the first decades of the 20th century and created several major firms, including Dominion Construction Corporation. His companies undertook some of the most difficult projects in eastern North America, including railways, tunnels and hydroelectric dams.[7]

By the Second World War this "giant" with the "nose of a Roman senator" was giving "away with enormous wrinkled fists more money in personal charity than any Canadian before him."[8] During the war years, he went around as the mysterious "Mr. X" handing out money to servicemen at the Christie Street Hospital and Union Station in Ottawa. As a *Globe* article on November 9, 1943, reported, he had "tossed away $5,000 in $100 bills" that fall.[9] While his generosity was

legendary, sometimes his manner of giving was a little odd. On March 30, 1944, for example, he threw dollar bills and quarters from his hotel room window in Windsor, Ontario, to the street below, and when he ran out of cash he started writing cheques on "blank forms which the lavish-handed millionaire called for and signed after they had been made out to the Toronto branch of the Bank of Toronto."[10] It was estimated he wrote $45,000 worth of cheques that day, and those who had received them waited excitedly to see if the bank would honour them.

Don Taylor, a longtime employee at Toronto's Royal York Hotel, also remembered McLean's antics: "Guests were sitting around reading the morning paper.... McLean stared around at the loafers, and then he shouts, 'Get up off your asses, you lazy bums, and go to work!' ... All of a sudden, H.F. reaches into his pockets and begins throwing money down from the mezzanine. He hollered, 'Scramble for it, you boobs!' And they did, reaching and grabbing for the bills he pitched at them."[11]

Having been born and raised in the United States, John Bogie had only heard bits and pieces over the years about McLean but these were enough to make any pilot nervous. While he was running the airport at Saranac Lake in New York State, he heard stories from a captain for Colonial Airlines, Lou Orton, about flying the famous Harry McLean:

Lou told me that he used to fly Harry before the War in Harry's Waco.[12] Harry would get on a bender every now and again with scotch. And Lou said, when he did, he'd disappear.

Lou told me, "So I'm out in Chicago with him and when I went to bed I took his clothes into my room because he'd been drinking pretty heavily and I didn't want to lose him. I called his room the next morning when I hadn't heard from him and there was no answer, so I worried that maybe he'd died during the night. So I got the desk clerk to come up and open up the room – and no Harry! So I called Toronto and told them he was missing – he'd disappeared. I finally got a call around twelve, twelve-thirty from Minneapolis/St.Paul – and it's Harry McLean.

"Lou, what the hell are you doing down there?! Why don't you come up here and get me?"

And Lou said, "Harry, how'd you…?"

And Harry replied, "I'm up here and you come up and get me!"

So Harry told him where he was, and Lou got the airplane and flew up there. It turned out that Harry had had his bathrobe and his pyjamas and he'd shoved his airline credit card into the pocket of his bathrobe when Lou had taken his clothes. Then he'd gotten out of the hotel, asked to go to the airport, and the taxi had taken him. He'd wanted the first plane out and the first plane was going to Minneapolis/St. Paul, and that's where he'd ended up. And Lou said, "I had to go up and get him."

"Another time," Lou told me, "I flew him to New York to see the owner of The Globe and Mail – a friend of Harry's – who was going on a world cruise. Harry wanted to go and say goodbye to his buddy so, as Lou said, "I stayed at the hotel and I get this phone call and it's Harry and he said, 'Lou, meet me in San Francisco in twenty-three days.' So Harry bought a room on the ship to go with his buddy. Lou said, "I flew to San Francisco and Harry was waiting there ready to fly back to Merrickville."

After John moved north to Ottawa to be a pilot for Laurentian in 1950, he heard similar stories from Laurentian's dispatcher, Eddy McIntyre. As John recalls, Eddy told him about how Laurentian used to take care of McLean's Waco and how he would sometimes hire the company to fly it. By this time, McLean had given away most of his fortune and retired to his home in Merrickville, Ontario, outside Ottawa.

One day, Eddy called John Bogie to tell him that Harry McLean had contacted Laurentian. As John remembers:

Harry's Beaver was at de Havilland Canada getting some work done and he wanted to go to Chapleau, Ontario, north of Sudbury, to see his brother. So Eddy said, "Take the Beaver, go down to Merrickville and he'll meet you at the dock." And so I fly down to Merrickville and there's the dock and there's a guy sitting on it with the limousine and chauffeur up behind him. And he's in a tam-o'-shanter, and a bathrobe, with a fifth of scotch in his lap.

I get out of the airplane, tie it up and he yells at me, "Where the hell have you been, you damn pisspot?"

And so I said, "Are you the fellow that wants to go to Chapleau?"

"That's right!" So he gets in and he sits down beside me in his bathrobe with his fifth of scotch in his lap. His chauffeur throws the baggage in the back and we head off.

We're going up the Ottawa River and we go by the atomic energy plant on the road to North Bay – a restricted area. I swung around and Harry says, "What are you changing direction for?"

I said, 'That's Chalk River, you can't fly over."

Harry said, "Land there!"

And I said, "I can't!"

This went on for awhile. Finally he laughs and

Laurentian's dispatcher, Eddy McIntyre, waits outside the Uplands hangar for customers in his shirt and tie while fellow employee Stan White takes a break. (JB)

the next thing I know he says, "We're having a hell of a time, aren't we kid?" Then he kisses me in the ear so I gave him an elbow in the gut. And he sat back and he said, "We're having a party, kid!"

So we get up and we get half way to Sudbury and the weather goes down: fog and drizzle. I had to turn around and land at North Bay. And so I asked him, "Do you want to stay overnight here and go on tomorrow?"

And he said, "That'll be alright."

We get out of the airplane – of course he's in his pyjamas and it's about two in the afternoon. And we check in at the hotel. By this time Harry had drunk all his scotch and the chauffeur didn't put a spare bottle in because he knew he'd better not.

Harry gets on the phone in the hotel room and he keeps yelling out the window "Who cares!" – that was one of his favourite expressions. He gets a hold of an old railway guy in North Bay that he knew. It was a Sunday and he asked him if he had any liquor. And his friend said, "All I got is part of a bottle of rye."

And Harry said, "Well, that'll do. I'll send my pilot up to get it."

So I go out and get a taxi and go up to this poor guy's house and he was nervous as a deuce. He said, "Where's Harry? Where's Harry?"

And I said, "He stayed at the hotel."

"Oh, thank God," he said. "You know, my wife's not too well and you know how he is when he's drunk."

And I said, "I'm learning!" So I finally get the bottle and go back and Harry said, "Well, this isn't the best of stuff but I'll drink it anyhow."

In the meantime he's got those matches that'll light on anything and he's lighting them off the wall, leaving a big black streak. And he's still yelling out the window, "Who cares!" He decided he wanted to go chase the maids down the hall and I said, "No, no Harry."

So I struggled with him to keep him from getting out of the room. And he said, "God, kid, you're strong." It was all I could do to hold him.

Finally he says, "Let's get ourselves something to eat." And I said, "That's a good idea."

So we go downstairs and the manager of the hotel comes out and says, "You fellows have been in this hotel about two and a half hours and you've made more noise than anyone we've ever had. You're going to have to leave."

Harry says, "I've been kicked out of better hotels than this. I could buy this hotel if I wanted to." And so Harry went into the room and the manager was going to call the police.

Harry said, "OK, we'll get out of here. Kid, get our clothes." I was afraid of losing him, so when he went outside I dashed up to the room to get the bags.

When I came down he was out in the street talking to some kids. By this time he'd put on a pair of pants and a shirt. A taxi came along and the driver said, "Where do you want to go?" And Harry said he wanted to go to Merrickville. So I figured that was it, I'd be rid of him. But he insisted I come with him.

The driver said, "If I'm going to Merrickville I'm sure I can get a better car and you'd have a nicer ride."

And Harry said, "What's wrong? Why can't you go now? I want to get going!" It turned out the owner of the taxi company knew Harry and when we got back to the taxi place the owner came and chatted with Harry. He gave us a brand new car to drive down to Merrickville.

Harry gets in beside the driver and I'm in the back seat. We're going down the two-lane highway in North Bay, which wasn't too good in those days. And the driver would be doing about 40 or 50 mph and a car would come towards us and he'd slow up. And Harry would say, "'What are you slowing up for? What's the difference if you hit him at 30 or 70 – we're all going to be killed!'"

"But," he said, "Try to miss him!" And then Harry put his big foot on the driver's foot and shoved the accelerator right down to the floor. And the driver just hung on.

We got down the highway and Harry had to go

to the washroom. And so he told the driver to stop. He got out and opened up the trunk and reached in; he had a case of expensive cigars in his bag called Pandoras. He took a big handful of these – he must have had about eight of them – and he flung them along the side of the highway. "There," he said, "Some poor bugger comes along and if he wants to smoke he can have a smoke."

We got back in the car and we arrived in Merrickville at 1 a.m. He'd told the housekeeper we were coming and she had a nice ham and so the driver and I had a good meal. He was going around the house trying to find liquor but she'd hid it all. So there was Harry with a bottle of soda water, drinking straight soda water. Before we left he gave each of us a $100 tip and then the taxi driver went back to North Bay. He dropped me off at the seaplane base and I spent the night in the airplane. The next morning I flew back to Ottawa.

And that was my one and only experience with the famous Harry McLean.

While McLean had grown increasingly eccentric and his antics in later life at times over-shadowed his achievements, he was a generous philanthropist. Among other donations, he pro-vided the intial financing for Wilbur Frank's re-search into pressure suits for fighter pilots at the beginning of the Second World War. McLean's money allowed Frank to buy the materials for the first anti-G suit as well as a tailor to fashion it. He was also an aviation enthusiast, owning and piloting a Stinson Reliant, Waco and Beaver during his lifetime.

Harry McLean was not the only colour-ful passenger John Bogie flew in the early 1950s. During the fall of 1951, he went to fly a Laurentian Beaver chartered by Bill Hall of Hall's Air Service in Val d'Or, Quebec. One of his main jobs was to fly to Chibougamau, Quebec, "a bustling mining town with no roads or railroads." As he later wrote, this job was "an eye opener": "our loads were food, supplies,

diamond drills, liquor, beer, mine executives, miners, and 'ladies of the evening.'" During the winter months, he hauled furs for the fur buyers east of James Bay and Hudson Bay:

This area had no published maps so we made our own and used a sextant – that I had learned to use in the Navy – and a compass to locate the position

CANADIAN OWNERS AND PILOTS ASSOCIATION

John Bogie co-founds COPA in 1952

"In the fall of 1952, I was speaking with Margaret (Marg) Carson in the Ottawa Flying Club's lounge. Marg owned a Seabee at the time and said that what we needed in Canada was an association like the Aircraft Owners and Pilots Association (AOPA) in the United States. I had joined AOPA in 1945 and knew of the work that they were doing for private aviation, as general aviation was known then. We held a small meeting – that I chaired – in December and the group decided to hold an organizational meeting right after Christmas.

"We talked to many private pilots and aircraft owners in Ottawa, Montreal and Toronto, and they all supported us. One evening in January 1953, we held another meeting in the Château Laurier Hotel in Ottawa. Marg and I paid for the room, and about 60 pilots and aircraft owners showed up from these cities. Marg and I had invited Doc Hartranft, the president and one of the founders of the Aircraft Owners and Pilots Association in Washington, to attend and ex-plain how they got started and how they had helped the Australian AOPA and the AOPA of Hawaii to get started. We ended up choosing the Hawaiian format and called ourselves the 'AOPA of Canada' but later broke off, changing the name to 'The Canadian Own-ers and Pilots Association.'

"I was elected the first chairman and later president of COPA and Ernest G. Warren became vice-president. Marg, who set up an office in her heated garage off her Rockcliffe Park home, became the first secretary-treasurer."

This fine sequence of photos shows testing a canoe rack on one of the Beavers Laurentian bought in 1953 (the "x" on the tail indicates experimental work). Carrying an external load such as a canoe is considered a design change requiring formal approval because of possible effects on the aircraft's flying qualities. The shots also provide good views of the Beaver's wheel-skis. (JB)

of the Native camps. We found them by finding the smoke from the fires they always kept going in the tents. I would take a shot on the sun and mark my position so I could find them again. I made many trips hauling food in and furs out.

Laurentian continued to do a lot of flying for timber companies north of Ottawa, including "servicing fire towers, fire fighting, timber cruis-ing, etc.," for commercial firms and protective associations in the area.[13] One particularly active area at the time was Fort-Coulonge, Quebec, and, as operations manager Doug Pickering related to the Secretary of the Air Transport Board in a letter, Laurentian was often asked to "transport men, supplies and equipment" from that site.

"He won't kiss you in the ear, anyhow!"

Another service Laurentian provided for these companies – and one that Doug did not mention in his letter – was body transport. As John Bogie recalled in an interview, on two separate occasions he flew to a lake north of Fort-Coulonge to pick up the body of an E.B. Eddy cook who had died in the bush and needed to be flown out to Ottawa. The first time, John said, he

pulled into the dock and there were some logging people there. I got out and tied up the airplane and looked down and there's a guy down there looking up at me through six or eight feet of water. They'd stored him in the lake! So they fished him out and put him in his sleeping bag and put him in the back of the plane. It was in the summer – July. All our communication back then was through radio contact and sometimes the radio didn't work too good.

Bill Peppler: Surviving solo

In the early days of bush flying, pilots always carried a mechanic along for two reasons: the government required that all commercially licensed aircraft had to be inspected and signed off as being "airworthy" every 24 hours by an air engineer; and the air engineer could patch any holes or fix any mechanical problems that came up. I had my ratings both as a pilot and an air engineer and in the 1950s there weren't too many commercial air pilots with both qualifications. So I was one of the rare pilots who generally flew alone.

Bill Peppler, pilot for Spartan Air Services in the 1950s and longtime manager of the Canadian Owners and Pilots Association, in more recent years. (COPA)

This made some situations difficult, as one incident in November 1952 illustrates. It was getting cold enough that it was time to convert the DHC-2 Beaver I was flying back to skis for winter operations. Many companies hired Laurentian to do spring and fall changeovers on their aircraft, so as I approached the Ottawa River to make a landing at Laurentian's Rockcliffe seaplane base, I called the Ottawa Control Tower and asked them to phone over to Laurentian with a request for a power-boat to transport me from the Beaver (which would be moored to a buoy in the river) to shore.

Upon preparing to land, I noted that the temperature was below freezing and the wind was blowing from the west. This meant I'd be landing against the river current flow and into the wind. So prior to conducting my approach to land, I had to reach back into the cabin floor and grab a hold of about 30 feet of nylon rope which I coiled up and placed on my lap. I touched down on the water fine and proceeded to taxi up to the orange-coloured buoy which was swaying back and forth due to the current and wind. I taxied as slowly as I could into the wind and up-stream with the left pontoon just grazing the buoy. I went about 20 feet past it and then with one end of the rope clenched in my teeth – and when I thought I had the timing just right – I cut the engine and the prop stopped.

Then I quickly scrambled out of the cockpit onto the left float with the rope in my hand and mouth, and I tied the free end of the rope to the front strut as the aircraft began to move backward with the wind and current. The

He'd been there near a week, I guess. He was in better shape than had they left him out of the water.

This type of service was not that out of the ordinary for Laurentian, John recalls. A few years earlier, John and Doug Pickering went down to Atlantic City in the Goose. "The undertakers brought him out to the Goose," John remembers, "but we couldn't get the coffin in the airplane. We had a stretcher in the airplane, so we took the body out of the coffin, put it on the stretcher, covered it up and were on our way."[14] While transporting a body might not have been the most pleasant job, there was a positive angle, as one of John's colleagues reminded him: "He won't kiss you in the ear, anyhow!"

Prospectors and geologists

During the winter of 1951, John was flying quieter – but still live – passengers for Laurentian on a contract with Spartan Air Services. That winter Spartan was hired by U.S. Steel to survey the area north of Baie-Comeau, Quebec, for potential mineral deposits and brought Laurentian into the project. As John remembers, he was contracted out with one of the Beavers to "supply the stakers – the fellows who were staking the land" as well as those up on Mount Wright, near Labrador City. He and the other workers, he recalls, were "based at Manicouagan Lake, at the headwaters of the river north of Baie-Comeau. Now there's roads all up back there for the huge Hydro-Québec facility, but there was nothing back then."

top of the pontoon was a sheet of ice due to the spray of near-freezing water, so I had to wrap my right arm and hang on for dear life. As luck would have it, the Beaver brushed the buoy going backwards and I prepared to tie up. So with my right arm still hugging the strut and the end of the ¾" rope clenched in my teeth to keep my hands free, I reached my numb index finger out to grab the ring on top of the buoy as the aircraft drifted by. Then the fun really began.

Now my right arm was wrapped around the airplane strut and my left finger was attached to the buoy ring – in the middle of a fast-flowing river. I felt like my shoulders would pop out of their sockets, but I hung on. Then through sheer force of will I was actually able to pull the aircraft to the buoy and very quickly pushed the end of the rope through the eyelet on the buoy and looped it into a temporary knot – all using only one hand. Then I climbed back intro the cockpit and waited for the boat to arrive with several crew, who fastened additional lines from both pontoons to the buoy.

Bill Peppler performs the daily ritual of sweeping snow and ice off Beaver CF-DJI in November 1952. The photo was taken shortly before his adventure bringing this aircraft in to Laurentian's Ottawa base to change it from floats to skis. Peppler, a pilot for Spartan Air Services, was flying on a James Bay development contract, hauling fuel for Spartan's Bell 47G2 helicopters, which were hopping from lake to lake measuring water levels.

The Beaver's unusual paint scheme was done by Spartan employee Frank Pynn. Peppler believes the Beaver belonged to Spartan as both he and another Spartan pilot, Gord Townsend, flew it from 1951 onwards. He does note, however, that aviation companies leased each other aircraft from time to time. Available records state Laurentian purchased the Beaver in 1949 from DHC with the intention of operating it for Ottawa-based Atlas Aviation Ltd. It is possible Laurentian then leased it to Spartan in 1951. (COPA Archives)

Bill Peppler was a pilot and air mechanic for Spartan Air Services on that contract and became good friends with John. Bill remembers one time that winter John was flying three passengers from Manicouagan Lake down to Baie-Comeau: "They were forced down just before darkness to spend a very cold night in the cabin of their Beaver aircraft. It was only then that they discovered that there were four people but only three sleeping bags. So they had to somehow join these three sleeping bags together and then the four bodies more or less wrapped themselves up in it. All night they had to listen to passenger Bill deLaurier utter superlatives complaining how cold it was!"[15]

Another of John's trips from Manicouagan

Lake was more successful and certainly more profitable for the young pilot. At the end of January in 1953, John was flying two U.S. Steel employees – a geophysicist and a geologist – from the base up to Mount Wright. As he recalls, the conditions were less than ideal:

It was snowing and it was low. It's what they call snowfog: snow coming very light but you can see the sun up through. If the sun got obscured up in that country I'd head back or find a place to put in, but as long as you could see the sun you knew you were OK. So we're going up and I said, "Holy, geez – my compass is spinning!" Airplanes have got a gyrocompass – you have to set it because after a while the bearings will change. So you got to check

One of Laurentian's Beavers on Tessialuk Lake in northern Labrador, during the Brinco contract in 1953. (JB)

John Bogie with one of the company's Beavers on wheel-skis. (JB)

it against your magnetic compass and readjust it. And the magnetic compass was going around and around.

I can still hear the geophysicist shouting, "Where are we? Where are we?"' And I didn't know where we were, so I put a big circle on the blank map we were working on. There were no maps in those days and so we'd draw in big lakes and any special hills or mountains.

We went up to Mount Wright where the prospectors were staking and then the weather closed and we stayed with the prospectors in their tent. When the weather broke I could see these rolling hills roughly where I had put the circle on the map so I went and flew down there and eventually over one of the hills my compass started spinning again and the geologist had an earth's magnetic compass which has a big dip needle that gives you the earth's magnetic pull. His dip needle went down and pointed right to the hill.

U.S. Steel gave me $2,500 dollars as a finder's fee which I thought was pretty nice because my total salary for the year was $3,500. A good shot in

the arm! I'd probably have done better if I'd gone in there myself and staked the land, but I had witnesses in the plane![16]

After John's passengers returned to base, they used Spartan's survey aircraft, an Avro Anson Mark V, to get better readings. In the end, as John notes, U.S. Steel spent $365 million in the 1950s developing the site (later named Gagnonville) and in 1961 it was the "main ore deposit of Cartier Mining Corporation."[17]

In March of 1953, John Bogie went south to get married and Bill Peppler took over on the Beaver. Bill would fly into Baie-Comeau weekly on a mail run and to pick up supplies for the base. He still recalls how secretive he and others working on the contract had to be during these forays into town: "Mining explorers were always working hard to try and find out where a competitor was searching for an ore body. They would do almost anything to find out. During wintertime taxi trips from the airport into town, none of our crew was allowed to engage in conversation as the taxi driver had his ears wide open listening for clues that might reveal the whereabouts of our activities." As it turned out, even with these precautionary measures, some determined prospectors were able to learn of U.S. Steel's exploration activities. Bill remembers the Walsh brothers in particular, "a couple of bushmen," who "heard about the bush activity and set out by dog team and then canoe" up to the area where Spartan and Laurentian aircraft were involved in surveying work. Then, Bill figures, "because they could see or hear the bush flying aircraft they started staking claims in the hopes that my boss would want to buy their claims where they butted up against each other. This was all done on sheer speculation, without any proof of mineral deposits."

Brinco and black flies

The early 1950s was a time of speculation: Canada was in the midst of a mineral boom and everyone wanted a share.[18] Joey Smallwood, the premier of Newfoundland, decided mineral exploitation was the way to stimulate economic development in his province, provide jobs, and maybe show both the Canadian and British governments that "the Rock" was a hot commodity.

In August 1952, Smallwood went to London and stated at a press conference that he was there to offer the British people the "biggest real estate deal of the present century."[19] He met with Winston Churchill and other top British decision-makers to win backing to develop Newfoundland and its adjoining territory, Labrador. He told them about the "vast iron-ore discoveries in Labrador, which were then beginning to be developed" and "expressed his confidence that there were other virtually limitless mineral resources as yet undiscovered." But, he warned them, appealing to patriotic sentiments, it was "American capital" that was currently trying to open Labrador's mineral vaults.[20]

It was likely the economic facts rather than Smallwood's rhetoric that won him support, but either way, he found the financial and logistical backing he needed. The British Newfoundland Corporation was born, although as Philip Smith, who wrote a book on Brinco's creation and major projects, notes, it did not exactly have legal standing when it first began the process of staking its claims in Labrador.

In March 1953, Brinco hired Dr. A. Paul Beavan, "a consulting geologist who had worked all over Canada" as exploration manager. He was charged with the task of surveying Labrador to advise his bosses where to select Brinco's 50,000 square mile concession from

A group of workers on the Brinco contract in Labrador circa 1953. Laurentian pilots Paul Saunders (at left) and John Bogie (centre with red and black check shirt and yellow hat) flew Beavers CF-EYT and 'EYU. (JB)

Beaver CF-EYT in Labrador on a chilly July day. (JB)

the 70,000 or so square miles that were available to them.[21] As Smith wrote, "The sort of survey Beavan envisaged – indeed any sort of exploration in Labrador – could be accomplished only with aircraft, using skis in winter and floats in summer. Before he returned to Newfoundland, Dr. Beavan negotiated a three-year contract with Laurentian Air Services in Ottawa for the charter of two new de Havilland Beavers, at $88 an hour each for a minimum of eight hundred hours a year."[22]

It is not surprising Dr. Beavan chose Laurentian for the Brinco contract in 1953. Its pilots were used to flying over unmapped regions in uncertain weather conditions and its Beaver aircraft were perfectly suited to flying company personnel and all the equipment they would require in the bush. It appears from available correspondence, however, that another company already on Brinco's books might have suggested them for the job.

In 1952, Brinco had signed agreements with Spartan Air Services to provide helicopter services and Eastern Provincial Airways Ltd. to fly supplies, equipment and people. The records suggest that Spartan Air Services requested Laurentian specifically, much to the chagrin of Eastern Provincial Airways, who felt it had the matter in hand. To appease Eastern Provincial, Gérald Morisset, the Secretary of the Air Transport Board, wrote a letter to Doug Pickering letting him know that Laurentian would be restricted in its operations in Newfoundland and could only fly for Spartan "providing Eastern Provincial Airways Limited cannot, upon reasonable request, provide the service requested in any particular instance."[23]

It is not surprising Spartan recommended Laurentian for this work. After all, the two companies had close ties. Both were based at Ottawa and Laurentian had been overhauling Spartan's engines for years.[24] Furthermore, Barnet Maclaren was instrumental in helping John Roberts and Russ Hall get Spartan started as an aerial survey company in the late 1940s. According to Bill Peppler, who flew for Spartan at this time, Barnet provided some financial support. John Bogie recalls that Barnet also purchased Spartan's first helicopters. Initially, Barnet was considering purchasing them for Laurentian

A pair of Laurentian Beavers at a camp in Labrador in the early 1950s and, at right, another Labrador scene in June 1952. (JB)

for topographical work. As John notes, though, Barnet was "an old fixed-wing pilot" and after the demonstrator pilot flew him backwards across the hangar in an impromptu show of the machine's versatility, Barnet was so rattled that he told John Roberts, "I don't want any part of them if they can do a damned fool thing like that fellow just did!"[25] Roberts, on the other hand, was thrilled to have them for his aerial photography and surveying work.

In the end, all three firms collaborated on the Brinco contract, each bringing specific strengths and aircraft to the project. Spartan had two Bell 47 helicopters and an Anson Mark

Members of the Newfoundland topographical survey take a break after climbing Gros Morne in 1952. (JB)

Mercy flight

During the three-year Brinco contract, John Bogie and Paul Saunders had the chance to fly over parts of Labrador and Newfoundland that few other "Mainlanders" had seen and were often only accessible by air. "Now you can drive to Goose Bay," John notes, "but back in the 1950s the only transportation was by plane or dogsled."

John still gets anxious thinking of the snarling sled dogs in summer at the native community near the base: "We were way up the Lab coast in a little town. In those days there were no skidoos so the native people had dogs for sleds. In the summertime they'd chain them and throw the odd fish to them. You wouldn't dare go near them!" On one occasion a little girl strayed too close and was viciously attacked. Luckily for her, Laurentian's pilots were on hand with one of the Beavers: "This was late in the afternoon. So Paul and I flew down to Goose Bay and arrived about 10:30 at night. We landed at the harbour there and got the child over to the ambulance – they knew we were coming. Luckily the little girl survived, but she was really chewed up."

V survey aircraft and Eastern Provincial Airways transported fuel in its Canso for Laurentian. As John Bogie recollects, the pilot would load "empty drums in the cabin" and then "fill one wing with our fuel. Then they'd fill the drums, throw them in the water, and float them to shore, where we'd pile them up." Laurentian supplied two Beavers – CF-EYT and CF-EYU – which the company bought new from de Havilland Canada. Laurentian also provided its own pilots. As John recalls, initially he was not supposed to fly on the Brinco contract, but the first pilot Laurentian hired to work with Paul Saunders had a bit of trouble: "He was supposed to be an experienced pilot but he landed a Beaver too close to shore and ended up on the beach – knocked the floats off from under it. It was salvageable but they had to bring in new parts and everything. That's when Laurentian bought a third Beaver [CF-EYN] for the Brinco contract. I flew it down and spent the rest of the summer flying it."

As in the U.S. Steel contract, John and Paul were mostly flying geologists that year. Because of the mineral boom across Canada, finding geologists willing to work on the Brinco survey was apparently tough going.[26] By April 1953, though, Beavan had two parties in the field – one in Newfoundland and one in Labrador at Northwest River, near Goose Bay. The parties did most of their work during the following three summers, but an advance party was sent in February 1954 to gather information so that "the summer parties could concentrate their work on the critical lower areas." As Philip Smith notes in his book, "They would fly in to the [Churchill] falls each day in ski-equipped Beavers, two engineers and a guide to each plane…. At all times the Beavers carried emergency rations and camping equipment; and whenever the men were left on the ground, even for only a few hours, the vagaries of the Labrador weather were respected and they were equipped with enough supplies to make them self-sustaining for several days."[27]

While Labrador winters are harsh, the summers could be equally torturous – especially to newcomers. John and Paul had been living and flying in the back country for years and knew what to expect. As John recalled during an interview:

We would dress for bugs up there. The mosquitoes and black flies could be pretty bad. The poor Englishmen – Brinco had all their geologists from the London School of Mines in England. They came to Canada and landed in Goose Bay, and we took them to the bush. That was the only part

Wintry Labrador scenes from Brinco work in the mid-1950s. (Left) A Laurentian Beaver, tied down in case of high winds. Tree boughs outline the make-shift landing strip. (Below) A Laurentian Beaver, its engine protected by an engine tent and heater, and a Spartan Air Services Avro Anson Mark V. (JB)

of Canada they ever saw. And of course, in the bush they were eaten by the flies – they didn't have proper fly dope or anything. We had to get it for them. I remember two of them said they'd never come to Canada again. "It's a terrible country," they said. "Terrible country."

They may have endured tough conditions, but the geologists' work was not fruitless. According to Philip Smith, during the summer of 1953 "the ten Brinco men exploring for minerals in Labrador had reconnoitred about 52,000 square miles. They had found indications of iron ore, ilmenite (titanium), chromium, nickel and cobalt."[28] During the course of their surveying, they also discovered that Labrador's Churchill

Falls held tremendous potential for hydroelectric projects, and within a decade Brinco would discover that hydroelectric power could prove even more profitable than minerals.

Through Barnet Maclaren's well-planned expansion Laurentian was able to participate in Canada's mineral boom and share in the country's post-war prosperity. Life was good at Laurentian: the company had a growing clientele, a new base in Maniwaki and a reputation among mineral exploration companies. Looking at the flying picture in 1955 it seemed as if this good fortune would last forever. Unfortunately for Laurentian and other Canadian aviation companies, a slowdown was on the way.

LOSING ALTITUDE

5

The early 1950s was an exciting era for Laurentian and other Canadian aviation companies. The mineral boom meant profit, expansion and, for bush pilots, adventures in territories like Newfoundland and Labrador. In January of 1956, *Canadian Aviation* magazine asked leaders in the aviation field to predict how business would fare in the coming year. F. H. "Tom" Wheeler, the president of Wheeler Airlines, wrote: "1955 proved to be our busiest year, and, from present indications, 1956 could well exceed those operations."[1] In his opinion, the outlook for charter work "lends much encouragement" and forestry "looms large on our program." Like Laurentian, Wheeler Airlines had a range of aircraft types which could operate on skis, floats and wheels and its president felt confident that "with the pace of northern development steadily increasing" there would be many opportunities for bush operators.

In 1956, Barnet Maclaren was feeling pretty confident about his company's future as well. While Laurentian was wrapping up the Brinco contract it had a solid business out of Ottawa and Maniwaki flying for forestry companies as well as for sportsmen and tourists. Although John Bogie left the company to fly for mining magnate M.J. Boylen that year, Laurentian still had a top-notch roster of pilots and was hiring more to fly its ever-increasing fleet of airplanes.

By the next year, though, John Roberts,

president of Spartan Air Services, was already talking about "a leveling off in the Canadian air transport industry"[2] and within a few years Laurentian and other Canadian aviation companies were suffering from the economic slowdown after these boom times. During the post-war excitement a number of new companies had begun operations while those already in existence had acquired more aircraft and hired personnel to meet the demand. As this demand began to stagnate, however, the increased competition and overhead spelled harder times for many. In *Canadian Aviation's* May 1959 issue its editors discussed the Air Transport Board decision to manage competition "where it will result in financial deterioration of the established carrier to a point requiring subsidy" and cited statistics from the previous year indicating that Canada's "industry operating income" was "a long way off the totals" from the height of the boom.[3]

Barnet Maclaren may have influenced the board's focus on overlapping services. In 1958 he submitted testimonials, reports, maps and letters explaining how his company, which had been in existence for 20 years, was being choked by new competition. This correspondence was largely intended to block Bertrand Airways' proposed base at Fort-Coulonge, Quebec, but it is apparent that this was simply the tipping point for Barnet; if he did not start pushing back against encroaching firms, Laurentian, already operating at a deficit, would have to cut personnel, sell off airplanes, reduce services, or possibly even shut down operations entirely.

John Gill joins Laurentian

While in Newfoundland during the Brinco contract, John Bogie had flown M.J. Boylen and his partners in Laurentian's Goose, CF-BXR. After Boylen bought a Goose of his own, CF-IFN, he hired John to be his executive pilot. Before he left Laurentian and Ottawa in 1956, though, John had perhaps inadvertently encouraged a teenage boy in his aviation dreams by letting him come along for rides in Laurentian's Beavers when he ferried customers to cottages and camps. Little did he know, but that young man, John Gill, would begin flying for Laurentian during his absence.

John Gill had grown up around some of Canada's aviation pioneers and, as he wrote in an unpublished autobiography in 1997, "aviation was always discussed around me." Consider-

ing how close-knit the aviation community in Ottawa was during the 1930s and 1940s, it is not surprising that his parents were also friends with Barnet Maclaren.[4] Perhaps this is why, by the time he was a teenager, "one of my favourite haunts was the Ottawa New Edinburgh Canoe Club" where Laurentian anchored its airplanes. John Bogie and the other Laurentian pilots liked this young man who would help "Americans carry their luggage down the hill" in the hopes of getting a free airplane ride.

According to Gill, his only ambition was that "by hook or by crook, I would someday fly for that company." In 1956 he achieved that dream. He had worked for nine months with Pulsifer Bros. in Nova Scotia in 1955 and had logged about 600 flying hours when he approached Laurentian for a job. In the spring of 1956, when Gill was 23 years old, Doug Pickering checked him out on Laurentian's Cessna 180, CF-HPQ. As Gill remembers, "I was safe enough handling their old Cessna 180, even though it took me

Mining magnate M.J. Boylen circa 1960, and (below) his Grumman Goose, CF-IFN, flanked by one of Wheeler Airlines' Curtiss C-46s on the left and Trans-Air United's Canso on the right in Great Whale, Quebec. Boylen bought the Goose in 1955 and two former Laurentian pilots flew it for him: John Bogie from 1956-61 and Reg Phillips from 1966-72. Phillips said when it was time to leave 'IFN he felt "sort of like a cowboy saying goodbye to his own horse." John Gill also worked for Boylen for several months during the summer of 1957, flying his Beaver, CF-JKH. (JB)

John Gill joined Laurentian as a pilot in 1956, flying for the company full-time for a year and then part-time until the 1990s. Here he describes the yearly changeover to floats:

"The first picture shows Laurentian's fleet in spring 1956, having just been serviced in the hangars at Uplands, changed over to floats and then flown over to the water base near Rockcliffe Airport. From there they would fly out all over Canada to various job sites for the summer's work.

"Changing to floats in itself was quite a tricky job. The planes newly mounted on floats were put on four-wheel dollies at the airport, and you had to be careful not to lift off, or even try to, until you had flying speed, as the dollies would stop very quickly and leave you suspended in mid-air. I apparently got the job after one of the pilots lifted off too soon and

landed the floats on dry pavement.

"In the fall, it was again quite exciting as we tried to wait until the first snow fell, and then we would fly the planes up from the river to the airport and land them with their floats on the grass. It was a very sudden stop but it seemed to work okay.

"The second photo is of me with Beaver CF-JKH in 1957 in Newfoundland, where I was flying for M.J. Boylen's mining enterprises in Baie Verte and on the Burin Peninsula."

After Laurentian closed down, John Gill went into aerobatic competitions and instruction for ten years. The photo at left shows him near Gatineau in his Zenair CH-180 aerobatic aircraft. (JG)

ages to get it off the water. But despite the slow take-off, I was hired by Laurentian, at the excellent salary of $400 per month, whether I was flying or not."

It did not take long for Laurentian to put Gill to work, sending him to fly for the Ottawa River Forest Protective Association (ORFPA), "a group formed by various timber companies to protect against forest fires." The ORFPA territory covered approximately 100 square miles stretching from the Gatineau River in the east to the Ottawa River in the west and south and north almost to Val-d'Or. His first job was to "take the technician and fly him to all the inaccessible places and help him install radios in the fire towers – a three-day job only, as long as I helped by carrying the radios up the long bug-swarmed trails. It was good practice though, and within a couple of days I was using up much less lake during landings and take-offs." While the two men were installing the radios, "severe electrical storms started several large fires that covered almost a quarter of our total area," helping to underline the importance of both his current task and Laurentian's fire-fighting work.

"The three-day job of installing radios in fire towers turned into 32 days" of work, Gill remembers wryly. During that month of flying charter for ORFPA in the Cessna 180, he experienced the full range of Laurentian's work for lumber companies. While this had consisted mostly of flying aerial fire patrols and shuttling executives to back-country locations in the past, Gill notes in his autobiography that Laurentian's pilots were increasingly charged with flying in fire-fighters (both professional and volunteer) along with all their equipment.[5] He was still flying a near-daily patrol of the whole area, but if "smoke was reported, or I spotted a fire, I would head for the nearest supply camp and fly a crew – complete with pumps, shovels and food – to the lake nearest the fire. Always remembering, of course, to report where they were and when they were expecting to be picked up. It wouldn't have been the first time people were forgotten in the woods. And of course I always carried full emergency equipment in the back, including a sleeping bag, as I often stayed in different places at night." In those days, he remembers,

All the pilots were deputy wardens for Quebec. We could fly into any camp (or cottage) and demand the occupants leave what they were doing and come and fight fires. I never had to do that though because, in practice, word spread quickly and we picked up most of the men where they gathered to wait for us – in a tavern in Fort-Coulonge, about 75 miles northwest of Ottawa.

A Laurentian Beaver demonstrates its water-bombing abilities circa 1956. It was equipped with two 45-gallon tip-over water-tanks, which, as pilot Tim Cole notes, was fairly advanced for an early system but not very effective as you had to be flying very low. He only used them once in the 1970s to test the system, and found they really only worked on small spot fires or for lightning strikes. (JB)

Longtime Laurentian customer and friend Barb Stayman, with one of the company's Cessna 180s, CF-HPQ, on wheel-skis circa 1959. Laurentian purchased this aircraft in 1955 and operated it for many years. The Confederation College of Applied Arts and Technology in Thunder Bay acquired it in 1986 for its aviation flight management programme and owned it until 2004. (DP)

We would land and taxi up the river for half a mile and tie up right outside the pub. Within only a few days we had flown in hundreds of men – as many as eleven in a Beaver and eight in a Cessna. You would certainly not be allowed to do that these days, as the men were often fairly hung-over – if not still drunk – and they just sat on their loose haversacks on the floor. No seat belts or anything like that.

My main problem was trying to keep them from getting sick in the plane, and I sometimes had to land so they could get out onto the floats and throw up. I almost got a standing ovation once when I deftly grabbed a fedora off a guy behind me, and managed to get it under the face of the man beside me, just in time! They all thought it was a great joke – even the owner of the hat. Another lad on the same day seemed totally out of place so I asked him why he was up fighting fires. He replied that he had been a waiter at the Ritz-Carlton hotel in Montreal up until the day

before. He had accidentally spilled a tray-load of drinks all over the owner of the hotel and had been promptly fired.[6]

Doing this work allowed Gill to really perfect his take-offs and landings in small back-country lakes. As he says, "I found myself going into smaller and smaller lakes to unload supplies, and taking off with only ten or fifteen feet beneath me to spare became routine. Once I landed on a very small river, gave the fire ranger his new supply of food, and took off while winding down the stream bed. It was really fairly hairy and I had just resolved never to go into that particular spot again, when I noticed I had forgotten my sunglasses in his hut. So I had to go back for them, and go through the whole process all over again."

When Gill got a weekend off to go to a wedding in Ottawa, Laurentian's chief pilot, Paul Saunders, took over his duties. "Upon my return," Gill notes, "he gave me a list of three places I was *never* to go into again. He said he'd damn near killed himself a couple of times, flying what I, by then, considered my customary routes." As the chief pilot knew, though, if something went wrong in some of those tight squeezes, Gill and the aircraft would be goners. The summer before on the same ORFPA contract, Laurentian pilot Jack Fleming was flying the Cessna 180 when a piston broke on take-off. As his wife Betty noted during an interview, it was fortunate "the take-off was from the Ottawa River and he was able to land straight ahead. He would never have survived if it had broken on either the previous or following take-off, as he was flying in and out of a small tree-rimmed lake."[7]

Gill also learned the importance of "getting to your destination before dark." As he notes in his autobiography:

It's very difficult to land in a place with no lights and no runway in the middle of the night. You'd find yourself trying to put the plane down on a pitch black lake, rimmed by trees, and dotted with rocks and islands and other invisible hazards. The only instruments you could use were an artificial compass that ran off a gyro, so it didn't jiggle all over the place, which helped you keep a straight heading. If you knew you needed to head 30 degrees to make a landing, and you were landing in fog or dark or anything else like that, the only way to keep yourself straight was off your gyro compass. The only other instrument that might help

in landing at night on a dark lake was the vertical speed indicator, which tells you how fast you are descending. The vertical speed indicator was also handy for other tricky landings.

About a year into his work for Laurentian, he forgot that daylight savings time had ended the previous night and found himself trying to land the Beaver on Mont-Laurier lake at twilight. He was flying several doctors from the Department of Health and Welfare back to Ottawa after a visit to the Grenville Mission. They left a little later than expected and halfway into the 200-mile trip he made the call to land at Mont-Laurier instead of chancing a night landing on the log-packed Ottawa River. As he said, it worked out, because they "pulled up to shore near a road, found a house with a phone, and called a taxi which drove the doctors the 100 miles back to Ottawa that night. Another lesson well learned!"

There were also times when he had some daylight but conditions made bush flying difficult. Fog was an obvious hazard: "One evening I was closing up a fire camp, had already taken out all the equipment, and left the two men there for the last trip. I was held up, but had promised to go back and get them before dark. By the time I picked them up it was after sunset, a cool breeze had come in, and when we got to our destination at Maclaren Depot, there was only enough light to see that 20 feet of fog had hidden the whole lake. Luckily, the fog was the exact shape

From left: Engineer Bill Dennis, Doug Pickering, Laurentian director and attorney Gordon Maclaren, and Barnet Maclaren. (DP)

Goose CF-BXR at Quebec's Lac Désert Fish and Game Club in the 1950s. (JB)

of the lake, so with only one island to avoid, I had a strip about 150 feet wide in which to land." While he managed to land safely, he notes, "It did take quite a while to find the dock though!"

Gill also describes a condition he encountered called "glassy water," where "all you can see is the reflection of the sky. Many aircraft still crash because of this phenomenon." As he notes, to land safely when you have no idea how high off the land or water you are is tricky: "The only way to land successfully under 'glassy water' conditions is to lower about 20 degrees of wing flap, put the aircraft into a slightly nose-up attitude, and ease off on the throttle enough so that by watching your vertical speed indicator, you can lower the plane at the rate of about 200 feet per minute. At 200 feet per minute, you can touch down quite safely, even if you don't know when you're going to land. Once you feel the touch down, then you pull off power." He used the same technique to land in foggy conditions.

Aside from the sometimes harrowing flying conditions, he faced other dangers while flying for Laurentian in the 1950s. Chief among these was apparently the food, which was unappetizing and did not always make for balanced eating. At the main camp, Osborne Depot, which was about 40 miles north of Fort-Coulonge, he says,

the pilots were up each morning at 4 o'clock for a rotten breakfast consisting of dried mash potatoes and pork cooked in fat. The fat to soak the potatoes a bit and give the men lots of grease. After a couple of days of that, I always made sure to "liberate" cans of fruit from the fire fighters' supplies, and every now and then I'd land and be served a freshly caught pike or lake trout cooked over an open fire. By the time we got our logbooks and way-bills up to date it was usually past midnight, and the pilots' only refreshment was on those occasions I happened to get to Rapides-des-Joachims and pick up a case of beer.

One sunny fall day in 1955, he was enjoying a homemade sandwich on the beach at Lac Dumoine when he encountered another hazard of bush-flying: the local wildlife. As he writes in his autobiography,

I had just finished lunch when I looked up and saw a moose a few hundred yards away, trotting towards me. Well, a male moose at any time of the year is something to avoid, but in the fall, presume him to be deadly. I ran for the floats, jumped in the door, primed and started the engine, and pulled out into the lake with a great roar just as he went galloping past the tail, hell-bent on rape as far as I could tell! The plane didn't even look like a moose, but he sure as hell would have made an awful mess of it and perhaps of me at the same time!

"In retrospect," Gill remembers, "the fire fighting was very interesting – taking supplies into the fire camps, and evacuating the men and equipment if the going got too hot. Or dropping 45 gallon fuel drums off the floats into ponds too small to land on – fuel needed mostly for the fire pumps." It was also during the fire-fighting season that the DHC-2 Beaver became his favourite aircraft, and it remains so to this day. As he writes, "Everything imaginable was carried on the floats – mostly boats and canoes, but even sides to construct fire observation tower huts. I had to get smart one day and try to put four sides of a hut on the Beaver instead of two, and it was only because it was a magnificent machine with a hell of an engine that I even got the plane into the air enough so that I could turn around and land safely to unload it."

John Gill would get the chance to fly one of Laurentian's Beavers quite a bit that winter, once the forest fire season was done and Laurentian refocused on providing services to mining companies. He was sent to Maniwaki after freeze-up with an engineer and another Laurentian pilot, Pierre (Pete) Arpin. The two were flying one of Laurentian's Beavers, "supplying mining camps with food and gas and men." According to Gill, Arpin taught him some very valuable lessons about bush flying in the winter. The

Pilot Pierre (Pete) Arpin, who was always happy to teach Laurentian's new pilots about bush flying, in later years. (IB)

first day, they marked "a runway on the snow with little pine trees lined up on each side. Pete would then make me practise taxiing in and out of the pine trees, and taxiing on skis can be even harder than on the water." Arpin also taught his young co-worker about protecting aircraft during the cold months and making sure they could be flown safely. As Gill notes,

Only an eighth of an inch of frost on a wing can destroy the air flow enough that all "lift" is lost, and any attempt at flight ends in disaster. So in the morning there was the struggle with the wing covers, and also to fire up the Herman-Nelson heater to blow hot air onto the engine. If it was going to be a very cold night, even having the heater in the morning would not be good enough. We would have to remove the battery into our hut, to give it a little extra protection. We also diluted the engine oil with gasoline to make it thinner. This protects the engine on cold morning starts. But even after running for five minutes the engine would not be up to proper operating temperature so take-off was a delicate affair. Once in the air the engine warmed quickly, and the gas would vaporise off from the oil and all would be normal.

Gill did appreciate some things about the winter season. For one, there were no bugs. "There were times during the spring," he writes, "when we almost made ourselves sick by having to spray bug-juice throughout the cockpit. And we would have to scrape the inside of the windshield to clear a hole big enough to see out of for take-off. Once in the air we could open the window and most of them would be blown out." The colder, denser air of winter, he notes, also "provides greater lift" which could make flying easier.

Many of the things Arpin taught him applied year-round. When they were up flying in the Beaver, for example, Arpin would make him "keep one finger on the map all the way. Within a few days he was making me call out the next landmark I was looking for during the flight – with no map allowed. Every now and then we would find ourselves pushing weather, or daylight, or both, and it was vital that we could find our way almost blindfolded."

While flying for Laurentian Gill also picked up another year-round skill that proved very useful for a bush pilot: scuba diving. As he recalls, this came about by accident when one day he was "flying a fishing party into a lake" in the Beaver and he "dropped the pilot's door into the lake and had to fly home without it." It was certainly useful that the doors could be removed "to facilitate loading and unloading" but in this case, it worked a little too well and Laurentian charged him "$400 – a month's pay – to replace it." Not wanting to lose this large sum of money, Gill went in search of a diver who could retrieve it. While this diver spent half an hour underwater looking, he said the "visibility was impossible and we should give up." Gill was now out $400.

"A few months later," Gill remembers,

another pilot did the same thing. Me, knowing everything, said I could find the door and borrowed the equipment of the diver who had helped me out. We were both pretty stupid – me for borrowing it, and he for lending it – I didn't have the first clue about how to scuba dive. But what the hell. I got up to the lake, donned the equipment and dove in. Luckily I was able to find the door, but came up about 30 yards from the plane, completely out of air. Too stupid to think of turning on my back, I struggled a lot, and feel that I only just made it back to the aircraft alive. Laurentian thanked me, and asked me if they owed me anything for the door. Of course I answered $400, which – I'm happy to say – they paid.

Deciding it would be more efficient – and much safer – to learn the proper techniques involved in scuba diving, Gill took some courses and received his certification. Laurentian then used him to check its concrete anchors in the Ottawa River and he later dived for the Ottawa police looking for drowning victims.

In 1957, Gill was "sort of fired" by Paul Saunders, Laurentian's chief pilot. According to Gill, the owner of the hotel in Rapides-des-Joachims wanted her son-in-law to be rehired for the summer season and put the pressure on Saunders. With a remarkably generous spirit, Gill showed no hard feelings: "This didn't worry me a great deal as I was unable to get a Class 1 medical rating because I wore glasses. In those days the scheduled airlines did not hire pilots who wore glasses, as it was considered unseemly for a pilot wearing glasses to walk up the aisle to the cockpit. There were also so many pilots back from the Korean War who didn't need glasses, they had no need to hire pilots who *did* wear glasses. I really didn't want to spend the rest of my life in the bush, and decided that, apparently, full-time flying was not meant to be for me." He would continue to fly for Laurentian on and off for 40 years, though, and spent many hours flying as a jump-plane pilot and performing aerobatics.

The Bertrand Airways affair

By 1957, the year John Gill was "released" from Laurentian, Barnet Maclaren was becoming increasingly frustrated with the aviation picture in Canada and worried about his company's ability to withstand the changes. Twenty years earlier when he had launched one of Canada's first commercial aviation companies, there had been little competition (other than from the RCAF on occasion). Just a decade before – as J.L.G. Morisset of the Air Transport Board noted in a speech on November 4, 1957 – the "main problem" was "to find enough carriers and sufficient equipment to provide the proposed services."[8]

Laurentian's Beaver CF-EYT at the company's hangar at Uplands circa 1973 with its new paint job before being delivered to Ace Service Inc. Air Kipawa, Anaconda American Brass, and Geoterrex all operated EYT before it was written off in 1981 and disappeared from the register in 1982. (JB)

Now, in addition to "the many new forest roads being built" (which reduced the amount of air services needed), Morisset observed that "the crowding process becomes even more apparent" and an "increasing number of complaints [were] received by the board during the last few months. It has been said by a few that the industry is over-equipped. I would prefer to say that due to the termination of the defence construction program and a slower economic tempo we are going through a period of readjustment."

Morisset's careful rhetoric did nothing to comfort Barnet, who was battling overcrowding first-hand at his Maniwaki base. Laurentian had established Maniwaki as a protected seaplane base in 1952. By December 1957, though, Joseph Bertrand of Bertrand Airways had applied for a licence at Fort-Coulonge, only 30 to 35 miles from Laurentian's bases, and a mere 11 miles from another commercial air service in Pembroke, Ontario. Apparently nothing was heard of the application for "nearly one year" and Barnet "considered the application had been refused or

withdrawn." That was not the case, however: in November 1958, Barnet "ascertained that Mr. Bertrand's application was being pressed again. It is now going to be heard and we understand it is being supported by political friends."

Barnet immediately objected to this application and set about filing reports with the Air Transport Board, "giving an analysis on all the flying done in the general area of the Upper Ottawa and the Laurentians by his company, for the period 1953-57 inclusive." He also sent "testimonial letters from some of the lumbering and power companies and other associations that have used Laurentian's services" and who "objected to any new licence that might curtail such possible service" in the future.

From the evidence, it looks as though Joseph Bertrand's application was simply the last straw for Barnet. As he wrote to the Air Transport Board, in the past he had not "objected very vigorously" to the "other licensed air bases, either protected or unprotected, [which] have been established in the very near vicinity" and had even overlapped Laurentian's work out of Ottawa and Maniwaki. Nevertheless, these other companies had "cut deeply into the business established and built up by Laurentian Air Services" in the region. To illustrate his point, Barnet attached a map showing all the protected and unprotected air bases in eastern Ontario and western Quebec, as well as all of Laurentian's fuel caches in this part of Quebec. From this point forward, he argued, the Air Transport Board should deny new applications for the survival of existing businesses like Laurentian and "the good of aviation in general."

Barnet was especially worried since during the early 1950s he had increased the number of aircraft and personnel to meet demand. As he told the board, "additional fixed wing aircraft have been purchased to suit all feasible needs of transportation in the district so we can see no reason for duplicating same when there already is a surplus of aeroplanes licensed in the district, on wheels, skis and floats." In his opinion, Laurentian's seven Beavers, Cessna 180 and Grumman Goose were more than sufficient to service the area's needs and they were all equipped with radios, so that local companies could contact them at a moment's notice. As he pointed out, "No company or other person wishing to charter an aircraft from Laurentain Air Serivces Limited … has had to wait long for said service, unless all aircraft were busy on fire work or there had been a period of bad flying weather." If Joseph Bertrand and other applicants were approved, however, Laurentian would be forced to sell "excess aeroplanes and discharge excess pilots and employees. In other words, cut overhead and give less service and less employment."

As Barnet explained in his letters, he was not out to make a fortune with Laurentian. His first priority was to provide "good, safe and efficient aviation" and this way of doing business, he admitted, "is not a money maker." To ensure the highest quality and safety standards, he "kept on over the winter months … nearly all the employees and pilots" even though most of Laurentian's flying took place during the summer months. For safety's sake, Barnet also paid a set salary per month. As John Gill notes in his autobiography, this "was a very unusual practice in our industry, as most pilots were paid for the number of hours they flew. Over the years I came to realize that many accidents were caused by pilots flying at times they had no business flying, trying to earn some extra money."

1958 was a particularly "poor year and this company undoubtedly will operate at a considerable deficit," Barnet wrote. He was confident, though, that "This deficit can be surmounted and the good service continued, but not if excessive overlapping and 'fly-by-night' competition is permitted."[9]

Declining demand for engine overhauls

Laurentian's engine overhauling facility in Ottawa was also losing money by the late 1950s. Barnet explained to the Air Transport Board that he had begun the facility during the Second World War at the request of the Canadian government, "employing a large staff of licensed engineers." Laurentian continued to operate this facility "for the benefit of itself and the aviation industry, although there is not now adequate demand to keep it fully occupied, yet staff are maintained the year around as part of Laurentian's services."[10]

The engine overhauling facility had been incredibly busy during the war years and Barnet had every intention of keeping it going once hostilities ceased. Laurentian continued to market its services to the Canadian government, as can be seen in a letter Barnet wrote to the Superintendent of the Air Regulations branch on October 2, 1945: "It is our intention to provide permanent employment for as many of our present staff and returned personnel as possible and to maintain our overhaul facilties to serve this section, and feel that we are fully qualified to do so. Situated as we are, next to your centre of operation in Ottawa, we feel that we can be of service to your Department and we would be pleased to quote you on any work that you may require in this district."[11] The Superintendent assured him in his reply that he would send Laurentian tenders for work when the company's services were required.[12] There is evidence that over the next decade Laurentian overhauled several engines for the Department of Transport.[13]

Laurentian also marketed itself to other aviation firms and beginning in 1949 was listed in *Canadian Aviation*'s directory of "Enterprises Approved to Overhaul, Repair, Manufacture, and Suppy."[14] For example, in December 1945, the company overhauled a former RCAF Ranger Engine that Leavens Bros. of Toronto, Ont. had purchased.[15] It also overhauled engines for the Quebec North Shore Paper Company and, of course, for Spartan Air Services, among other companies.[16]

For the most part, Laurentian had a stellar reputation in Ottawa. There was one incident on May 3, 1953, however, that caused major headaches for chief engineer George Beveridge and could have spelled disaster for a Dr. H.T. Mount and his Bellanca Cruisair Senior, CF-EQL. According to the records, Dr. Mount had to force land "due to engine failure shortly after takeoff" that day. An investigation into the failure was launched which revealed that "the engine showed beyond doubt that No. 5 connecting rod big end had seized solid to the crankshaft, that the crankshaft throw was badly burnt and gouged, and that the remaining throws were bone dry. Only lack of lubrication could produce this condition."[17]

D. Saunders, District Superintendent of Air Regulations fired off an angry letter to the Director of Air Services on June 19, 1953, saying that "the only possible deduction regarding the cause

of engine failure is that this aircraft was permitted to depart with insufficient oil. You will note, from paragraph four of Mr. Bell's memo, that Mr. Beveridge made a verbal statement to Mr. Bell that the oil had been changed a week prior to the date of crash, but there was no entry or certification in the engine log book to back up the statement, which is regrettable." Saunders goes on to note that "it is our considered opinion" that Laurentian, "who were responsible for the maintenance of aircraft CF-EQL, have been most careless in this regard" and stated that George Beveridge had demonstrated an "obvious lack of co-operation."[18]

The Department of Transport wanted to pursue disciplinary action, but as W.M. Johnson, Inspector for Civil Aviation noted, it lacked "accurate proof of individual responsibility." Nevertheless, he warned Laurentian to be more careful in the future and wrote to Inspector P.S. Walker that "Toronto district might do well to keep a close watch on Laurentian's engineering practices."[19]

As no other records pertaining to Laurentian's engine overhauling business exist for this period it is impossible to say exactly what impact this incident had. The Department of Transport had been one of Laurentian's first and steadiest customers, but several other commercial firms also relied on the company's overhauling expertise. We do know, though, that in 1958 Barnet wrote to the Air Transport Board that demand for engine overhauling services had dropped and the facility was losing money.

By the end of the 1950s, Laurentian was dealing with a general slowdown in the aviation industry after the boom earlier in the decade. Barnet Maclaren was becoming increasingly frustrated with overcrowding at Laurentian's bases and the drop-off in the number of engines his shop was overhauling. He was also getting older and had decided he was ready to hand control of Laurentian over to someone else.

Paint schemes and markings over the years

Central to Laurentian's initial aircraft markings was a circular crest featuring a Waco flying over a typical southern Quebec landscape. Even after Laurentian began acquiring new aircraft and painting their fuselages lighter colours, the crest remained. In fact, as late as the early 1960s it could be seen on many Laurentian aircraft, with the addition of the company's name across the tail or body.

The photos that exist of Laurentian's first Standard Cabin Waco (above right) do not clearly indicate the paint scheme. John Bogie thinks he remembers the fuselages being painted a dark blue with a white or yellow stripe. This scheme would have complemented the early crest, seen in the luggage tag. (PG)

When Laurentian first acquired its Grumman G-21A Goose, CF-BXR, from the RCAF it was unpainted. Within a few years the company gave it the paint job seen here. John Bogie

recalls it being a light grey with a stripe down the fuselage that became a sort of lightning bolt or zig-zag in front of the door. (PG)

Laurentian, like other bush flying companies, generally did not have all its aircraft in the same colours. It often leased or operated other companies' aircraft for short periods and so had aircraft that appeared to be part of the fleet with differing paint schemes. Also, when it bought an aircraft, it generally needed to put it to work right away and a full paint job would wait until business slowed.

The photo at left of three of Laurentian's aircraft at the Knob Lake base near Schefferville in 1965 shows several paint schemes co-existing: (left) Otter CF-JFH purchased in 1962 from Shell Avion, (middle) Beech 18 CF-RRE with the colour scheme and stylized "LAS" on the tail introduced in the mid-1960s and (right) Beaver CF-GCW, still with the 1950s-era paint job it was given when Laurentian bought it in 1952. (JB)

Otter CF-VQD at left clearly shows the blue and white paint scheme John Bogie introduced circa 1965, the stylized LAS on the tail, and the company's newly-adopted bilingual name. (JB)

In this photo, which was taken at the Maniwaki base in 1972, several of Laurentian's aircraft can once again be seen with very different paint schemes. On the far right is one of the green Widerøe Flyveselskap Otters the company had imported from Norway the year before. Laurentian needed to put the aircraft to work immediately after they were delivered and barely paused long enough to write the registration on the fuselage. There are also two of Laurentian's early Beavers (CF-GCW and likely 'FHR), sporting the paint scheme introduced by John Bogie circa 1965. Finally, there are two Cessnas: to the right of the dock is Laurentian's Cessna 180H, CF-BTK, which it had just purchased that year, and to the left a 1970 model Cessna 172L, CF-CWX, which Laurentian's Cessna dealership owned and the company used for fire patrol out of Maniwaki for the summer season before selling it that winter. (JP)

Laurentian's subsidiary Air Schefferville had a similarly eclectic history of markings. In its 15 or so years of existence, its paint schemes changed several times, often appearing simultaneously as can be seen in these photos. In the first photo, Otter C-GLAB, which Laurentian purchased in 1974, is seen with Air Schefferville's original paint scheme, while the Beaver in the background shows the distinctive "Rainbow Air" colours John Bogie introduced circa 1984. (JB)

Twin Otter C-FCQL, at right, has a variation on the "Rainbow Air" paint scheme. "I chose something that could be easily spotted in summer and winter," John Bogie says. "I'd just seen photos of a Beaver that had crashed in the bush and it blended right into the rocks and trees around it and if you didn't know what you were looking for, you could have easily missed it flying overhead." No one could miss these bright colours! (JB)

Finally, two Beech Queen Airs: C-FIAQ (right), recently purchased from Labrador Airways, still sports that company's paint scheme, and C-GCST (left), with a different set of markings circa 1983. (JB)

NEW BLOOD AND
NOUVEAU QUÉBEC

6

By Laurentian's 25th anniversary in 1966, big changes were underway. Barnet Maclaren had enticed his nephew, John Bogie, back to the company as executive vice-president, with the promise that if he could make it profitable again, he could purchase it. John Bogie's attempts to turn the company's fortunes around meant taking risks, expanding in new directions and heading north to Nouveau Québec.

"I knew the business."

John Bogie had been working as chief pilot for mining magnate M.J. Boylen in Newfoundland for five years when Barnet approached him to rejoin Laurentian. Barnet was not just looking for another pilot, though. As John recalls, "Barnet made me the offer to buy the company if I could turn it around. It was losing money and Barnet didn't want to sell me a loser. His children weren't interested in it and he knew I was, and that I knew the business." And so, in 1961, John returned to Ottawa from Newfoundland as executive vice-president of Laurentian. Barnet stayed on as president and the two would "talk occasionally about any decisions as to what to do here and what to do there," John says. "He was pretty good at giving advice, but I guess he wasn't supervising Laurentian closely in the 1950s: the engine shop was losing money every time they

M.J. Boylen's Grumman Goose, CF-IFN, in the foreground with its new retractable wingtip floats, with Laurentian's Goose, CF-BXR, with the original fixed floats. Laurentian provided all the servicing and modifications for 'IFN and retained a lease on it in the 1960s, when Boylen was using it less, in case 'BXR was inoperable. (JB)

The main street in Schefferville in the late 1950s. (JB)

sold or overhauled an engine. They didn't run their costs properly." John hoped to maintain what was great about the company – its safety record and commitment to customer service – while finding ways to make it profitable again.

When he returned to Laurentian, he was working with many familiar faces: Doug Pickering was still general manager; J.P. McIntyre was secretary-treasurer; and George Beveridge was chief engineer. The aircraft had not changed much either: Laurentian owned several Beavers, one Cessna 180 and CF-BXR, Laurentian's golden Goose. The company was still involved in many of the same services, too. According to an ad announcing John's impending return to Laurentian published in *Canadian Flight*, the company provided air frame modifications and overhauls; engine service and overhaul; radio sales and service; engine, parts and accessories sales; refuelling; aircraft storage; float and ski repairs; and a number of services connected to charter flying.[1]

John knew that he would have to start making some changes if the company was going to get back onto solid footing. As he said during an interview, a memory from his time working for Boylen convinced him getting Laurentian involved in Schefferville's mining boom could be profitable:

I remember walking into Boylen's office when I started working for him back in 1956. There were hundred-dollar bills stacked a couple feet high on his desk and covering the whole surface. Some guy had sold a whole bunch of mining claims and it was all in cash. He started giggling with all this money in front of him. Must have been damn close to a million dollars there. I'll never forget that. When I saw things starting up in Schefferville I thought, "Well let's move up there and get a little involved with it."

John saw an opportunity to expand the company's operations. While Schefferville, which was about 900 miles northeast of Montreal, had a seasonal population of between four and five thousand, local industry relied heavily on air transportation because there was no road. Furthermore, the railroad from Sept-Îles was still under construction and, once it was built, might actually increase demand as more people would require air service to "the surrounding area for mining, exploration, survey, hydro projects and sportsmen fishing and hunting."[2] The increase in scheduled air service between major Quebec centres and the mining town had certainly led to a demand for more charter services.

In 1961, John hired Reg Phillips to provide flying services to mining companies like Anaconda American Brass and the Iron Ore Company, as well as to the Department of Mines and Technical Surveys.[3] Reg was an ideal candidate for flying in remote, largely unmapped areas with unpredictable weather conditions. Since his solo in 1947, he had worked for Austin Airways, Bradley Air Service and A. Fecteau Transport Aérien Ltée in northern Quebec and Ontario, and even on Ellesmere Island in Canada's high arctic.[4] He had flown the Noorduyn Norseman, Fairchild Husky and other large bushplanes. His wife, Edna, was also willing to move with him to Schefferville – always a bonus.

During the summer months, Reg flew Laurentian's float-equipped aircraft from Schefferville's seaplane base, Squaw Lake. In winter, those same aircraft were put on wheels and flown in and out of Schefferville's airport at Knob Lake. When the company first began operations there in 1961, Reg would fly customers in one of the Beavers or the Cessna

180. Soon John Bogie was acquiring new aircraft to accommodate the needs of mining companies as well as prospecting and survey parties. In 1962, for example, he purchased a Beech C18S, CF-DXN, for use on the Anaconda American Brass contract, as well as Laurentian's first de Havilland DHC-3 Otter, CF-JFH, which he bought from Shell Avion.[5] As John knew, though, mining was a fickle business. While working for Boylen, an experienced prospector, he learned that the man had made and lost his first million by the age of 21.

The advertisement Laurentian ran in COPA *Canadian Flight* magazine in 1961. (JB)

Announcing...

LAURENTIAN AIR SERVICES LTD.

COMPLETE ONE-STOP SERVICE ON OTTAWA'S UPLANDS AIRPORT

- ✔ AIR FRAME MODIFICATIONS AND OVERHAULS
- ✔ ENGINE SERVICE AND OVERHAUL
- ✔ CONTINENTAL, FRANKLIN & LYCOMING
- ✔ SPECIALISTS ON P & W R985 & 1340
- ✔ RADIO — SALES AND SERVICE
- ✔ ENGINE SALES
- ✔ PARTS AND ACCESSORIES
- ✔ IMPERIAL OIL DEALER
- ✔ 24 HOUR SERVICE
- ✔ LINE SERVICE AND COURTESY CAR
- ✔ AIRCRAFT STORAGE
- ✔ CHARTER FLYING SERVICES
- ✔ FLOAT & SKI REPAIRS
- ✔ SEAPLANE FACILITIES AND SERVICE
- ✔ "BEAVER" SPECIALISTS SINCE 1948
- ✔ SERVICING INTERNATIONAL & DOMESTIC AIRLINES, EXECUTIVE AIRCRAFT, AND PRIVATE OWNERS.

Mr. A. B. Maclaren, President of Laurentian Air Services Ltd., Ottawa (Canada), is pleased to announce the appointment of Mr. John M. Bogie as Executive Vice-President and Director.

Laurentian Air Services Ltd. has been the fixed base operator and Charter Air Service on Ottawa's Uplands Airport since 1936. They sold the Uplands Airport to the Department of Transport in 1937 and in 1940 opened their engine overhaul shop which has turned out 6,000 engines to date of all sizes up to 800 hp. Laurentian Air Services is also one of the oldest aviation dealers for Imperial Oil having handled their products since 1936. Mr. Bogie has been associated with the aviation business since 1943 and is one of the founders, the first President and is presently a Director of the Canadian Owners and Pilots Association. He held the position of Operations Manager and Director of Laurentian Air Services 5 years ago when he left to take over the position as Chief Pilot of the M. J. Boylen mining interests in Toronto.

JOHN BOGIE

LAURENTIAN AIR SERVICES LTD.

New Postal Address

P.O. BOX 4070, STATION "E", OTTAWA, CANADA — PHONE TA 2-2002

D. PICKERING — *General Manager*   G. L. BEVERIDGE — *Chief Engineer*

Visiting old friends: the Maclaren Power and Paper Corp. chartered Laurentian's Beech 18 along with pilot John Bogie (right) and co-pilot Garland Ericson (left) to fly several top executives down to visit the Wolf family in Columbus, Ohio, circa 1962. Next to Ericson is Barnet Maclaren, chairman and CEO of Maclaren Power and Paper as well as Laurentian's president; Jim Thompson, the Maclaren Corp.'s president, holding the Wolfs' going-away present (a batch of Bloody Mary mix – the ice was already in the aircraft); and A. Roy Maclaren, vice-president of Maclaren Power and Paper. (JB)

All this meant that during the early 1960s John was careful about keeping Laurentian's operations diverse both in terms of services offered and locations. At its Ottawa base, Laurentian retained its engine shop, although John raised prices so that the company was no longer losing money on every overhaul. In 1965, Laurentian also became a Cessna dealer for eastern Ontario and western Quebec. John hired Gerry Taillefer to head up the sales department and later Bernie Scobie, a gifted salesman, came aboard. "For awhile we were the biggest Cessna dealer in the area," John remembers, "and we did pretty good at it." As for flying services, Laurentian was hired by several firms, such as Crawley Films Ltd., to conduct aerial photography in and around Ottawa.[6] The company also continued charter services for hunters and fishermen, flying them out of its bases in Ottawa as well as Maniwaki, Lac des Loups, and starting in 1966, from Rapides-des-Joachims.

In addition to this work in southern Ontario and Quebec, Laurentian participated in two major projects in Newfoundland and Labrador. Starting in 1963, the federal government undertook a topographical survey of Newfoundland to create accurate maps of Canada's newest province. Laurentian was largely hired to move personnel from one location to another and John Bogie still remembers flying around the head of the department for the survey as well as the senior field engineer, Howard Spence. In the 1960s, the British Newfoundland Corporation (Brinco), which had hired Laurentian in the 1950s to do aerial survey work, began development work on the hydro power project at Churchill Falls in central Labrador.[7] During construction of the dam and infrastructure – the largest construction project undertaken in Canada to that point – Laurentian aircraft could be seen regularly at the Twin Falls airstrip.[8]

Laurentian's northern home

As the decade progressed, John's decision to get into Schefferville was proving to be a good move. By November 1964, Laurentian decided to set up a permanent base and applied for protected status. According to its application to the Department of Transport, the company had begun by leasing "buildings and dock facilities from Department of Mines and Technical Surveys at Squaw Lake for seaplane operations" and subsequently purchased a "building as an office, warehouse and shop … located on the airstrip

Laurentian pilot Reg Phillips hooking a big one in Schefferville circa 1965. (JB)

for winter operations." Laurentian also established radio facilities and proposed additional infrastructure that would benefit the community, including an access road. In all, Laurentian reported, it had invested approximately $31,000 in its operations in Schefferville and, through its marketing efforts, had received about "400 inquiries from potential tourists."

Laurentian was not the only company operating out of Schefferville, however, and its application was opposed by its competitors. According to the DOT records, Baie Comeau Air Service and Northern Wings only objected to Laurentian's request for a protected base. Larivière Air Services, however, "the only existing base operator" there, argued that the granting of the application would deprive them of "its entire source of income and that there is insufficient traffic" for multiple companies. DOT's reports show that Larivière only owned one aircraft, a Cessna 180, and "that its revenue charter hours reported at Schefferville totalled 125 in 1963 and 277 in 1964."

Wheeler Airlines, which had been flying charter services in and out of Schefferville since 1950, was also applying for the same operating licence and protected status and therefore tried to block Laurentian. The Air Transport Board considering both Laurentian's and Wheeler Airlines' applications noted the following:

It appears to the Board that Laurentian Air Services has been far more enterprising at Schefferville than Wheeler Airlines, although this latter carrier

has served the point for the past fifteen years. Laurentian Air Services designated Schefferville in 1962 but has shown more active promotion to stimulate air service; it is the main supplier of service with Group B [gross weight 2,500-12,500 lb] aircraft in the area and the statistics show that this air carrier's charter hours as reported using Group B aircraft, totalled for the years 1963 and 1964, 1,030 hours and 1,585 hours respectively, including operations under contract to and from other points but all originating and terminating at Schefferville.

The board went on to say that neither carrier had "submitted any evidence to show that there is any demand for Group C [over 12,500 lb gross weight] aircraft at Schefferville." In August 1965, both carriers' applications for that group of aircraft were denied (although a few years later the Air Transport Commission would allow Laurentian to use these aircraft for a charter commercial service). But Laurentian still came out on top: it was granted permission to operate a Class 4 Group B charter commercial air service from a protected base at Schefferville. Wheeler Airlines, on the other hand, had its application for this

At a party in Schefferville in 1963. Back, from left: Laurentian pilot Reg Phillips, unknown, Department of Transport employee Ivan Manuel. Front: June Baker, Edna Phillips, unknown woman, Mrs. Manuel and Keith Baker. (KB)

Keith Baker in the early 1960s testing ice thickness. (KB)

visual geographical problems of the glacier-scoured landscape that was miles and miles of similar lakes, moraines, tundra, stunted trees, and eskers that made it very difficult to navigate because there were no distinctive visible reference points.

The weather also caused difficulties, Keith remembers, as the "Northern Quebec and Labrador plateau was affected by five weather systems so the weather was uncertain and could change very rapidly." In an interview Keith recalled one time he and Reg were flying a group of native caribou hunters back to their village. When they were flying at altitude the skies were clear and the sun was out, but "below was a dense cloud-like mass." It turned out to be a whiteout – "flat white snow moving along with the wind, several feet high." In order to land, Reg and Keith radioed ahead to the village and told them to prepare bonfires in a line on the frozen lake so they would know where to land. As Keith said,

same licence denied. By December of that year, Laurentian's bases at Squaw Lake and Knob Lake were fully licensed and operational.

While Schefferville was becoming a transportation hub, in the early 1960s it was still under what one person dubbed "primitive flying conditions." Keith Baker worked in Schefferville from 1961 to 1963, running the Upper Atmosphere Physics and Ionospheric data gathering station that his employer, Dartmouth College, had set up during the International Geophysical Year of the Sun and continued to operate. Baker and his young family were Reg Phillips's neighbours in Schefferville's trailer court and he – a self-described "frustrated would-be pilot" – was more than happy to strike up a friendship with Reg.[9] Not only did the two men get along well, but it allowed Keith to get "lots of time in the right hand seat of some of Laurentian's aircraft" and Reg got an experienced assistant to "handle radio communications and navigation in some of the worst flying conditions in Canada." As Keith explains:

There were almost no radio aids such as beacons and Radio Direction Finding stations for navigation of aircraft and the magnetic compass "spun like a top" because of the anomalies caused by iron ore deposits. Adding to those problems was the

They made a bunch of bonfires and lined them up in a way so that when the smoke rose up through the whiteout we could see exactly where to set down. Once we were down we only found them by the sound of their voices: you can barely see your hand in front of your face during a whiteout. Afterwards, we got lined up with the fires to take off again. Risky business, but Reg didn't think anything of it. It was just the way things were up there.

Flying out of Schefferville in the early 1960s often required making split-second decisions. One day Keith was flying with another of Laurentian's pilots at the time, Lester Best. They had made a delivery to a mining camp and left later than expected. With night coming on fast, Lester took off in the Cessna headed back for Schefferville, but the aircraft started to ice up. As Keith recalls,

We ended up coming in very fast and very heavy and landing on a lake for the night. I had no real concerns about our safety, but I was concerned

someone would start an air search, which is very expensive, time consuming, and can put other pilots at risk. So I thought to myself, "How could we subvert that?" So I turned the transmitter on for the tower at Knob Lake and Lester stood on the aircraft with a canoe paddle up above his head and the antenna wire trailing.

Careful not to use any of the emergency signals, I sent Morse code on a phone frequency to my friend, the operator at the Knob Lake tower, by pushing the microphone button. I sent the message three times: "We've decided to stay out at the camp." The operator phoned my wife to tell her not to worry and we managed to avoid people coming out to search for us.

Then we ate the sandwiches I had brought, pulled out the sleeping bag and went to sleep for the night. The next morning the ice had started to separate from the skin of the aircraft and with some careful fist poundings we managed to get it off. Then we started the aircraft and headed back. My operator friend should have reported my lie, but he agreed that I had done the safest thing for everyone. I could have lost my radio operating licence for that one, though!

The long hours, tricky flying conditions and hard work all took their toll on the bush pilots in northern Quebec. As Keith remembers, "guys would get dozy because they had to try to cram as much as they could into the daylight hours because of the visual flight rules in effect. They could get completely bombed out – robotic even." The pilots often relied on those in the right-hand seat to take the controls so they could grab a quick cat-nap. This was fine with Keith, who loved flying. Even without a licence, he knew how to maintain altitude, check the instruments and what to watch out for in weather and other possible dangers. Also, as he explained, the airspace around Schefferville at that time was pretty quiet: "There was pretty much zero chance of running into another plane at that altitude!" One day, though, his skills would be tested.

He and Reg were flying CF-JFH, Laurentian's Otter, back to Schefferville after unloading at one of the camps. "He hadn't fallen asleep on the way out," Keith remembers,

so on the way back he took a snooze. He gave me the altitude and the heading and everything I

John Gill continues to fly for Laurentian

"Several years after I joined London Life, Laurentian and its owner, John Bogie, became good clients of mine. Desperate to fly, though, I asked John once if I could do something useful and was given the job of ferrying new aircraft from the Cessna plant in Wichita, Kansas, back to Ottawa for sale. Laurentian at the time were dealers for Cessna, and they happened to need someone.

"The first Cessna I flew back from Kansas was fairly primitive. It was a new two-seat model primarily for training – the C150. It was slower than advertised, but other than almost running out of gas trying to reach Fort Wayne, Indiana, it flew rather well. I spotted a small airfield and refuelled there; but the refuelling held me up and it was dark as I was heading up the south side of Lake Erie. The aircraft had fairly basic instruments but I intended to fly on to Ottawa that night.

"As I approached Cleveland most of my instruments quit, and I was left with only one very weak radio. I called the tower for an emergency clearance and they brought me in between two large jets, and I was able to stay at the airport hotel for the night. A front was coming through the next day and the weather was unflyable, but despite this and no instruments the tower gave me special clearance to fly over to a small field with a radio shop about 10 miles away. This sounds simple, but when they lost another plane trying to do the same thing, I was routed out over Lake Erie using only "needle, ball and airspeed" until it was safe to return to shore, find the smokestacks I was to look for and land. The electronics were subsequently fixed and I eventually got home.

"The next two planes were Cessna 180s on amphibious floats – working bushplanes that were much more fun to bring back because of the vast increase in power."

Pilot Reg Phillips fuelling Laurentian's first DHC-3 Otter, CF-JFH, at the Squaw Lake seaplane base near Schefferville circa 1963. (PG)

needed to know. For awhile I flew along without any trouble, but then I started to recognize landmarks that indicated we were nearing Schefferville. Reg still wasn't awake, so I went through all the radio routine and called in to the tower. There was no traffic and so I said we were coming in and that we were ten miles out. And that was it.

We were flying with wheel-skis and I had to pump the wheels down to be able to land on the runway. It was a hydraulic system and it took several hundred stokes on this handle to get the gear up or down. Because I was in the right-hand seat and I'm right handed, I had to pump with my left hand, which got tired pretty quickly. I was also struggling to steer the Otter – which was empty and getting buffeted around by the wind. I kept thinking that Reg would wake up at any moment, but he just slept on.

Soon I was a mile out from the airport and

preparing for the approach with the nose down, throttle back, flaps down. It was only then that Reg woke up. I still admire his unflappable nature. He just looked at me, looked at where we were and what I was doing and said, "Ok, I can take over now." Later he said to me, "You'd have landed the damn thing, eh?" but he was so nonchalant about the whole thing.

Creating Laurentian Ungava Outfitters

In 1963, Laurentian's unofficial pilot and navigator Keith Baker left the sub-arctic tundra to move back south. Reg Phillips stayed on for three more years to manage Laurentian's interests in Schefferville, and pilot Paul Saunders often joined him to help fly passengers. The two were still doing some flying for mining companies, but increasingly they returned to Laurentian's specialty: flying sportsmen to

One of Laurentian's Beavers, CF-HOE, and two Inuit kayakers share the water off the Belcher Islands in Hudson Bay. Ted Bennett was flying this aircraft on a topographical survey contract circa 1953 when this photo was taken. (JB)

Laurentian Otter CF-JFH with a canoe lashed to the float, waiting at the Squaw Lake dock with Beaver CF-EYN, circa 1962. (KB)

remote locations. To take advantage of this growing business, Laurentian did something it had never done before, it created Laurentian Ungava Outfitters, Ltd., a subsidiary company, to fly visitors to hunting and fishing locations near Schefferville; it also obtained hunting and fishing leases throughout the area and began creating its own camps.

Laurentian was just one company among many tapping into what Barrie Martland called a "new and growing market" in a May 1963 *Canadian Aviation* article. According to Martland, "sportsmen [were] anxious to penetrate

sportsmen to lodges and camps owned by other businesses, as indicated by a May 1965 *Ottawa Journal* article. According to it, Laurentian aircraft regularly flew from the company's various Ottawa-area bases to "Big Moose Hunting and Fishing Club, O'Sullivan Fish and Game Club, Iredale Club, Charlie's Hunting and Fishing, and Scott's Hunting and Fishing Camps."[11] During the fall moose hunting season alone, the author stated, over 100 hunters hired Laurentian to fly them from Rapides-des-Joachims, Maniwaki, or Lac des Loups to local hunting camps.[12]

The remote regions accessible from Schef-

First Nations caribou hunters pose with Otter CF-JFH after a successful trip in March 1962. For decades Laurentian flew groups of First Nations hunters on their winter caribou hunts. Pilots had to be careful to hose down the interior of the aircraft after transporting the carcasses as the blood would quickly corrode the belly of the airplane. (KB)

the well-stocked preserves of Canada's backwoods" and were "leaving the car behind and flying to fishing areas inaccessible by road. A similar scene is replayed at the opening of the deer and moose season and it all adds up to one thing to the air charter service operator – big business."[10]

Laurentian had been founded largely to provide air services to sportsmen and 30 years later it remained a central part of the company's operations. It was still primarily flying

ferville, however, were not nearly as developed as the Ottawa area, where hunting and fishing camps had been established in the late 1800s. There were lots of opportunities for Laurentian to obtain fishing and hunting leases and in many ways they had their pick of spots to set up camps.

Marc Terziev, a former bomber pilot and Syracuse lawyer, became one of Laurentian Ungava Outfitters' first and most loyal customers. An avid fisherman, his hobby, as he wrote in a July 1964 *Outdoor Life* article, was "exploring the Canadian bush for new fishing spots." In that article, he reported on a fishing trip he and three buddies from New York had taken the previous summer. They had flown northwest of Schefferville to the Caniapiscau River in search of "the famed landlocked salmon which Quebec calls the ouananiche … considered by many to be eastern Canada's sportiest game-fish."[13] After a 900-mile airplane trip from Montreal to Schefferville that cost the group $125 per person, they were met by Reg Phillips. At this time, bookings were made by mail and the group of fishermen had written ahead to Reg with a grocery list. When he picked them up in one of Laurentian's floatplanes at Squaw Lake,[14] he had a 10-day food supply and camping gear aboard, as well as a "20-foot square-stern canoe lashed over one float." Each member of the fishing expedition had also brought about 50 pounds of clothing, fishing tackle and a sleeping bag for the week-long trip.

On July 20, 1963, the group flew out from Schefferville to the Caniapiscau River, "one of the largest and longest rivers of eastern Canada, with an extensive headwaters basin of lakes. The river contains many spectacular falls and rapids in its lower course, including breathtaking Eaton Canyon, one of the sights of the Canadian North."[15] The terrain, Terziev went on to remark, was "hard rock and well forested. The climate seems milder there, and numerous trails of the woodland caribou lace the muskeg." Terziev and his group were in search of prime fishing, though, and so set up camp on a large island in the river itself:

A stretch of deep, smooth water along one side of the island seemed to be the only suitable landing spot…. The end of our landing run brought us just to the tail of the current below a wide area of fast water, and, as we drifted off, the float on the canoe side hung up on a rock shoal just under the surface. Reg cut the engine. "We'll take the canoe and

Barnet Maclaren and John Bogie at one of Laurentian Ungava Outfitters' camps in northern Quebec circa 1965. (JB)

some of the load off," he said, "and I think she'll float loose." A quick reconnaissance convinced us a beach about half a mile downriver was a better spot than the first one we had picked.

When the men had reached the spot, they pitched a tent, made coffee and a snack and set up camp. "With things pretty well organized and an hour or so of light left," Terziev wrote, "Phillips decided to head back to his base where he had an early flying appointment. 'I'll try and get in and check your luck in a couple of days,' he told us, 'and, in any event, I'll figure on picking you up next Saturday in time to get the afternoon plane back to Montreal.'"

By the time Reg and his chief mechanic, Ben Byl, came by midweek to check on the group, the men had "ouananiche fever." Their reports were so enthusiastic, in fact, that Reg "decided to bring in a load of lumber and additional equipment to make a more permanent site for future parties. When he came for us Saturday morning, he had a full load in the plane, including two Montagnais Indian boys and an extra pilot to supervise them. They were hard at work as we pulled away from the beach."

Terziev and his friends enjoyed themselves so much they returned to Schefferville several times in the coming years for more fishing – and not just for landlocked and Atlantic salmon, but for brook and lake trout, arctic char and pike as well. They also ventured to other fishing destinations in the Ungava Bay basin such as Tasiuyak Bay, George River and Whale River. Terziev continued to write about his exploits, helping to publicize Laurentian Ungava Outfitters' services to an American audience. His descriptions of "snow-patched mountains in August," "giant walled fiords," "icebergs" and "leaping silvery fish" captured the imagination of readers in New York state and beyond.[16] Terziev's confident assertion that "Schefferville is probably the most accessible and versatile spot in North America today for fishermen from 'down south'" didn't hurt either, and he reported in September 1964 that there "were people fishing the area from such nearby points as Potsdam, Elmira, and Oneonta, New York, to as far away as Michigan and Virginia. All were having the time of their lives."[17]

By 1965, Reg Phillips was flying some pretty big names from the northern U.S. up to Ungava Bay for fishing excursions. One day, he and Terziev went to the Knob Lake airport to meet the daily flight from Montreal and three Michigan VIPs who were going to test out Laurentian's new fishing adventure package deal: Howard Grimes, department-store president; Morrie Henderson, a shoe-company owner; and Morrie's partner, Ray Crouse.[18] Terziev was at loose ends and Grimes invited him to accompany the group on a once-in-a-lifetime fishing trip in Laurentian's Grumman Goose, CF-BXR:

The plan was to fly a 1,200-mile circuit covering forested lake country, towering mountains, and iceberg-guarded fiords. We would land and camp at spots that looked good, and refuel periodically at a couple of far-northern airstrips. Constant radio contact with the base would be maintained. We aimed to complete the tour in about five days, allowing a couple of extras for delays caused by

weather. Trophy trout, salmon, and arctic char were prospectively on the menu.[19]

Paul Saunders, who had just flown 'BXR up from Ottawa, was to be the pilot on this expedition. As Terziev wrote, Paul flew the aircraft "as if she were a part of himself" and had "been into practically every landable piece of water up and down the length of this rugged area, a background that was to prove extremely valuable to us. Paul is also a competent guide and woodsman, a superb cook, and a good working geologist." When Morrie Henderson pulled a muscle while unloading gear, Paul even offered to give him a massage!

Outdoors enthusiasts like Terziev were happy to "rough it" out in the wilderness in a tent. Some operators had extensive services resembling what writer Barrie Martland called "a plushy African safari." Not Laurentian Ungava Outfitters; its initial hunting and fishing sites were quite spare, which

Laurentian pilot and Schefferville base manager Ted Bennett circa 1966. (JB)

was welcomed by the majority of its customers. Even so, the northern landscape and climate were harsh. As Nicholas Karas wrote in *Sports Afield's Fishing Annual* in 1966, when he flew north to Schefferville in the second week of July, the "ice had broken up only three weeks before." The weather during his trip was hardly summery and while fishing on the Caniapiscau River, he momentarily questioned his decision to go: "The wind was laden with rain and sleet and pelted my hood and rainsuit, creating a din that rivalled the roar of the river. Long before,

On the far right is Marc Terziev, an avid fishermen from New York State, who wrote several articles on Laurentian Ungava Outfitters in the 1960s. These photos were taken on one of the yearly fishing trips north of Schefferville. Beyond the tents in the view below can be seen the engines and wings of Laurentian's Grumman Goose, CF-BXR. (JB)

my hands and face had become red and raw; this was no weather in which to be fishing. Shivering almost beyond control, I made the first cast of the trip into the cold, dark pool and had taken no more than a few turns on the spinning real when the line jerked taut."[20]

With his first catch, a 16½-pound grey trout, Karas quickly forgot his discomfort and let himself be carried off by excitement. Later during the trip, Reg, who "knew about my dream of fishing where no one else ever had before," took Karas up in a Cessna 180 floatplane and "hopped from rapids to rapids. We fished several rivers that didn't even have names, and he swore that no one had ever tried them before." While Karas enjoyed himself immensely, he was constantly re-

minded of the region's restless weather patterns:

One day while I fished, it snowed for a few brief moments. Then the sky cleared, and the sun bore down. Within the hour we were shedding clothes, and the temperature rose to almost 60 degrees. By afternoon of the same day the weather had changed again, and a gentle, springlike rain was falling.... Ground frost is always melting in the summer, and when you walk across the moss-covered ground, water quickly wells up in your tracks."

Mosquitoes were also a nuisance, "moving about in gray clouds" and causing real annoyance when the wind died down or you were on the beach. With their two Innu guides, Phillipe Laurent and Joe Dominique, and "a short rotund

Canadian" camp cook named Lucien Ferguson on hand, though, Karas and his party were well fed and well looked after.

In 1966, Reg Phillips, who had been instrumental in building Laurentian Ungava Outfitters, decided to follow in John Bogie's footsteps and went to fly for M.J. Boylen as pilot of his Grumman Goose, CF-IFN.[21] By then, Laurentian's Schefferville operations were well staffed and Reg left feeling that Laurentian Ungava Outfitters was in good hands. Pilots Paul Saunders, Robert Burke, Don Routhier, Delbert Thompson and Jim Irvin were all under the watchful eye of new base manager and fellow pilot Ted Bennett. In addition, there were several engineers and mechanics, including Carl McIntosh, Hank Vaisanen, Ben Byl, Martin Vanderheid and Roger Guay. The following year, however, Bennett and Laurentian Ungava Outfitters would be faced with an alarming situation in Labrador's wilds.

"Lost for Nine Days: Ordeal and Death"

Fishing and hunting in Canada's northern regions continues to be popular, and there are numerous companies that offer fly-in services to remote camps. Visit these companies' websites – or northern tourism websites in general – and you will find most contain information on preparing properly for a trip to these beautiful, if unpredictable locations. Underestimating the conditions can lead to discomfort at the very least, or, in the case of one group of Laurentian's customers, even death.

In September 1967, a group of four friends from Michigan went north to hunt for Quebec-Labrador caribou.[22] The men, ranging in age from 21 to 35 years old, were young, strong and excited about bagging some trophy bulls. There was Don Barnard, a fire fighter for the Michigan Fire Department; Guy Beauregard, a dispatcher at the communications centre of the department; Terry Brandon, a steel worker; and Bob Hammond, a journeyman pattern maker. "Don was the organizer," Guy wrote in an article detailing the experience. "He was the most experienced outdoorsman in our group. He'd made many big-game hunting trips to Wyoming and Idaho, and he'd become a nut on trophy hunting." Bob was also an experienced caribou hunter, having travelled to the Brooks Range of Alaska in pursuit of the sport. The other two men had been hunting and fishing since their early teens, but this was to be their first "wide-ranging big game hunt" and their first trip to the north.

The planning for the trip had begun the previous November when Don contacted Laurentian's new manager at Schefferville, Ted Bennett. Ted apparently told him, "The bush up here is very remote. The area supports hordes of caribou. There are no facilities or accommodations. When you go in there, you're on your own. Shooting a trophy bull should be easy in late September. Let me know when you want to hunt, and I'll fly you in and fly you out." Don and the group booked for the following September and began preparations for the five-day hunting expedition.

On September 17, 1967, the group packed all their gear into Don's van. As an experienced camper, Guy wrote, "Don owned a complete camping outfit" including: a wall tent with double floor; three-burner gas stove for cooking; a gas heater; a gas lantern; an axe; ropes; knives; cold-weather sleeping bags and air mattresses. Full of anticipation, the group began the 950-mile drive from Detroit to Saint-Siméon,

Lost for Nine Days

ORDEAL and DEATH

Our wilderness caribou hunt became a nightmare of terror and tragedy

By GUY BEAUREGARD

Quebec. By the next afternoon they arrived at Sept-Îles and boarded the train for the 350-mile journey to Schefferville. In addition to seeing a lot of scenery along the way, the group saved money by driving and taking the train instead of flying to Schefferville. They had also decided on another budgeting measure – rejecting the option of hiring a guide – which would cost more than they could imagine.

On the morning of September 20, 1967, Ted Bennett met the men at the dock, where they loaded their gear and themselves into one of Laurentian's floatplanes. By 8 a.m. they were heading northeast to the remote spot Bennett had selected for their hunting adventure, less than an hour's flight from Schefferville. As they flew, Guy remembered looking out the window: "Below us, sunshine flooded a region that seemed to be more water than land." Ted landed on one of these innumerable lakes and taxied toward the group's campsite. After helping them unload their supplies, he took off again, wishing them good hunting.

It was still early in the day, and after setting up camp and eating sandwiches, the men decided to spend the afternoon scouting for caribou. As Guy wrote:

The sky was a deep blue and the weather was warm and clear, so we dressed in light hunting clothes. There was no reason to pack lunches or foul-weather gear. We each pocketed a couple of chocolate bars and then walked away from camp. I should add that we had no maps of the area, but this lack was not an oversight. We'd asked for maps in Schefferville and were told that none were available. The area we were hunting is only a few hundred miles from the northern line of tree growth, and most of it has never been accurately mapped.

The men paired off, Don and Guy waving to Terry and Bob as they headed off in different directions. Don yelled, "See you in a few hours," and the two "took off on a northwesterly course."

About a mile or so away, they could see a high ridge. Don suggested they climb it, so "we can look around from up there and take compass readings on landmarks." The two men soon discovered what Reg Phillips and Keith Baker had learned from years of flying over the region: it is very difficult to distinguish landmarks. As Keith noted during an interview, he would have to keep his finger on the map and figure out where they were by calculating distance and speed. When he lost his bearings he would tell Reg and "he'd fly a 360 until we'd somehow or other locate the direction we were meant to be going in. There are so many lakes – it's just like a paisley pattern in that you can't distinguish things."

Don and Guy were not concerned, though. It was still warm and there was lots of daylight left. When they spotted seven caribou, including "one good bull" about a half mile away, their excitement kicked in and they stalked the herd for five miles. Their happiness knew no bounds when they "blundered into the midst of a much larger herd" and Guy shot and killed a big bull. They "cut out a part of the hindquarter meat and Don caped out the head" and, feeling pretty proud of themselves, they headed back to camp.

By this time, the sun was getting low on the horizon. They knew they had to go southeast, Guy wrote, so "we took a compass bearing on a faraway high ridge that we guessed was the same one we'd climbed" before.

When we reached it, we looked down on a lake that we were sure was the lake we were camped on. In the lowlands of pine and spruce the going got tough, and darkness came on fast. Don decided it was senseless to stagger around in that jungle when we couldn't see where we were going. 'We can't be more than a mile from camp,' he said. 'But we'd better say here for the night.' We built a roaring fire, sliced some meat, and cooked it on forked sticks. Even without salt, those steaks tasted great. After eating, we made beds out of pine boughs, built up the fire, and went to sleep. I woke up shivering in the middle of the night. I built the fire back to a roaring blaze and went back to sleep. In an hour I was up again. I couldn't relax, though Don was sleeping soundly.

At daybreak they headed out toward camp but "what we had thought was our campsite lake turned out to be a strange lake." During their five-mile overland trek the day before, Guy figured they must have changed direction ten times and it was becoming clear they had lost their bearings in this maze of rocks, water and brush. Their naiveté in heading out for an afternoon's hike under-equipped was also becoming apparent as "the sky clouded and a heavy wet mist filled the air."

They thought they "spotted another lake to the north that looked like ours, so we walked fast." Or, as fast as they could, as the "swamps and bogs" in the lowlands "made traveling extremely tough." As Guy wrote afterwards, "We reached the lake about noon only to find we were wrong again. We'd been walking for eight hours and we were bushed." By this time "rain began coming down in sheets, and we decided to dry our clothes. We broke large branches off pine trees and shaped a lean-to near some rocks. Then we built a big fire. By the time we cooked some meat, the afternoon was well along and the rain was still pouring. We decided to stay right where we were for the night." That evening, they heard "three series of three shots" fired by their friends and answered with "two series of two shots." When Guy spoke to Bob and Terry afterwards, though, he discovered that they hadn't heard the returning shots. The frantic friends, who were safely at the camp, also had "no way of getting word out that we were lost" since they hadn't brought two-way radios.

"The next morning," Guy wrote, "three inches of snow was on the ground, the temperature was in the low 20s [about -5 degrees

Photo: DP

The Maniwaki slush incident

In the early 1960s, Joe and Barbara Stayman had become close friends of Doug Pickering and they often flew together in one of Laurentian's aircraft. In March 1963, the three were in one of Laurentian's Beavers on their way to the Pythonga Club and Maniwaki. As the Staymans' son, Web, recalls from his parents' stories, "it was a very clear, sunny day" and all were enjoying the flight. When Doug came in for his landing on Lac des Oblats near Maniwaki, he employed "the standard procedure for landing on a virgin frozen lake surface: Doug made an immediate turn upon landing to look at his ski tracks."

As Web remembers: "When he saw slush Doug hit the power and started to take off. Unfortunately, the prop picked up a wad of soft snow and killed the engine and the plane was brought to a quick stop in the thick slush.

"They got out of the plane and Dad took pictures of the skis in the ice and the ice all over the engine cowling. Dad and Doug started shovelling a path in front of the skis, knowing that once the sun went down the Beaver would be fully frozen in position. I guess the heat of the engine melted the engine intake snow and Doug was able to get the engine started, and horse the plane loose.

"The flight back to Ottawa was very low and slow and Doug had to work hard to keep the Beaver in trim. Upon landing, we could see that the reason for the Beaver's poor performance was a couple of hundred pounds of ice stuck to the under-belly of the plane. I think rather than a 'forgettable incident' the episode shows what a remarkable, resourceful and skilled pilot Doug was."

Celsius], and Don had developed a bad cold. Though we had huddled together all night, we'd slept hardly at all, and our strength was fading fast." The day brought more disappointment as they continued to misidentify the surrounding lakes and ridges, and Guy became increasingly worried about his friend, who "looked awfully sick." Guy also became convinced he had seen "a tent and a beached canoe," only to discover after wading across an ice-cold stream that it had been a hallucination.

By day five, after having spent the night in a small cave without a fire, Don was "critically ill" with pneumonia. Guy helped Don to a clearing where searchers would be able to spot them better, built a large fire and sat down to wait for help. By this time, Terry and Bob had managed to find Ted Bennett, who had flown in on the agreed-upon date. "Ted got on his radio," Guy wrote, "and the search was on within hours. "I learned later that the Royal Canadian Air Force had sent search planes and a search helicopter out of Goose Bay, Labrador. Several ground par-

ties totalling about 20 men had joined the search after being flown out of Schefferville. But that's a huge country; nobody came close to finding us."

It took three more days for searchers to finally find the two men. Those days, Guy remembered, "were horrible nightmares of snow, rain, awful cold, and hopelessness. Don couldn't get to his feet and hadn't eaten for days." He "must have known he was slowly dying, but he never mentioned it, and he never gave up." On the ninth day they heard an outboard motor nearby and "screamed like two crazy men" to attract attention.

While they were found, Don sadly did not survive the ordeal.

This tragedy did not deter other sportsmen from making the trek north to Schefferville for hunting and fishing expeditions. Marc Terziev, for example, continued to be a loyal customer, as did others.[23] In fact, by Canada's centennial in 1967, John Bogie's instincts about going north had paid off. The company was back on its feet and John was poised to become its new president.

General manager and pilot Doug Pickering in the cockpit and, at right, in the hatch of Laurentian's Goose, circa 1965. (DP, JB)

Laurentian's first Beech 18 with the cargo door modification, CF-OII, at the New Edinburgh Canoe Club on the Ottawa River circa 1960. As Larry Milberry notes in *Air Transport in Canada*, CF-OII spent its final days with Ignace Airways in northwestern Ontario and ended up in a Kenora scrapyard, where it is being slowly overtaken by the vegetation. (DP)

Bogie at Beechcraft: John Bogie poses with Laurentian's new Beech C55 Baron, CF-URO, in 1966. The company used this aircraft to fly Anaconda American Brass personnel and executives all over eastern North American. Below it is pictured in October 1966 with one of the company's Beech 18s and its Grumman Goose, CF-BXR. (JB)

Laurentian operated this Super Canso, CF-MIR, from September 1964 until the following year, when it sold the flying boat to Survair in Ottawa. It began as an amphibious model 28-5A PBY-5A Catalina (the RCAF called them Cansos) and was delivered to the U.S. Navy in 1944. Eight years later it was withdrawn from service and bought by a New Jersey company. In 1956 Miron & Frères Ltd. in Canterville, Que., purchased it and had it converted to a model 28-ACF Super Canso 1000 by Noorduyn Aircraft in Montreal in 1960. Modifications to make it "Super" included more powerful engines and greater tail surface area. It was last noted at Super Catalina Restoration in the UK in 1999. (JB)

Beech 18 CF-RRE seen above on Bristol 5100 wheel-skis and below at Schefferville with a canoe slung beneath. Laurentian bought CF-RRE from the RCAF in 1964 and in 1969 sold it to St. Félicien Air Service, which had the 800-lb 5100 kit installed. CF-RRE was one of only eight Beech 18s with this modification, but St. Félicien only got four years out of it: CF-RRE was lost in a crash in September 1973. (JB)

TALES FROM THE BOARD-
ROOM AND THE BUSH

I n 1971, Laurentian celebrated its 35th anniversary. By now John Bogie had been running the company for ten years, first as executive vice-president, then, beginning in 1968, as owner and president. At the start of the 1970s, Laurentian had 18 aircraft, 6 bases in Ontario and Quebec, a staff of 65, and had logged over 500 million charter passenger miles.[1] The first 35 years had certainly proved challenging at times, but in the late 1960s and early 1970s Laurentian, like Canada more generally, seemed to be enjoying an exciting time of growth fuelled by baby-boomers whose ambition equalled their ability to have a good time.

Sharing the joy of flying

One of Laurentian's newest endeavours in the late 1960s was a flying school in Schefferville. In a November 1967 application to the Department of Transport, general manager Doug Pickering

wrote that people had been contacting Laurentian in northern Quebec looking for flying training. "Schefferville is the site of iron ore mining," he stated, and "employees [are] fairly high salaried." Furthermore, "being isolated, [there is] not much opportunity for recreational activity." The Iron Ore Recreation Club supported the idea and agreed to provide office space free of charge in the former Mid-Canada Line buildings. It also "offered to subsidize part of the costs" of running a flight school, as Laurentian would have to pay salaries to an instructor-manager and maintenance engineer as well as insurance, fuel, landing fees and so on. Other groups in town were similarly enthusiastic: the Schefferville Flying Club, for example, was "prepared to construct a double T hangar" where Laurentian could lease space.

On April 1, 1968, the Air Transport Committee approved Laurentian's application, noting

Otter CF-VQD was the last one manufactured by de Havilland Canada and Laurentian took delivery of it on June 16, 1967. Here it is pictured at Schefferville the following year earning its keep. (JB)

it "would be in the public interest" for three reasons: "Schefferville is an isolated community which reportedly lacks sufficient recreation facilities"; "some 38 persons have already indicated that they wish to take flying training"; and "the nearest carrier offering such a type of service is almost 300 miles distant." Schefferville's town manager, Raymond Poitras, wrote Laurentian that month to let it know that the city would "provide, free of charge, an adequate room for approximately 15-20 students for ground lessons." Soon Flamand Clermont was hired as an instructor and joined the other Schefferville staff: base manager Ted Bennett, engineer Keith Maxsom, engineer helpers John Harssama and Eddie Patten, as well as several other men including Alphonse Grégoire, Dick Desrosiers and Sandy Hart.

It was not until October, though, that an official agreement between Laurentian and the Crown to form a flying school was signed. After almost a year of applications, inspections and correspondence, Laurentian's Schefferville flying school was finally in business![2]

Meanwhile, in Maniwaki, a growing number of residents were also interested in learning how to fly. In a January 1968 application to operate a flying school, Doug Pickering noted, "A group of interested people have acquired a property south of Maniwaki and have had it approved by the DOT for development of an airport and plans are underway to develop runways and build accommoda-

tion." Because the residents were interested in being trained for all seasons, Laurentian proposed using a Cessna 150 on wheels, a Cessna 172 on wheels and floats, and a Piper PA-18 Super Cub on wheels, floats and skis.

By March, internal memos were floating around DOT's Civil Aviation branch discussing the application. Then in August 1968, Laurentian was granted permission to operate a flying school out of Maniwaki pending inspection reports.[3] A year after the initial application was submitted, a DOT agent wrote, "Teaching personnel, material and classroom facilities at Maniwaki found satisfactory for the DOT approved course of private pilot flying training."[4] Laurentian hired Pierre Riopel – who was qualified to fly single, multi-engine, land and sea Class II instructor and Class II instrument – as instructor. Jean-Guy Lejeune was listed as base manager and Roger Guay as engineer. The aircraft Laurentian initially proposed, however, were not all approved: the Piper Super Cubs, CF-PUZ and CF-LHQ, were fine, but the Cessna 172s (CF-OSJ and CF-VBQ) were "not suitable for the type of flying sought until

One of Laurentian's two Piper PA-18 Super Cubs that it used for forest fire patrols and flying training at Maniwaki circa 1968. (JB)

A few Laurentian employees take a break from routine work on light aircraft at the Uplands hangar in 1971. (JP)

the airstrip is built." However, both aircraft could be used at the company's Schefferville flying school until then. Even so, that spring Laurentian had its operating certificate in hand and could operate a private flying school with DOT-approved courses.[5]

Continued expansion

Laurentian's operations in the late 1960s still centred mostly on providing flying services out of its Ottawa, Maniwaki, Lac des Loups and Schefferville bases for fishing and hunting.[6] The latter place was also a major jumping-off point for aerial surveying and support on large development projects. Much of this expansion into new areas was John Bogie's doing. Since 1961, he had been executive vice-president of Laurentian, running the show with Barnet Maclaren's occasional input. His decisions had paid off, and by the mid-1960s John Bogie had begun turning Laurentian's fortunes around. As John said, "About '68 the company started to make some money and so we finalized the deal." That deal was Barnet Maclaren's 1961 promise to John that as soon as the company was back on its feet he would sell his nephew the company.

In May 1968, the Air Transport Committee approved the transfer of shares and John officially became Laurentian's owner and president.

At this time, Laurentian's staff and fleet were its largest since its founding.[7] It had 16 aircraft: a DHC-3 Otter, five DHC-2 Beavers, a Grumman Goose, a Cessna 180, a Cessna 185, three Cessna 172s, a Beech D18, a Beech Baron C-55 and two Piper PA-18 Super Cubs. To take care of all these aircraft, it had a large engineering and maintenance crew. George Beveridge, who had been with the company since its beginning, was still the chief engineer. He had two supervisors, Bill Dennis and Roy Smith, working alongside him to keep the staff organized: Roger Guay, H. Jac, Keith Maxsom, Hank Vaisanen, Martin Vanderheid, J.H. Logan, A. Arseneault, Roger Gagnon and 12 engineer apprentices.

To help John keep the company running smoothly were general manager Doug Pickering, flight manager Don Routhier and sales manager Gerry Taillefer. While these men still had their pilot's licences, they left most of the flying to Laurentian's younger pilots: Doug Argue, Ben Byl, Barry Chamberlain, Tim Cole, Jim Irvin, Jean-Guy Whiteduck and chief pilot Paul Saunders.

A daring rescue and an unwanted one

Paul Saunders left Laurentian and joined the DOT in accident investigation soon after John Bogie became president, later founding the Vorlage Ski Resort near Ottawa.[8] Before he left, though, writer Deane E. Bostick witnessed Paul's daring as a bush pilot.[9] According to Bostick, one frigid day at Laurentian's Ottawa base:

Paul was playing gin rummy haphazardly and glaring morosely at the greyness of the large window in the pilot's lounge when the telephone rang. He answered, listened, replied in a terse voice then hung up. The others in the room watched as he walked to a clothes rack and began pulling on flight suit, parka, and fur-lined boots.

Tom Muir, his mechanic, yelled, "Wadda ya think you're doing?"

"Getting dressed. There's a trapper disabled off the Dumoine River and I think I'll go get him."

Apparently two trappers from Hull, Quebec, Thomas Mathias senior and junior, had ven-tured out into the bush northwest of Ottawa to tend their trap lines, even though the father had "had a premonition that they should delay the trip into the woods." As Bostick wrote, the two "pressed deeper" into the bush as the temperature dropped. A snow storm struck and they were forced to seek shelter. The father began gathering firewood and his son started to build a lean-to. While he was chopping wood, though, his numbed fingers lost their grip on the axe; it slipped and cleft his right foot in two.

The elder Thomas Mathias quickly applied a tourniquet. He finished building the shelter, cut a supply of firewood and "put all the supplies within his son's reach." Strapping on his snowshoes, he headed back out of the bush, braving the intense cold. After walking for 56 hours in

Laurentian pilots Jean-Guy Whiteduck, Jean-Guy Lejeune and Tim Cole with Beaver CF-FHR at Lac des Oblats, Maniwaki, in 1971. (JP)

A rescue story 40 years in the making

Peter (Lou) Goodwin went to work for Laurentian right after he graduated from high school in May 1966. This young pilot with "peach fuzz, hoping for the best" started out flying the company's Super Cub, moving on the next summer to a Cessna 180 for a few weeks flying out of Lac des Loups until he was needed on a Beaver. He was only 19 years old and looked pretty young. In fact, he laughs as he remembers customers coming down to the dock and asking "Where's the pilot?" while looking straight at him.

At the beginning of his third season with Laurentian, Goodwin was sent north to Schefferville to fly one of the Beavers on contract with the Hydrological Survey of Quebec. On June 20, 1968, Goodwin had an experience that would take 40 years to play out completely:

"That day I was steaming down from the other side of Kuujjuaq and was passing by a little lake we called Snowball Lake, when I saw someone throwing all these things into the water: canoes, paddles and other unidentifiable things. I called Ted Bennett, the base manager, and asked him if I should check it out. He said yes, so I landed the Beaver, shut off the engine and got out onto one of the floats.

"There were two guys standing there, and they started moving forward, looking at me strangely. I could see they were in rough shape. I went to shore and one of the guys came right up to me, grabbed my face in both hands and said, "He's real, he's really real." He told me that I was going to fly them out and I didn't argue.

"I got them and some of their stuff into the Beaver, and the one who spoke English came and sat up front with me. He told me his name was Elijah Watt, that he was Inuit from Kuujjuaq and his companion was Cree from somewhere in northern Ontario. They had been up there staking a claim for a big mining company and one of the other bush flying outfits had dropped them off in the fall. They were supposed to have been picked up before breakup months earlier but no one had come.

"The two men had gone through all their supplies but, skilled as they were at bush living, had managed to kill a black bear and caribou. It turned out that they had given up on being picked up and so had decided to leave the next morning on foot to find the Pons River, from which they would get to the Caniapiscau River. There they were going to build a raft to try and get back to Kuujjuaq. Their departure imminent and their fate unknown, Elijah had carved a message in Inuktitut on a stump: 'My name is Elijah. I'm Inuit. My wife's name is Mary, we have one daughter. Goodbye.'

"I flew back to Schefferville and brought them to the hospital there. The medical staff called to let me know they were okay, but when I checked back in a few days later (when I had a spare moment from flying) I discovered they'd left. They'd headed back to Kuujjuaq. And you know what? A couple of weeks later I was flying around up there and landed on a lake – and there they were, back in the bush. I went up to Elijah and asked what on earth he was doing there after all he'd been through and he replied simply, 'Gotta eat.'

"The last 40 years I've regularly flown up north, either with Laurentian or my company, Wilderness Wings of Canada. I go up to Schefferville, Kuujjuaq and Baffin Island. Every time I'd go up through Kuujjuaq I'd ask if Elijah was there, but he never was. He would either be out on the land or working someplace else, but I kept asking.

"In the summer of 2008, I was on a trip up to Baffin Island with three aircraft and the winds got really bad around Kuujjuaq, so we decided to set down and make a day of it there. As usual, I went in search of information on Elijah. I headed to the municipal offices and saw on the door that the mayor was named Larry Watt. I figured that couldn't be a coincidence and I was right. It turned out Larry was Elijah's son. The next thing I know, Larry, his brother David and I are on our way over to Elijah's house and we had quite the reunion – exactly 40 years to the day since I'd picked him up at Snowball Lake."

Forty years after their initial dramatic meeting, former Laurentian pilot Peter (Lou) Goodwin reunites with Elijah Watt and his two sons in Kuujjuaq in 2008. From left: David, Peter, Elijah and Larry, who is the mayor of Kuujjuaq. (Photo courtesy Dr. Beverly Goodwin)

Laurentian Beaver CF-HGV, circa 1969, having its engine warmed up by a Herman Nelson heater before starting it. Laurentian operated 'HGV for a short time before selling it to Wilderness Airlines in Dawson Creek, B.C. (JB)

-50°C temperatures, this "frozen spectre staggered into an isolated trading post on the Dumoine River." The storekeeper quickly called the Canadian Forestry Service installation 20 miles away and informed them of what had happened. There, game warden Henry Madone contacted headquarters, which in turn called the authorities in Ottawa.

The young man's only chance for rescue was a bushplane. The problem was all aircraft were grounded due to the adverse flying conditions. When Paul Saunders learned of the injured trapper, though, he decided to risk it. Tom Muir, his mechanic, followed his lead, "pulling on overclothes" and following "his boss to a de Havilland Beaver." Then he "started the engines and began scraping ice too thick for the defrosters to cope with off the windshield." When Paul radioed to the tower, "flight control refused permission for take-off." Undeterred, Paul "ignored them and taxied his plane down the runway and disappeared into the frozen murk. His plane skimmed over the trees at less than a hundred feet then skipped over the roof tops of Hull." As Bostick went on to write:

Saunders navigated strictly by familiarity with the terrain and in less than an hour he covered more than the distance it had taken Père Mathias two and a half days to travel on foot. The Beaver was landed on a frozen lake and Thomas Mathias was bundled inside after the pilot and his mechanic fought off a pack of wolves as in a Jack London story of the North. Half an hour later the casualty was delivered to a waiting ambulance at Ottawa Municipal Airport and taken to a hospital where his foot was saved and he fully recovered from his ordeal.

In contrast with Bostick's colourful prose, Paul Saunders apparently played down the whole incident. When asked by Bostick about the young trapper's dramatic rescue, Paul is reported to have said, "I've seen worse."

After Paul left Laurentian, Tim Cole took over as chief pilot. He had joined the company in 1967 and was quickly sent north to Laurentian's Schefferville base. As Tim recalls, "The first year I was married, I was away for nine months

Train rescue

During the winter of 1970, Laurentian pilot Tim Cole was called up by an Ottawa man to rescue his wife, who was stuck aboard the Ottawa-Montreal train. The train had become snowbound near Hawkesbury, Ontario, and Tim was dispatched in a Beaver to pick up this woman and several other passengers.

Two views of the Turbo-Beaver, CF-RDA, Laurentian operated circa 1969. De Havilland Canada introduced the Turbo-Beaver, with its increased efficiency and payload, in 1963 but only completed 60 as it was a very expensive aircraft compared with its piston counterparts. After Laurentian, 'RDA was registered to Ptarmigan Airways Ltd. in Yellowknife from 1976 to 1989. For almost two decades it hopped back and forth across the border until 2007 when it returned to the States, taking up residence with Beaver Aircraft LLC in Missoula, Montana, as N812LT. (PG, JB)

in Schefferville!" During his seven-and-a-half-year stint flying for Laurentian, Tim returned to Schefferville often and had many interesting experiences in the region. Like Paul, Tim was concerned about the safety of his fellow man. So, when

Paul Martineau at the controls of Cessna 180 CF-VXB. Martineau, who came from Buckingham, Quebec, worked the 1969 and 1970 float seasons with Laurentian, first on fire patrol in a Cessna 172 and then as the Cessna 180 pilot in Schefferville in 'VXB. As Tim Cole remembers, "He had great hand and feet coordination and could do awesome landings with that aircraft. He was probably the best Cessna 180 pilot I've come across." (PG)

he was told about "an old doctor who had been holed up on an island" and hadn't been heard from in quite some time, he flew out to check up on him. The doctor's colleagues told Tim he should be on the lookout for two people, as they had heard a research assistant had gone to help the doctor out. When Tim got out to the island, he remembers, the research assistant "turned out to be a young woman. They had a black lab and were living together quite cosily. The doctor was furious he was being taken off his island!"

Summer of '69

During the summer of 1969, Tim was in Schefferville flying Laurentian's Turbo Beaver. According to Paddy Gardiner, who spent a week in Schefferville that August, this "earned him the nickname 'Turbo Tim.'"[10] Paddy was a jack-of-all-trades who created technical drawings on a freelance basis for companies like Laurentian. "I would go out to such and such an airplane," he explained, "and figure out a method to reinforce it, then I'd communicate that to an aeronautical engineer and prepare a set of drawings. Then I'd send in the drawings along with a bill. Laurentian was always good about paying promptly!" Paddy had a solid background in aviation: before his freelance career, he had apprenticed as a mechanical engineer in his native England and, once arrived in Canada, went to work for Canadair in Montreal as part of the Avro Arrow's landing gear design team. One day, sick with the flu, he showed up late for

Fred Burke, one of Laurentian's pilots circa 1970, with Cessna 305 CF-XBX. This aircraft was developed from the Cessna 170, the main difference being the 305's two tandem seats (as opposed to the 170's four seats) and angled side windows to improve ground observation. Laurentian used it on a survey contract with SOQUEM (Société québécoise d'exploration minière). The U.S. Army designated this aircraft the L-19 Bird Dog. (JP)

Otter CF-CEE near the George River in northern Quebec, 1974. 'CEE was manufactured in 1958 and delivered to the U.S. Army. Laurentian purchased it at the army's Atlanta depot in 1973 and, as Iain Bogie says, "We gave it a quick paint job at our hangar in Uplands and put it in service." (JP)

work just in time to be ushered into the cafeteria for an announcement that the project was being cancelled and the plant was shutting down! The next day he went to work for Personal Plane Service in Ottawa. His subsequent jobs,which he says he took "to make ends meet," also contributed to his understanding of aviation in Canada's north: he worked as base manager for Johnny May Air Charters in Kuujjuaq, as well as for Northern Bell Telecom and the Canadian Radio-television and Telecommunications Commission (CRTC) in northern Quebec.

In August 1969, Doug Pickering suggested Paddy accompany pilot Jim Irvin on his flight up to Schefferville in Laurentian's Grumman Goose. While Paddy wasn't paid for the trip and he didn't do any work while he was there, he did gather enough material to pitch several articles to the business editor at the *Ottawa Citizen*, who, Paddy recalls, "was only too happy to get his hands on an article to do with the aviation industry in Ottawa."

He also had an article published in *Canadian Aviation's* October 1969 issue that detailed Laurentian's Schefferville operations. As Paddy wrote, Laurentian primarily provided air services to fishing and hunting camps "that abound in the beautiful rugged landscape of Quebec." The tourist season lasted from about June to September and early each summer morning, Paddy wrote, "the communications radio starts

crackling its daily list of flight requests." Brad Mackic, who flew for Laurentian in Schefferville the summer of 1971, still remembers the morning ritual: "Upon entering the office, you would often see Ted Bennett down on one knee with his ear to the radio listening to static and weird guttural sounds, which he somehow interpreted into useful information." Paddy described in his article the next step in the morning routine: "Bennett would check the weather with the Department of Transport Meteorological Office and plan the day's flying to serve the customers best, while getting the maximum use of the aircraft. Cargo or passengers are quickly loaded, and one by one the floatplanes take off. Usually it is noon-hour before they are back, having covered anywhere from 400 to 500 miles."[11]

Paddy flew along on some of these trips, which generally involved shuttling fishermen or hunters in and out of remote camps. On one flight, he noted, he was aboard "a float-equipped Beech 18 carrying such diverse commodities as 4 × 8 plywood sheets and other assorted building materials, drums of gasoline, an outboard motor, cases of beer, a food freezer, and even canoes lashed to the floats!" As Paddy noted about bush flying generally, "The planes in those days were almost always overloaded." Jean-Guy Whiteduck, another Laurentian pilot, vividly remembers how in those days sometimes the "aircraft would just be crawling through the air. I don't know if it was our skill or our luck, but we always made it!"

Paddy also rode along on two mercy flights during his time in Schefferville. In the *Canadian Aviation* article he wrote about one of the incidents:

One night in the middle of supper the radio crackled with a request for a "mercy flight" to pick up an injured man in the bush. I went along with Tim Cole in his bright yellow Turbo-Beaver. Not knowing what state the man was in, we took a stretcher and headed out over the sparsely wooded landscape. The man was not so badly hurt as had been thought, but Cole brought him back to the mine hospital at Schefferville.

During an interview in his Nepean, Ontario, home in 2008, Paddy related the story of another emergency flight in Schefferville. While he was at the Laurentian base, a prospector called over the radio. "He had been bitten by black flies so badly that he couldn't walk," Paddy recalled. "We flew in around sunset and the water was like glass, which is always a dangerous time to come in for

a landing. I went along with Paul Martineau, the pilot, and helped him carry the prospector to the plane. He was in bad shape."

Although it was 1969, Paddy noted that working out of Schefferville meant "rough[ing] it just like the pioneers of old, fighting the black flies and the bush." The work was hard and the conditions were not cushy: the men lived in a "bunkhouse near the seaplane dock"; often worked from "sun-up to sundown" during the busy season; and were 800 miles away from supplies in Ottawa, which meant they learned "to save every nail or piece of scrap material in case it will find another use." This distance from major cities caused difficulties at times. As Paddy noted, "Electric power is supplied from gasoline-driven generator sets and everything to build the camp facilities, and supply it throughout the season, has to be flown in." When a rail strike on the line from Sept-Îles to Schefferville occurred in the late 1960s, all of Laurentian's aircraft but one were grounded after "gasoline supplies became exhausted" – only the turbine-powered

Pilot Jules Pilon and Cessna 180 CF-AJW, testing the ice at Fort Chimo (Kuujjuaq) in September 1972. (JP)

Laurentian's "Last Otter" CF-VQD in 1969 in Schefferville. Laurentian sold it to Sabourin Lake Airways in Cochenour, Ontario, in 1977, which operated it for nearly two decades. Since then it has been registered to Black Sheep Aviation & Cattle Company Ltd. in Whitehorse and Eagle Aviation in Manitoba, which converted it to a turbine Otter with a Walter engine and continues to lease it out. (PG)

(Right) Cessna 180 CF-VXB with Paul Martineau on the Whale River in northern Quebec in 1969. (PG)

Beaver could be kept going on coal-oil. "The only thing," Paddy wrote in 1969, that the Laurentian workers did "not suffer is poor food. Chef Paul Kelly produces meals that would be a credit to any good hotel."

Laurentian pilot Jean-Guy Whiteduck remembers the long hours and hard work:

The working conditions were difficult and the company could be pretty demanding sometimes. We would leave in the spring – breakup was about the 15th to 20th of June in Schefferville – and come back in the fall. We worked seven days a week. Conditions were no better than they were in the 1930s. We had a base and better communications and the aircraft were a little bit better, but the rest was pretty rough.

One spring coming in to Schefferville there was almost half a million pounds waiting for us on the dock. We'd put in 10 or 12 hours a day flying when there was good weather – which is illegal now but we did it back then. Guys put in a lot of hours. We were all under visual flight rules. You got to know the terrain so well – you had to! We'd leave on a 200-mile trip and you'd get 50 miles from base and not have enough fuel to turn around. You'd get to know every creek and spring that could get you in and so you were able to get around pretty safely. We used to push it pretty low. Sometimes I wonder why I stayed so long – I guess I did it for the glory!

Jules Pilon, seen at the controls of an Otter in 1974, was a keen photographer of the scenes he encountered in the north, including caribou crossing a stream in northern Quebec, the Torngat Mountains of Labrador in winter and a polar bear hurryng across the tundra. The scene below shows one of the Cessna 180s Jules flew during the summer of 1972 at one of Imperial Oil's camps. The company was conducting exploratory drilling northwest of Kuujjuaq and Jules would transport employees from the main camp at Lamda Lake to its other camps, as well as other errands. "I guess you could say I was the link between the camps and civilization," he says. (JP)

The conditions were rough, but not everyone minded. Jules Pilon, a young pilot for Laurentian, "liked working in the north. I moved my family up there. Laurentian provided a trailer for us." Carmen VanDette, who is now Jules' wife, lived in Schefferville with her first husband, Denis Pelneault, another of Laurentian's pilots. She lived there for one year, beginning in December 1974, and while it could get very cold in the winter and the bugs in summer were bad, "I liked the mentality up there: people enjoyed doing things together. It was a very social environment – big parties at Christmas. There was always someone to play tennis with or go swimming." Both Jules and Carmen also remember there being a decent nightlife in Schefferville in the early 1970s: there was Le Montagnais, Le Diable, the Relais SS and Le Royal.

Living and working in what Paddy described in his article as "bawdy conditions" did not appeal to all of Laurentian's pilots. Brad Mackie, for example, "wasn't all that excited" to go up to Schefferville in August 1971. Brad had received a phone call two months earlier from Jim Irvin asking if he would be interested in flying a Cessna 180 for them that summer. "Not knowing about Laurentian and the experience opportunities they offered," Brad recalls, "I said no thanks, I already have a summer job flying a Cessna 180." Brad's father, Lou Mackie, owned Kawartha Airways near Coboconk, Ontario, and Brad had spent the last three summers flying for the family company, "mostly doing sightseeing rides at a number of local lodges, and fire patrols for the Department of Lands and Forests." Jim was not to be put off, though, and after talking to the folks in Laurentian's maintenance department, told Brad he "could work year round for them, mainly in the hangar at Ottawa during the winter. I accepted."

Tim Cole, who at the age of 25 was Laurentian's chief pilot, checked him out on a leased Cessna 180, CF-APC, on McGregor Lake and the Ottawa River. "Tim seemed a little nervous with my full flap/power off landing," Brad remembers:

These were a standard for me, growing up flying with my father into his numerous small lakes, but most Laurentian pilots didn't spend much time using a Cessna 180 in this manner, and the resulting steep approach didn't seem to set too well with Tim, but always left me with a satisfying feeling of accomplishment, especially if it ended with a smooth touchdown. I modified my technique, however, and tried to conform to my new company standards, especially on check-out flights. A person is always concerned about fitting in okay, so I was relieved when Tim reported to Jim Irvin: "He certainly knows how to fly a 180."

After getting the thumbs-up from Tim, Brad worked out of Ottawa and Maniwaki – which "I considered practically paradise" – until August, when he was told he was going to Schefferville. Even though he "had never been there before," he "knew it couldn't be as good as Maniwaki. Sure, we had our fair share of black flies," he said, "but pilots mostly viewed their world from the cockpit of the aircraft, and left the passengers to enjoy contact with the flies."

"Upon arriving in Ottawa for my trip north," Brad noted, "Jim Irvin tried to placate me by saying Schefferville would be good experience. It sounded rehearsed." On July 22, 1971, Brad arrived at Laurentian's most northerly base in the company's Beech C55 Baron, piloted by Irvin. His first impression of Schefferville confirmed his worries: "I found it to be a desolate area of rock, surrounded by many lakes, and dotted with small spruce trees that looked like they had just been planted last week. The seaplane base was located a couple of miles northeast of the bleak town." After a "bumpy ride in the air service truck over a gravel road" to the seaplane base, he "immediately understood why they buoyed the aircraft out at night:"

The dock was fully exposed to about a four-mile run of open water to the northeast. I learned that wind could come up fast and furious here, slapping waves and aircraft up against the docking area. There were three buildings here belonging to Laurentian, plus a small aircraft maintenance facility. The first small building housed the company office. In the centre building there was a bunkhouse and small pilot lounge. In the third building, there was a dining room and kitchen with facilities for the cook and his helper. This was about the only amenities to encourage a fulfilling existence here.

Still taking it all in, he was anxiously greeted by Ted Bennett, the base manager, who wanted to bring the new pilot up to speed. Brad learned he "was to head out the next day to fulfill a contract with a company called Canex Aerial Explorations." After a night in the bunkhouse, Brad "was introduced to Cessna 180, CF-AJW, a rather new 1970 model." He "loaded her up with fuel, a case of oil, a portable HF radio, and my pack sack, and headed north for Fort Chimo [Kuujjuaq]. This was a two-hour flight which took me past the tree line." Once in Kuujjuaq he picked up Dr. Robert Sabourin, "who I assume was a geologist for Canex," and two other passengers. He flew them "northwest about 150 miles to Faribault Lake, a large lake where we would camp among the caribou moss and rocks

Three Laurentian aircraft in Schefferville circa 1969 after a late-summer snowfall: Otter CF-VQD, Turbo-Beaver CF-RDA and a Cessna 180. At right is another shot of the Turbo-Beaver taken on the same occasion. (JB)

Laurentian operated Otter CF-AYR in northern Canada for the famous Ottawa-area aerial surveying company Geoterrex beginning in 1970. The aircraft was initially owned by the United Nations, which used it in the Congo, Yemen and Egypt. More recently Alkan Air and North of Sixty Flying Services have counted it among their fleets. It is seen here at Sudbury in December 1973. (JP)

for the next two weeks, while I flew these fellows around to various lakes to chip away at rocks, I guess looking for something valuable." A short while later, Brad flew Dr. Sabourin to "Doublet Lake, east of Schefferville, to gather more rock samples." Dr. Sabourin "became one of my favourite customers," Brad recalls. "He was a thoughtful, considerate person, who accepted limitations in the weather, airplane performance, and capacity, with grace." He even sent Brad a note of thanks that fall. A rare passenger indeed!

During the weeks flying Dr. Sabourin north of Schefferville, Brad had a reprieve from the black flies, although he remembers "the mosquitoes were plentiful enough to literally drive a person insane. I walked around most of the time with my winter coat and hood, with gloves on to protect myself." Nevertheless, the black flies were patiently awaiting his return to Schefferville on August 6, 1971. As he recalls, "I was to learn the bugs didn't have any boundaries at Schefferville. They were thick at the base, swarmed into the aircraft, and generally joined you in any activity you might be trying to enjoy."

After his return to Schefferville on August 6, Brad was constantly in the air flying sportsmen, outfitters, exploration parties, and a few government agents checking navigation aids (which,

he adds, were few and far between up there). Laurentian's biggest customer base in early August was fishermen and Brad recalls that "people spent a lot of money to fly out of Schefferville for salmon fly fishing on the George and Whale Rivers, and at the many lake camps where they fished for pickerel and trout. The Tuktu, Montagnais, George River, Eaton Canyon Club and Ungava camps all had HF radios with which they sent messages regarding customer bookings and supply requirements." The fishing and hunting camps were good customers, but Brad remembers it was not always a pleasurable activity:

One of the camp owners had the worst smelling breath I have ever encountered in my life, and I dreaded taking flights with him to his camps. The only time I remember having a worse smell in an aircraft was during the caribou hunt, when we were late on pick-ups due to a couple of days of bad weather, and one of the hunting parties insisted on me flying out a caribou that was completely rotten. When we got back to Schefferville, they were made to throw it out, leaving at least one of the hunters practically in tears.

During the caribou hunting season that August, Jim warned Brad and the other Laurentian workers that "as we got backed up with the many

Two views of Cessna 305 CF-XBX, seen in the first photo on floats on the Manicouagan River. These shots show well the additional tail fins fitted because it was often on floats. As Jules Pilon notes, "Because the surface area is greater with floats these fins give extra longitudinal stability." He adds that "initially, XBX had clean wing tips – any survey work was done with internal equipment only. But at the end of 1972, the aircraft [second photo] was fitted with pods on the wing tips and behind the cabin [and a "Restricted" sign in the window]. That was part of the survey equipment added for a job with SOQUEM. I believe this was a one-of-a-kind modification for a Cessna 305 – I've seen it on bigger aircraft but never on one of these." (JP)

flights waiting, the door to the bunkhouse would be locked at night, because some of the hunters did not have any accommodation, and in the past, some had tried to barge their way into the bunkhouse.

"If you hear any banging or yelling at night," Jim said, "just disregard it."

Well, as it happened, a couple of nights later, his prophecy came true. We all lay there quiet as mice while someone began knocking at one end of the building, and gradually worked their way around to the back door, which faced the dining building. Then this voice started yelling, 'Let me in! Let me in!' Now this was at two or three in the morning, so I, for one, was not feeling too comfortable.

Well, Jim finally got up, and I heard him shout at the back door, "Who is it?"

Laurentian's Cessna 180, CF-BTK, at a very rickety-looking dock at Finger Lake in northern Quebec in 1972. Laurentian sold it in 1979 to Temair Inc. of Temiscaming, Quebec, and it has been operated by them since. (JP)

The voice said, "It's me."

This was repeated a few times until Jim finally responded, "Who's me?"

The voice answered, "Andy." and Andy, a young maintenance apprentice, was let in after spending a few hours out in the maintenance shed to study for his upcoming D.O.T. exams (without having let anyone know).

By the middle of September, long after the first heavy snowfall of the season, Ted Bennett let Brad return to the south. Brad was grateful

the Gatineau River, and little lush farms nestled in the hills. I never tired of the scenery in that area." Laurentian's main base was still on Lac des Oblats, in pilot Jean-Guy Whiteduck's community, Kitigan Zibi (near Maniwaki). "The lake was ideal from my point of view," Brad explains, "because there was no boat traffic on it and it was big enough to haul a full load out of comfortably, but not real rough in windy weather."

The base manager was Jean-Guy Lejeune, whom Brad remembers as "a friendly fellow in his early thirties – a conservative, no show-off

Laurentian Beaver CF-EGC on a winter langing strip near Ottawa Lake (about 100 miles north of Maniwaki) in 1973. In 1981, the company sold it to Calumet Air Services Ltd. – previously called Bertrand Airways – owned by former Laurentian employee Bob Burns. (JP)

for the "experience" (as Jim Irvin had phrased it). After all, he did get a lot of valuable time in the air and even got to fly the Grumman Goose once while "Jim crawled up into the big nose of the machine and fiddled with the radio equipment." Even so, he says he was "never happier to see trees with leaves on them again" and never did return to Schefferville for a second season.

"Back to my beloved Maniwaki"

Brad's next stop was to return to Maniwaki for the fall moose hunting season. He was ecstatic to be back in the region which, he says, "held some of the most beautiful countryside I have seen, with the Laurentian hills along the east side of

pilot." Lejeune was in charge of one of Laurentian's DHC-2 Beavers, CF-FHR, which was mostly on contract to Canadian International Paper (CIP) during the summer of 1971. Brad also recalls a 1965 Cessna 172, leased from an Air Canada pilot, and a recently purchased Apache Twin, CF-KJQ, were being used by Laurentian in Maniwaki that summer. The company could also easily bring in aircraft such as the ever-popular Goose for charters.[12]

Brad was flying with several other young pilots out of Maniwaki including Jules Pilon and Jean-Guy Whiteduck. "Whiteduck," Brad recalls, "was the most pleasant, calm and professional pilot you could ever hope to meet." Then there

Beaver CF-GCW pictured at Le Domaine on Lac des Loups circa 1968. In the background is O'Connell Lodge, which Laurentian rented when it still belonged to Herbert J. O'Connell, owner of a construction firm and associate of Quebec premier Maurice Duplessis. Even after the Quebec provincial government purchased the lodge circa 1958 and called it Le Domaine, Laurentian continued to provide flying services at this location. (JB)

was Jules Pilon. "Jules was out on fire patrol during the day," Brad notes, "and I didn't get to meet him until going to the hotel in town where temporary pilots stayed. I was given a room up on the 3rd floor of the old building and noticed a person resting with the door open in the room next to mine. 'Hi,' I said, 'you must be Jules. What are you doing?' 'Oh, just lying here listening to colour radio,' he said. I knew then that with a sense of humour like that he and I were going to be great friends."

It was both Brad and Jules' first year flying for Laurentian, but the latter was much more familiar with the company. While Brad had initially turned down Jim Irvin's offer of employment that summer, Jules "always wanted to work for Laurentian growing up. I had my first contact with the company when I was about eight years old: my dad would use Laurentian in his work at Eagle Lumber and I remember the pilots landing on the river at Rapides-des-Joachims (where I lived) to pick him up." The 22-year-old Jules got his childhood wish in 1971 when he was hired

as a navigator in the back of Laurentian's Cessna 305 CF-XBX. Soon he was flying Laurentian's Cessna 172s ('YEK, 'CWX and 'RRG) out of Lac des Oblats on fire patrols along with fellow pilot John Hamilton. By 1972 Jules was flying the Cessna 180s (CF-BTK and 'AJW) on fire patrols as well as taxiing fishermen around the Ottawa area before being sent to Schefferville and Fort Chimo (Kuujjuaq). At the end of September he returned to the south for the moose hunt out of Lac des Loups.

Lac des Loups

Laurentian had been building its air transport business for fishing and hunting outfitters for several years. In 1967, it had specific point licences for Camachigama Lake, Sullivan Lake and Lake Stramond – all places where outfitters had built lodges and were now in need of air services. By the late 1960s Laurentian had also established a successful seaplane base on Lac des Loups in Quebec's increasingly popular Parc de la Vérendrye, some 80 miles northwest of Maniwaki. The

Quebec Provincial Parks and Reserves Bureau had acquired it in 1964, and Laurentian, which had been active in the area when it was privately owned, was granted the right to provide air transportation on a designated point basis.

There were only 150 permanent residents in 1966 but, as in the Maniwaki area, large numbers of tourists and sportsmen came during the summer months.[13] The Quebec government encouraged this by building "dock facilities and [a] warehouse, hotel and cabins, [and] dining rooms" at Le Domaine, the government-owned lodge in the park. The government's efforts and Laurentian's marketing strategies meant a steady increase in customers: Laurentian logged 828 hours in 1966, an increase of 471 hours over the previous year.

By 1967, Laurentian had a licensed seaplane base at Lac des Loups and was looking to expand. Based on its success in 1966, the company decided "that the demand for service now warrants the establishment of a full-time operation on a year around basis [and] estimates that it will perform about 600 flying hours in charter operations yearly and in addition some 600 hours on forestry patrol." The following year it attempted to take over the operation of Lac des Loups airport from the Department of Transport but was unsuccessful. Rodair Inc. and Thériault Air Services also opposed its application that year for a charter commercial air service from a protected base at Lac des Loups, saying it would jeopardize their operations.[14] In the end, Laurentian was granted the charter licence but denied base protection.

Lac des Loups became one of Laurentian's busiest bases during the summer months. The company built an office and workshop in the spring of 1968 but, as Brad Mackie remembers, only one aircraft was based there full-time during the summer of 1971: Beaver CF-GCW, flown by Eddy Lord.

Eddy grew up in Clova, Quebec, (about 250 miles north of Ottawa) where his father worked for the local logging company. As a boy, he remembers "faking being sick so I could go to the dock and watch the bushplanes land. Then I'd get grounded for a week!" By the age of 14 he had already decided he wanted to become a pilot, although his math teacher and his parents discouraged him. First he tried to get into flying through the air force, but "the letter arrived a month too late" and so Jean-Guy Lejeune, one of Laurentian's pilots, suggested he go to Ottawa to learn English while getting lessons at the Ottawa Flying Club. After receiving his licence in 1968 at

Laurentian's base at Lac des Oblats at Maniwaki, Quebec, in 1971. (JP)

Laurentian pilot and Maniwaki base manager Jean-Guy Lejeune at the controls of a Beaver in 1971. (JP)

the age of 18, he applied to Laurentian; by that summer he was flying out of Schefferville and nearby Wabush, Labrador, as well as Laurentian's southern bases.

"Now Eddy – there was a man who loved to fly," Brad recalls. "He seemed to get enjoyment out of everything he did," including playing practical jokes on the other Laurentian employees. Brad notes:

The fires were bad during the 1971 season, and one day when Eddy was standing by at the Maniwaki base, he found an old set of water bombing tanks in the back of the shed, spent the whole day putting them on his aircraft, and then, taking me with him, picked up a load of water, flew down to nearby Blue Sea Lake where Jean-Guy [Lejeune] and friends were having a cottage BBQ party, snuck in and dropped the load of water on them. Not surprisingly, Eddy ended up as a water bombing pilot for the Quebec government.

Brad arrived at Lac des Loups in September 1971 just in time for the annual moose hunt:

Laurentian rented one of the nice varnished wood cabins complete with stone fireplace, and two or three other aircraft would arrive to help out, as they came back down from the north. Eddy had been provided with a 20-foot trailer, parked nearby. To the back of the main lodge office, there was attached a quaint restaurant, where great home-made food was available. The manager here was Phillip Davis, who was an avid fisherman, and a great help in accommodating the air service. Bob Burns, the company dispatcher, would come up at this time, to handle the transactions and scheduling of the many moose hunt flights. We were to become good friends.

The following summer, Brad was sent back to Lac des Loups, this time to fly one of Laurentian's Beavers, CF-GCW. Thinking back on the experience, he notes that "I couldn't have received better news. For me, this was the pinnacle of a flying career." Once again it was Tim Cole who did his checkout on May 11, 1972, out of the Rockcliffe seaplane base. Then he went to Maniwaki, where he spent about 20 hours flying with Jean-Guy Lejeune.

"The Beaver, of course, was a delight to fly," he remembers. "Laurentian had designed and certified a canoe rack for the Beaver that ran tubes from the side of the float, vertically up to the centre of the wing strut. It made loading canoes and boats a snap, and left the top of the float clear for walking fore and aft. I thoroughly enjoyed my summer at Lac des Loups, with accommodation in the little trailer, which could hold a surprising number of people for parties."

Labrador retriever

One day while flying alone in northern Labrador, Laurentian pilot Eddy Lord had to swim out to his aircraft in frigid water. He had beached his float-equipped aircraft on a sandy stretch to get to a gas cache, and by the time he reached the drum, the wind had carried the aircraft off. While he had anchors aboard the aircraft, he had not thought to use them. "I had to swim out in the icy water," he recalls, "and then climb into the airplane. This time, I dropped the anchor and went back to refuel. Good thing I always had a change of clothes with me!"

Young pilots and "grumpy engineers"

While Laurentian's Schefferville, Maniwaki and Lac des Loups bases were increasingly busy, its original base – Ottawa – was still a major centre of operations, especially during the winter months. When John Bogie officially took over the company in 1968, Laurentian had two hangars and the engine overhaul shop at Uplands Airport as well as a "complete radio shop, servicing tools and test equipment." Brad Mackie remembers that in 1971 Laurentian's head office had the engine overhaul shop on the ground floor, "with the offices upstairs. Immediately at the top of the stairs were the chief pilot's office, Bob Burns' dispatching office and Doug Picker-

Eddy Lord (right) with a couple of big ones and Cessna 180 CF-BTK, and (below) Brad Mackie with a Beaver at Rockcliffe, both in 1972. (JP)

ing's office." Then there was the "maintenance hangar, and the old Laurentian hangar nearby, which was used for storage and had an old office with an equally old Link trainer in it."

In 1970, Laurentian created a subsidiary

Laurentian and CF-FHB, the first Beaver

As Tim Cole notes, few people realize that Laurentian Air Services operated de Havilland Beaver s/n 1, CF-FHB. The company did not change the paint scheme as they were only dry-leasing it for a short period in 1968, but Tim logged about 400 flying hours on the aircraft. When Laurentian was done with it, Tim was told to fly it to Calgary. "I was a bit nervous," he recalls, "as I'd never flown over the prairies before and didn't know where the airstrips were. Then the radio quit on me, which didn't help!" All ended well, though, and after a long flying career, CF-FHB is now on display at the Canada Aviation Museum in Ottawa.

Chief pilot Tim Cole with the first production Beaver, CF-FHB, at Lac-des-Loups. Laurentian dry-leased the aircraft for a short period in 1968. For more information on this aircraft's amazing career and the fascinating story of its delivery to the Canada Aviation Museum, see Fred W. Hotson's *De Havilland in Canada* (1999) and Kenneth M. Molson's *Canada's National Aviation Museum: Its History and Collections* (1988). (TC)

company, Alliance Aviation, to represent its non-flying services. As Doug Pickering wrote a few years later, Laurentian hoped that by creating Alliance Aviation it would "simplify reporting requirements for the Air Transport Board" and perhaps encourage Laurentian's competitors in air services to use its engine shop, Cessna dealership and other on-the-ground services.

While the name had changed, the staff and services were still the same at the Ottawa maintenance hangar. This included engineer George Beveridge, now a 35-year-veteran with the company. Even after all those years, George had not changed much: Tim Cole remembers that he still disliked young pilots and wore a white shirt and tie to work. Pilots like Tim had a lot of faith in their engines because of his perfectionism. By the early 1970s, according to some of these "young pilots," George wasn't the only one who was impatient with them. As Jules Pilon recalled during an interview, Roger Guay was "another grumpy engineer." Brad Mackie gives the following description of Roger: "He was short, stocky, and usually looked like he could explode at any moment, especially if there were any pilots around. On the whole, I don't think he really liked pilots too much, and thinking back, I guess we were usually the cause of most of his problems." Brad remembers that the winter of 1971 "Jules and I in particular seemed to stir Roger up":

Incidents just seemed to happen when we were given jobs to do together. Like the time we were removing an Emergency Locator Transmitter from a Beaver outside. It was cold, and when you released the exterior mounted unit from the aft fuselage, it automatically started sending out a signal, until you inserted a little pin to hold the deploy lever in the off position. We couldn't get the pin in, and started to laugh, and the more we tried, the less success we had, and the harder we laughed. In the meantime, Roger received a call from the control

*tower, and came storming out to see what we were
up to.*

*Another time, early in the spring, four of us
were asked to move some heavy aircraft engines in
steel containers that had been purchased overseas.
We were using the hoist on the back of the monster
jeep, when suddenly there was a buckling noise,
and the main frame of the jeep split in two, making it look like a folded piece of paper. I had the
honour of informing Roger, who took one look out
the hangar door, clamped his lips together and
departed back to his office.*

On Friday, February 18, 1972, though, maintenance engineers and pilots all came together
when Laurentian's Ottawa hangar caught fire.
At 6:45 p.m. that evening, Ed Joines, the com-
missionaire for the gate at Canadian Forces Base
Uplands, noticed a glow coming from Laurentian's engine overhaul shop. He immediately
called the police, who notified both the Ottawa
and Uplands fire departments. George Beveridge, who was returning to the shop to fetch a
cylinder for an early pickup the next morning,
arrived to find firefighters at the scene. They had
already broken several windows to gain access to
the building and had cut a hole in the ceiling to
release smoke. They had also doused the place
with water and when Doug Pickering arrived at
7:10 p.m. there were several inches of water on
the floor, which quickly receded after firefighters
chipped the cement off the drains. It was a mess,
but Doug's quick thinking prevented more damage when the firefighters wanted to smash the
office windows to release smoke; knowing the
layout of the building by heart, he was able to
navigate the soot and smoke and
opened the windows from inside.

Once the smoke had cleared,
so to speak, it was obvious the
fire had been "confined to the
men's washroom and the area
immediately around it." In Doug

Pickering's statement to the Ottawa press he
reported that "no valuable equipment was lost"
and no one was harmed. Furthermore, it was
under control by 7 p.m. "but firemen remained
on the scene another two hours to clean up and
make sure it was out."[15]

John Bogie spoke with the employees and
tried as best he could to reconstruct the events
of that night.[16] According to his notes, George
Beveridge and Roy Smith had checked the shop
and closed it around 4:45 p.m. Then Doug
Pickering walked around the shop and men's
washroom at 5:30 p.m. When Jack McLean and
Barry Call left the office at approximately 6:15
p.m. the place seemed deserted and nothing
was amiss. On Sunday afternoon, though, Keith
Maxsom found a map in the men's washroom
smouldering and Brad Mackie remembers it was
"evidently caused by one of the workers throwing a cigarette into a trash can as everyone was
leaving at the end of the day."

While the fire itself did not have the chance
to cause much damage thanks to Ed Joines's
keen eyes, the incident did mean that everyone's
weekend was spent at the hangar. As John Bogie
recorded, Doug was concerned because the
furnace had lost power so he phoned Frank Risk
and Jim Wallace, who worked to restore power
until "well after midnight." Then Doug phoned
Jim Irvin (who was now flying operations director) to "round up as many pilots as possible."
Jim, Tim Cole and Brad Mackie "arrived in jig
time," according to John's notes.

Jim immediately went to Beaver Lumber
to pick up plywood to board up the smashed
windows. Then "Gerry Taillefer, Roger Guay, Jim
Hogan, Curry and Klaasen
all arrived and stayed until
after midnight" to put up
the plywood. After sleeping
a few hours they returned
at 5 a.m. to relieve Tim
Cole, who had stayed on

Page 4   Sat. Feb. 19, 1972

'Business as usual'
in air service fire

A fire in the building
housing part of the Laurentian Air Services operation

RUG
CLEANING
SPECIAL

Domestic
9' x 12'
Reg. $16.66

will not affect the company's service.

Douglas Pickering, gen-
eral manager of the firm, said
the fire—which erupted at
about 6.30 p.m. Friday—was
confined to a men's wash-
room and the area immedi-
ately around it.

The building is at Up-
lands Airport at the im-
mediate ...

Laurentian pilots (front to back) John Emmans, Tim Cole and Jean-Guy Whiteduck with Otter CF-VQD on June 22, 1970 before attempting a photo shoot that resulted in the picture on the facing page. As Tim Cole recalls, "Emmans flew Cessna 180 CF-VXB as the camera ship with the door off for the photographer, Hans Blohm. Jim Irvin flew the Goose, and Whiteduck flew the Beaver, which might have been CF-HOE. I flew 'VQD with the 180-gallon water-bombing belly tank on it. We were not used to flying in formation and we had a heck of a time getting the three airplanes in the same picture frame. To add to the difficulty, as the Otter had the water-bombing tank on it, the max speed was about 85 knots and at this speed the Goose was just about stalling out on Jim. In the end we got a pretty good picture and it was published in the *Ottawa Journal* in 1971 along with a story on Laurentian's 35th anniversary." (JB)

as night watchman. The Laurentian staff worked hard all day mopping the place and moving tables out of the way while George Beveridge supervised. One of George's "favourite" young pilots, Eddy Lord, arrived and stood guard until 8 p.m. when Brad Mackie relieved him, staying until Sunday morning. As Brad recalls, "It was a very strange feeling in that empty, dark building." On Sunday, Smith, Keith Maxsom and his father

Bellamy spent the day salvaging engine parts and other materials from quarantine stores to ensure they did not rust. Monday morning, after pilot Peter Gendron had spent the night guarding the hangar, contractors arrived to repair all the damage. With the cooperation of the whole Laurentian crew, within days it was business as usual at the Uplands facility.

Laurentian had a fine group of eager, young

Laurentian pilot Peter Gendron in December 1973. (JP)

pilots in the late 1960s and early 1970s. This is not surprising since it had become known as a company that trained its pilots well, provided top-notch maintenance for its aircraft and parts, and offered ample opportunities for advancement. Some pilots, such as Brad Mackie, only stayed a few seasons; in December 1973, he decided to leave the company. "Flying a Beaver in the Ottawa River Valley area was as good as it could get for me," he says. "I knew plans were in the works for me to return to Schefferville the next spring, flying an Otter. Most pilots would have considered this a natural progression in the trip to the top of the profession, but I was really not looking forward to it."

Instead, he left to work for another former Laurentian employee, Bob Burns, who had just bought Bertrand Airways in Fort-Coulonge, Quebec. Brad "was delighted when Bob asked me if I would like to come and fly for him the next summer. I think he was surprised a bit when I said yes." Brad flew for the company, renamed Calumet Air Service, in two aircraft that had been bought from Laurentian: a Cessna 180, CF-HLY, and a Beaver, CF-GIB. Bob became a client of Laurentian again when he purchased a new Cessna 180, C-GCAI, from sales agent Gerry Taillefer. In the early 1980s Calumet Air Service ceased operations and Bob went to fly

for other companies. In the 1990s he bought Bradley Air Services' old hangar at Carp Airport near Ottawa and renamed it West Air. In 2008, at the age of 71, Bob shut down his flying school and charter business and he is now pondering his next move. Brad, who left Calumet Air Service in 1978, went to work at Canadore College in North Bay as a technologist for the Aircraft Maintenance Program: "My maintenance licence finally paid off in a big way," Brad muses, "which I have my dad to thank for! And I still go out flying from time to time with my son, Scott, to get the rust out."

Tim Cole also left his full-time work as Laurentian's chief pilot in 1973 but continued to do some flying for the company. He is still a little

Tim Coles' logbook records that test water drops were made by Otter CF-VQD at Rockliffe on the Ottawa River on June 12, 1970, ten days before the formation shot described on the preceding pages. As he recalls, "We did a lot of fire support at the time, flying fire patrols and 'bird dogging' with our Piper Apache, CF-KJQ, and Cessna 305, CF-XBX, as well as transporting fire fighters to remote lakes with Beavers and Otters. Laurentian fitted Otter CF-VQD with a 180-gallon belly tank that the company purchased from Ontario Lands and Forests. The only operational fire I worked with this tank, though, was the Squaw Lake fire near Schefferville in 1972. I was simply more useful tending a Wajax fire pump while the firefighters I'd flown in fought the fire at the business end of the hose. After all, even though with 1800 pounds of water at 80 knots you could snap small trees, the water-bombing tank just wasn't that effective." (TC)

(Above) Laurentian's Goose at Uplands and (left) pilot Jim Irvin in the hatch of the amphibious flying boat, throwing a folding anchor onto the Schefferville dock, both circa 1970. (JB, PG)

Three of Laurentian's aircraft – an Otter, Beaver, and Cessna 180 – at the Rockcliffe base at Ottawa in 1970. (JP)

awed that in the early 1970s, at the age of 26, he "was in charge of 25 planes and 26 employees." During a recent interview he could not help but laugh when he recalled he "had as much hiring and firing responsibilities then as I did as director of Pacific Operations for the Department of Transport 30 years later!"

In 1974, Laurentian lost two of its jokers, Eddy Lord and Jules Pilon. Eddy went to work for Survair Ltd. in the arctic, flying Twin Otters, Cansos and Douglas DC-3s. His practice water bombing barbecues in Maniwaki paid off: he has been flying water bombers for 32 years and in the summer of 2008 he was off for a month to fly in San Diego, California. Jules also went north after leaving Laurentian, going to work for Bradley Air Services and Northern Wings. Then he went to work for Pemair out of Pembroke. In

2008 he retired as Regional Manager (Quebec) of Commercial and Business Aviation for Transport Canada in Montreal.

After logging about 10,000 hours for Laurentian, Jean-Guy Whiteduck also decided to move on in 1974. "I was elected chief of the band" at Kitigan Zibi, near Maniwaki and he remained chief for 30 years. "I have maintained my commercial licence, though," he told me, "and still do a bit of work around here, flying Beavers and Cessna 185s."

These talented pilots were central not only to Laurentian's ability to expand into new areas and bases, but to the company's growing reputation in the field of Canadian aviation. By the mid-1970s, however, Laurentian's involvement in "a million-dollar deal" would highlight the company's on-the-ground facilities.

GREAT CANADIAN BUSHPLANES

Since it began overhauling engines during the Second World War, Laurentian had developed a name in and around Ottawa for its first-rate overhaul, repair and refurbishing services. In 1970 John Bogie had created Alliance Aviation to represent this side of the business and began seeking opportunities to fix up used aircraft, primarily DHC-2 Beavers and DHC-3 Otters, and sell these reliable Canadian bushplanes to companies (and even a few governments) around the world. It turned out that these hard-working aircraft would only become more popular with time and that Laurentian had discovered a profitable enterprise.

Bringing CF-YOI home

In 1969, John Bogie ferried a Beaver Laurentian had just purchased 3,000 miles from Los Angeles to Ottawa. Writer Jack Leggatt rode along with John on the Los Angeles to Phoenix leg of the trip to develop an article for *Plane & Pilot* about the aircraft, Laurentian and the experience. According to Leggatt, this particular Beaver, CF-YOI, was manufactured in 1957 and first owned by the New Zealand government, which put it to work on exploration surveys in the South Pole. From there it went to Australia to top-dress arid agricultural land with fertilizer. A mishap there "put it back into the repair shop. Completely rebuilt, from propeller to tail cone, it was offered for sale."[1] This meant, Leggatt wrote, that CF-YOI had "zero time since rebuilding and zero time on the engine." At $32,000 it was also very reasonably priced: in 1969 the average price for a used Beaver in Canada (with much more wear and tear) was $40,000.

Four years earlier Hawker Siddeley (which then owned de Havilland Canada) had decided

Marc Terziev with Beaver CF-YOI, which Laurentian imported from Aerial Agriculture Ltd. in Australia in 1969. The company used it for three years before selling it to Columbia Airlines in Prince George, B.C. The aircraft was apparently booby-trapped in 1983 while registered to Vanderhoof Flying Services Ltd. in B.C., killing the company's owner and destroying the aircraft. (JB)

to stop manufacturing the "classic" piston Beaver and switch to a turbine-powered version. As Fred Hotson writes in his history of de Havilland Canada, "the extensive improvements along with the costly turbine, made the Turbo Beaver very expensive." After selling just 60 Turbo Beavers, Hawker Siddeley decided to shut down the production lines for both aircraft types in 1969 and change the company's direction.[2] Jack Schofield, writing on the Beaver's 50th anniversary in 1997, noted that "hindsight proves that de Havilland Canada quit building the Beaver too soon."[3] Far from waning in the late 1960s, the Beaver's popularity has continued to grow right into the 21st century.

This explains why Laurentian was willing to go to the trouble and expense in 1969 to retrieve a Beaver from Australia. 'YOI was crated "Down Under" and shipped across the Pacific, landing in Oxnard, California. One of John Bogie's friends, Phil Murray, "arranged to reassemble the airplane and make it ready" for the trip to Ottawa.[4] After a successful test flight at Oxnard, John called up Jack Leggatt to see if he wanted to "take a cross-country flight in his Beaver." As Leggatt writes, he did not have a moment's hesitation: "Every red-blooded Canadian would jump at the chance to fly a Canadian Beaver!" He met John at Van Nuys Airport, where he witnessed John land the Beaver. It "was not the best," Leggatt reported, "and it was not until some hours later I learned the reason. In Bogie's 7,500 hours of bush flying, of which 4,000 were in the Beaver, very few of his Beaver hours were on wheels."

Nevertheless, Jack happily climbed into the Beaver that day and set off with John and their good friend, Joe Gorman. During the flight he got to know the aircraft well: "'YOI was a basic airplane. No cabin heater, no radio, no omni, no ADF, no nothing. A Bayside portable VHF radio got 'YOI in and out of controlled airports, and that was about all." 'YOI also had an altimeter in

millibars, according to the Australian and British systems. This was confusing to John, an American by birth, who told him he would have to get "a new altimeter or a conversion card."

The first fuel stop was Palm Springs, 1 hour and 15 minutes after they had left Van Nuys. According to Leggatt, John was still perfecting his wheel landings: "Bogie's landing, with one-half flaps, was no better than his Van Nuys landing. Too high on approach, too far down the runway, and then he rounded out too high. He did make the turnoff, but only because the brakes worked real well." Responding to his friend's good-natured teasing, John told Leggatt after lunch, "You take it to Phoenix. Let's see how you make out.'" Not one to back down from a challenge, Leggatt took the controls, even though he had only flown Beavers on floats before – and was a bit out of practice at that. "Palm Springs tower had us taxi out to Runway 13, and I went through the cockpit check. Bogie sat unconcerned in the right seat – without rudder pedals, and without control wheel. Trusting soul." On Leggatt's first-ever wheel take-off, "the tail came up before I expected it to, we became airborne suddenly at 38 knots, we climbed sharply at 55 knots, and I dumped the flaps too soon and lost 300 feet in the process." His landing at Litchfield Park Airport near Phoenix proved to be a little rough as well. Even so, he wrote, "other than six or seven bounces because the tail was not low enough, we got in without too much commotion."

According to Leggatt, by August 1969 Laurentian had 'YOI on charter doing geological work in the Arctic Circle area. The company, John Bogie recalled during an interview, "also used it doing some experimental survey work down at the Toronto Island Airport. Then we sold it in 1972 to Columbia Airlines in Prince George, British Columbia."

Laurentian general manager Doug Pickering (right) accepting the last Otter manufactured (s/n 466), CF-VQD, from de Havilland Canada vice-president Russ Bannock on June 16, 1967. (DP)

Norwegian Otters

In 1967, Hawker Siddeley discontinued another famous de Havilland Canada bushplane, the DHC-3 Otter. In fact, Laurentian purchased the very last Otter, s/n 466 (CF-VQD), on June 16, 1967. The Otter was an excellent aircraft for Laurentian's operations in northern Quebec and by 1971 the company was looking to add more to its fleet.

During the summer of 1971, John Bogie and Joe Gorman headed to Norway to check out three Otters – LN-LMM (s/n 31), LN-BDD (s/n 138) and LN-BIB (s/n 201) – that Widerøe Flyveselskap in Oslo had for sale. Widerøe was founded in 1934 and was one of Norway's first and longest-running aviation companies.[5] In 1971 Widerøe had just changed hands and the new management was clearing out old inventory to make way for different

aircraft. On September 10, 1971, John put in a bid of C$200,000 for the three Otters as well as a number of Otter and Norseman spares.[6] To show he was serious, he included a $10,000 cheque as a deposit. John and Widerøe's vice president, Torfinn Hovda, negotiated by telegram for several days. From this correspondence, it appears "another Canadian operator was willing to go to $255,000" but Hovda found the "terms unclear" and told John he would "rather settle" with him.[7]

Once the deal was arranged, Fred Olsen Air Transport got to work at Widerøe's maintenance base in Fornebu, near Oslo, removing wings, floats, propellers and parts of the tail plane to prepare the Otters for crating. The company also made brackets for the main undercarriage and tail and fitted them to the aircraft. After all this its employees placed the different parts in containers ready for shipment.[8] From the correspondence between Widerøe and Laurentian in December 1971, it sounds as if the containers were like surprise Christmas gifts: no one really had any idea what was in them. As John wrote to a customs broker in Ottawa, he knew there were three Otters coming from Norway, but as far as spare parts were concerned he really had no clue. He had received a "list of parts that was not guaranteed accurate, as their inventory was

One of the Otters Laurentian bought in 1971 from Widerøe Flyveselskap in Norway is seen here in front of the Widerøe hangar at Boda airport. (JB)

poorly handled by the former owner.… Therefore we are going to have quite an inventory job cataloguing all the parts so we know what we got."[9]

John also did not know exactly when the various containers would arrive. He knew that they had been divided between two ships, the *Atlantic Causeway* and the *Atlantic Conveyor*, and that they had been loaded on three separate days in November 1971. From Göteburg, Sweden, the ships went to Halifax and then on to Montreal; after that, the containers were sent to Ottawa by rail. Not surprisingly with such complicated logistics, some containers went awry. Most of the shipment did arrive promptly, but on January 18, 1972, Laurentian was "still short one complete aircraft [s/n 31]," three sets of floats and two Pratt & Whitney R-1340 AN2 aircraft engines.[10] That spring all three aircraft were in Laurentian's possession.

Even with all the packing, shipping and customs fees, the aircraft ended up costing Laurentian less than the original price of a brand-new Otter, $95,000, but not by much.[11] Like the Beaver, the Otter was still in demand and used ones could fetch a decent price. According to Laurentian's final tally, Otter s/n 138 cost $90,226, Otter s/n 31 cost $94,145 and Otter s/n 201 $90,026. Laurentian also did well with its purchase of all Widerøe's spare Norseman and Otter parts. It had paid $16,000 for the lot of Otter spares and managed to turn a profit just by selling the three sets of floats.

John Bogie stayed in touch with Torfinn Hovda and in July 1972 sent him a photo of the three Norwegian Otters – now registered now registered CF-APP (s/n 138), CF-APQ (s/n 201) and CF-APR (s/n 31) – at the Schefferville dock. As he wrote to Hovda, "We finished licensing the last one the end of June just in time for the northern summer season, had a cylinder failure and forced landing on old LN-LMM [CF-APR], but no damage and had her flying two days later."[12] Unfortunately, the other two Otters

The Otters bought in Norway in 1971 went straight to work, still in their Widerøe green paint scheme. (Facing page) CF-APQ is shown over northern Quebec in 1972. CF-APR, seen in the second photo being unloaded at a northern camp, was the oldest of the three Otters Laurentian purchased from Widerøe. Peter Goodwin recalls that when he flew 'APR in the spring it would be on amphibious floats and was so high off the ground he could look down into the cockpit of a McDonnell Douglas DC-9 airliner on the tarmac. (JP)

(Below) CF-APP and CF-APQ are at Laurentian's Squaw Lake seaplane base at Schefferville in 1972. (JP)

had more serious accidents. As Otter enthusiast Karl E. Hayes notes, Otter s/n 201 (CF-APQ) ran into a spot of trouble in Esker, Newfoundland, on August 2, 1974. According to him, the accident report says the pilot "Selected unsuitable terrain, overshot, and incurred substantial damage." Laurentian was able to repair CF-APQ, however, and sold it to Direquair Inc. of Chibougamau, Quebec, in 1977. Otter s/n 138, CF-APP, was a write-off after its incident at Port Burwell, Nunavut, according to John Bogie: "'APP was on skis and we had built up the ice in places for it to land. One day, though, the pilot, Mervin Langil, taxied a passenger off the ice strip to

Laurentian imported Beaver VH-KWF from Australia in 1972 and shortly thereafter registered it as CF-CCJ. The company operated it until 1984 when it was sold to Pierre Brossard Ltée, and then went to Pierre Ferderber in Val-d'Or, Quebec, where it is still being flown. (JB)

see an iceberg and ended up on unstable ice. The fuselage crashed through the ice but the wings stuck up over it so at least the Mervin and his passenger were able to get out of the plane and back to shore safe."[13] Eventually, as Hayes notes, the aircraft became completely submerged and was never salvaged.

"Beaver king of the world"

By the early 1970s, Laurentian not only had ample experience importing aircraft from overseas but had also worked as an aircraft dealer for Fleet, Cessna and Beechcraft. This put it in a good position to take advantage of the rising demand for used Beavers, an aircraft that was still ideal for work in rugged, remote locations. In many ways, the Beaver was Laurentian's specialty: its engine facility staff had overhauled most of the Pratt & Whitney R-985 engines DHC planned to use in the original Beavers back in the 1940s and '50s, and the company had pioneered its commercial use in Canada.[14]

In 1971, Tom J. Watson, director and general manager of Aerial Agriculture PTY Ltd. in East Sydney, Australia, asked Laurentian to act on his

company's behalf for the sale of three Beavers, VH-AAS, VH-IDF and VH-IDX (serial numbers 144, 1434, and 1612 respectively). As a letter from Aerial Agriculture to John indicates, originally Watson was only going to let two aircraft go, but "at the last moment we decided to send you an additional older aircraft [s/n 144]."[15] Watson had the aircraft painted before crating them and then shipped them from Australia on September 25, 1971, aboard the *Lake Eyre*.[16]

Once they arrived in Canada, it did not take long for Laurentian to find buyers. In February 1972, Laurentian sold Beaver s/n 1434 (on floats) to Sainte-Anne-du-Lac Air Services in Sainte-Anne-du-Lac, Quebec, for $54,045. The following month, Cargair Ltd., based at Saint-Zenon, Quebec, purchased Beaver s/n 144 (registered as CF-BPC) for approximately $51,000. Laurentian kept Beaver s/n 1612 for its own operations and registered it as CF-BPA.[17] After the success of this venture, Laurentian continued importing Beavers on a piecemeal basis from Aerial Agriculture for sale in Canada. On April 27, 1973, for example, Laurentian sold another Beaver, s/n 646 (CF-TCW), to Norcanair of Prince Albert, Saskatchewan, for $39,000.[18] In all, according to John Bogie, he imported about six to eight Beavers from Tom Watson at Aerial Agriculture.

As Peter Marshall wrote in a *Canadian Aviation* article, in the 1970s Laurentian "scoured the world to recover serviceable and wrecked aircraft for resale and salvage." Marshall noted this was not surprising given that 25 years after the first Beaver was sold, there was still significant demand as bush operators discovered "that nothing replaces or matches a Beaver … except another Beaver."[19] The demand was such, Phil Hanson noted in 1977, that companies "will go to tremendous lengths to rebuild Beavers. They'll roll one in that seems to have been horrendously damaged and months later, roll her out again looking like new." In that year, refurbished Beavers were selling for an average of $55,000 (on wheels) to $80,000 for a pristine aircraft on floats.[20] Imagine John Bogie's excitement, then, when in 1973 he hit upon the opportunity to purchase dozens of well kept Beavers.

The seller was the U.S. military, which had been de Havilland Canada's biggest Beaver customer, ordering some 968 aircraft between 1951 and 1960.[21] The U.S. Army, which received the bulk of the aircraft, designated it the L-20 (and later the U-6), but it "was essentially an off-the-shelf civil DHC-2." After painting the Beavers "army green," they were shipped to Korea for service in early 1952.[22] As Carl Mills, tech rep for DHC in Korea in 1952 wrote, the Beaver "was a main form of transport for supply and communication along the front lines," including carrying a piano to one of the front bases when it was needed for entertaining the troops.[23] They were soon doing similar jobs in other locations. Neil Aird recounted during an interview that the Beavers "were used as communications hacks [taxis]; some carried under-wing stores for mortars with parachutes. They would also be used to

supply troops in the field who would be in tanks. The Beavers ranged around Europe during day-to-day military operations: from the islands in the Northern UK to Scandinavia – although none crossed the Iron Curtain."

By the early 1970s, the U.S. Army was phasing out the "flying jeep" and replacing it with the helicopter. To get rid of all the old Beavers, it began auctioning them off to the highest bidder on an "as is and where is" basis. John Bogie heard about one auction taking place in Mannheim, Germany. As John told Bob Ross of the *Ottawa Journal* in 1973, he only had "three weeks notice of the auction," which did not give him much time to get together capital. He approached Colin McOuat, whom he knew because their sons were friends, to partner with him in the venture. The owner of McOuat Investments in Lachute, Quebec, 45 miles from Montreal, McOuat was a good businessman and saw the potential for significant profit, as well as a boon for Lachute's flagging economy. At first, John explained to Ross, "we planned "to bid on just 10 planes. Then, two days before tenders closed, we managed to arrange financing for the entire package." He and McOuat had agreed to bid US$600,000 for the 64 Beavers; if their bid were accepted, they would form a separate company, B.M. Aviation Ltd., to purchase, refurbish and sell the aircraft. The details of the agreement were quite straightforward: McOuat Investments and Laurentian would both contribute to B.M. Aviation's capital, and Alliance Aviation (a subsidiary of Laurentian) would undertake the aircraft technical work and sales side of the business.[24]

After the sealed bidding, John and Colin discovered they had 54 competitors at the auction. They managed to win by a close margin, finding out later "that a West German bidder, who made the third highest offer, would have outbid us – at no cost to himself – if he had submitted his tender in German marks instead of U.S. dollars,

(Left) John Bogie, co-owner of B.M. Aviation, with one of the 64 U.S. Army Beavers he and Colin McOuat (right) had just purchased in 1973, and (below) some of the Beaver fuselages in B.M. Aviation's compound at Lachute, Quebec. (JB)

which were depressed by 10 per cent on the date of the sale." Such was the interest in the Beaver that the two men could have turned an immediate profit – as soon as it became public that they had won, they had several offers for the entire lot. The profit to be made if they brought them home to Canada to be overhauled and resold, however, would be much higher.

The Canadian media immediately publicized "the biggest airplane purchase of its kind ever." They also dubbed it the "million-dollar deal" because by the time B.M. Aviation paid a 12 per cent Canadian purchase tax as well as "packing and shipping costs of $2,500 per plane" the total cost of the aircraft would exceed the $1 million mark.[25] Luckily, the Canadian government agreed that the aircraft could be duty-free as long as they remained in B.M. Aviation's Lachute facility; this allowed the company to pay duty over time as each aircraft found a purchaser and helped the company afford the immediate costs of "completely stripping and overhauling the aircraft." Furthermore, to turn the L-20 back into a civilian aircraft, B.M. Aviation planned to make "a number of improvements and modifica-

tions." These included refurbishing the interior, improving the soundproofing, and slightly increasing the airspeed and payload.

This huge investment was guaranteed to return even larger profits. These Beavers were generally low-time aircraft: they had a "top of 4,500 hours airframe time." As John explained to Ross at the *Ottawa Journal*, "similar Beavers flown in Canada would likely have logged about 14,000 airframe hours." Once B.M. Aviation had completed its upgrades to the aircraft, John estimated they would sell for upwards of $40,000 apiece. He also foresaw "little difficulty in finding buyers. Enquiries have already come from Australia, Africa and the Middle East, as well as Canada and the U.S. Starting in mid-July the aircraft will begin coming on the market at the rate of about one a month." By the end of the venture, Ross wrote, B.M. Aviation was looking at potential sales worth over $2.5 million.[26]

To store, overhaul and sell 64 Beavers, B.M. Aviation needed a large facility separate from Alliance Aviation. The company decided upon the municipal airport at Colin McOuat's home town of Lachute. As McOuat told James Duff, a reporter for the *Montreal Gazette*, "This airport's been here for two years doing nothing, being used for nothing. I figured hell, we should use it for something."[27] The local newspaper, the *Watchman*, reported after the purchase that local industry boosters were excited at the prospects for the community, which had been suffering economic stagnation.[28] The company and the municipality worked together to create the "Lachute Airopark," the first industrial aeropark in Quebec, and B.M. Aviation was granted its management for 25 years.[29] As Pierre Vennat of *La Presse* noted, the company's private aviation base and facility would be the Airopark's anchor. By May 1973, B.M. Aviation's presence began attracting other businesses, which set up along the airstrip to have take-off and landing access.[30] B.M. Aviation also planned to hire a dozen local workers to start and would bring "highly skilled technicians and engineers" into the community. Together these workers would earn more than $250,000 in payroll annually, much of which would be spent locally.[31] The municipality would also receive $14,000 annually from rent.

During the spring of 1973, B.M. Aviation got to work bringing the 64 Beavers "home" to Canada. Gerry Taillefer, a long-time employee of Laurentian Air Services, had gone to the auction with John Bogie and in April he returned to Mannheim to supervise "the dismantling and packing of the aircraft" into containers. The crates would then be loaded onto ships at Hamburg and sent to Montreal or Halifax, before ending up at the wire-fenced compound at Lachute.[32] Once they arrived, chief mechanic Jean Girard was on hand to direct the rebuilding and overhauling.[33]

Within a month of receiving the Beaver shipment, B.M. Aviation sold its first rebuilt aircraft. According to the company's records, on May 15, 1973, it sold Beaver s/n 736 to Lac Seul Airways Ltd. of Winnipeg for $53,588. Girard and his team worked steadily to turn out a dozen rebuilt Beavers annually, and John Gill, who had been flying on and off for Laurentian since the 1950s, test-flew them and occasionally delivered them to their new owners. As he writes in his memoirs, these deliveries did not always go as planned:

Once, in March 1975, I took [my children] Alex and Peter (ages 11 and 9) with me to bring an aircraft I had already tested from Lachute to Ottawa…. In spite of having a brand new engine, it had been running rough most of the way home, and I had tried everything possible to smooth it out. Finally I called Ottawa tower from 25 miles out to report my position, to which they answered, "We know, we can see the smoke." I gulped, and decided not to tell the kids so as not to frighten them, and considered landing, but we were mostly over swamp. As I could see no sign of fire, I continued on a "straight in" approach to runway 22 and was met by five crash trucks halfway down the runway.

As John goes on to note, it turned out that "One bearing had seized in the starter crank, and I had lost 4.5 of 5 gallons of oil which had streamed out behind the plane through the exhaust. If we'd been in the air another five minutes, the engine would have seized, and we would have had to make a forced landing wherever we were." After the Beaver was re-checked, John was scheduled to deliver it to its new owners in Vancouver. He made it to Kamloops, British Columbia, and even though it was dark,

everything was working well and I thought I'd carry on. After about 15 minutes I realized what a damn stupid thing it would be to tackle the mountains with only a hand-held portable radio. I turned around, landed at Kamloops and found a hotel for the night. When I came out the next morning there was a large puddle of oil under the engine. This time it was the propeller seal which had broken, and it's fairly sure that I would have lost everything in the middle of the night and

Dozens of wingless U.S. Army DHC-2 Beavers awaiting rebuilding are seen in B.M. Aviation's compound and hangar at Lachute. Colin McOuat is the man in the light-coloured trenchcoat in the photo at left. In the photo below, crated parts are reassembled. (JB)

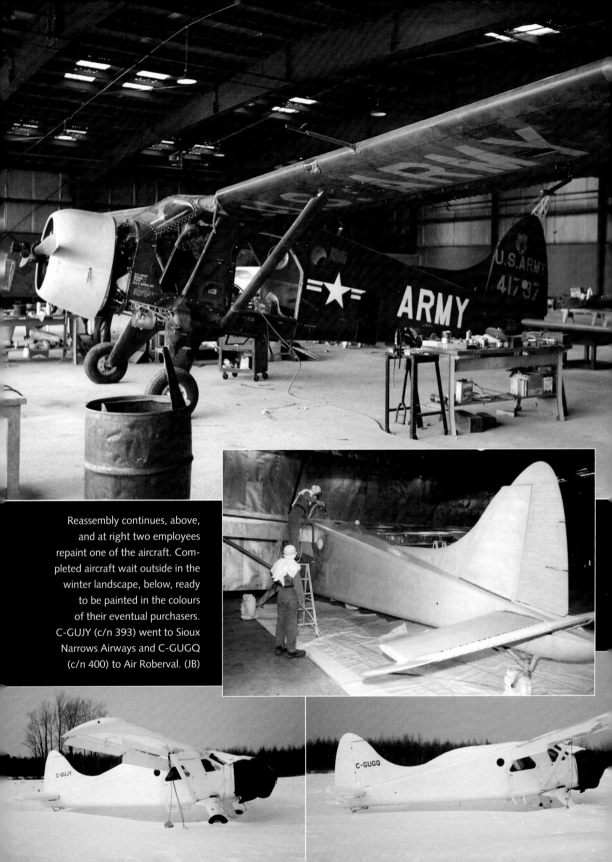

Reassembly continues, above, and at right two employees repaint one of the aircraft. Completed aircraft wait outside in the winter landscape, below, ready to be painted in the colours of their eventual purchasers. C-GUJY (c/n 393) went to Sioux Narrows Airways and C-GUGQ (c/n 400) to Air Roberval. (JB)

All the ex-U.S. Army Beavers on these two pages were refurbished by B.M. Aviation at Lachute, Quebec. John Bogie, president of Laurentian and co-owner of B.M. Aviation, poses at left with the first overhauled aircraft, CF-DUW, which it sold to Lac Seul Airways of Winnipeg in May 1973. (JB)

CF-DSG in 1973 before it was sold to Wilderness Airlines in British Columbia. It is now registered as C-FDSG to Pacific Coastal Airlines in Richmond, B.C. (JB)

CF-JRO, shown at Laurentian's hangar at Uplands, went to Ranger Oil of Calgary in 1973. Since 1993 it has been registered to Ranger Air Charter in Whitehorse. (JB)

C-GMAY, seen here on wheel-skis circa 1989, went first to Fastener Corporation of Franklin Park, Illinois, in 1974. It later returned to Laurentian to be refurbished for Johnny May's Air Charter of Kuujjuaq as "Pengo-Pallee". (JB)

VP-FAV (c/n 1233) before it went to the Falkland Islands government in 1976 along with VP-FAT (c/n 1098). Both were hit by British small arms fire in 1982 during the Falklands War. 'FAT was demolished while 'FAV was damaged but the Falkland Islands Government Air Service still reported it as serviceable. In 1989, however, its fuselage was sighted in a quarry at the far side of Port Stanley Airport. (JB)

C-GAJU went to Canadian Voyageur Airways of Fort Frances, Ontario, in 1977. It is currently operated by Pine Air at Sioux Lookout, Ontario. (JB)

SE-FUH (c/n 268) went to a Swedish buyer, Turistflyg i Arjeplog AB, in 1975. In 1989 it was exported to a U.S. owner, returning to Canada in 1993 with Nestor Fly-In Outposts in Ontario. (JB)

C-GUDZ before Laurentian sold it to Sabourin Lake Airways Ltd. in 1976. In 1981 it crashed and was destroyed. (JB)

DE HAVILLAND BADGE
COURTESY
FRED W. HOTSON

One of the Otters Laurentian bought from Widerøe Flyveselskap in Norway in 1971. Here, CF-APQ, is pictured on the George River near Schefferville in 1972. Laurentian sold it in 1977 to Direquair in 1977. It was last registered to Rapids Camp Lodge in Alaska. (JP)

been forced down in the dark. I had made a good choice. The only people with a repair depot on the field were the Mounties, and they were able to get me on my way by noon the next day.

John Gill loves to fly, but even he was not willing to "get caught up in some South American revolution" when it came time to deliver two of the Beavers, s/n 1098 and 1233, to the Falkland Islands in October 1976. As he explains in his memoirs, he simply "couldn't afford to miss much work!" The delivery went off without incident, but the two aircraft, which were sitting outside the floatplane hangar, were eventually demolished by British small-arms fire in April 1982 after the Argentinian invasion of the Falkland Islands.[34]

By October 1976, B.M. Aviation still had "about half of the original batch" left in its possession.[35] After successfully rebuilding and

selling most of the aircraft, Jean Girard was diagnosed with cancer. When he passed away in 1978 there were still 12 Beavers remaining. As John Bogie said during an interview, at that point "We decided to shut the thing down. We sold the rest to Kenmore Aviation near Seattle, Washington." Even with this sad and seemingly incomplete ending to the venture, B.M. Aviation had still rebuilt and sold 52 Beavers, delivering them to just about every province and territory in Canada, as well as to the neighbouring states of Alaska and Washington.

Before the "million dollar deal" Laurentian Air Services already had a reputation as "the local centre of de Havilland Canada DHC-2 Beaver activity"[36] and as "the senior commercial operator of Beavers in Canada."[37] The purchase of 64 Beavers put Laurentian on the international map and led one writer to refer to John Bogie as "the Beaver King of the World."[38]

Beaver CF-EGE, pictured here in Schefferville, was one of the aircraft Laurentian imported from Aerial Agriculture Ltd. in Australia in 1972. It has had many owners over the years and is currently with Viking Air Ltd. in Sidney, British Columbia. (JB)

For its part, 60 years after it was first manufactured, the Beaver continues to be a sought-after aircraft. In 1987, the Canadian Engineering Centennial Board chose the Beaver as "one of the most outstanding engineering achievements in Canada in the past 100 years."[39] In 1997, writer Dirk Septer estimated there were still 900 to 1,000 Beavers left in the world, "still daily earning their keep." In Canada in the early 21st century, Beaver expert and "hunter" Neil Aird told a CBC reporter that one of those Beavers could cost you anywhere from $250,000 to $600,000 for an "as-new or better than new condition [aircraft] with all the bells and whistles."[40] Quite the increase from the original asking price of $25,000-$35,000.

Neil Aird credits John Bogie with helping to keep many of these Beavers in the air: "The Beavers wouldn't be as prevalent as they are if John hadn't bought them. They would have probably been scrapped." After meeting John at a conference in Victoria a few years ago, Neil did some research on the veteran pilot and businessman. Afterwards, he said, "I thought to myself, 'Here's just as important an icon [in the history of the Beaver] as Russ Bannock and George Neal.'"

Temptation strikes

After the three Norwegian Otters arrived in Ottawa, it was discovered that one had an inflatable raft in a big duffel bag. One day, according to Laurentian pilot Brad Mackie, some of the staff were sitting inside the hangar lunch area when Eddy Lord walked in. "Eddy walked around that bag with mounting fascination when Roger Guay, one of the engineers, spotted him," Mackie remembers. "Roger said, 'Don't you even think of inflating that raft in here, Eddy.' And then proceeded into the hangar. Well, the whole thing was too much for Eddy and a moment later a loud *phoofsheee* sound was heard."

CHANGE
IN THE AIR

Laurentian's involvement in B.M. Aviation was a major undertaking, but the company was certainly not restricted to overhauling and re-selling Beavers in the 1970s. It also became one of many contractors on the massive James Bay hydroelectric project in northern Quebec, flying cargo and personnel in its newly acquired Douglas DC-3s. These DC-3s were also put to work for the Canadian International Paper Corporation, flying forestry workers to and from logging camps several hundred miles northeast of Montreal.

The company may have spread its resources too thinly, however; it was during this period that its fatality-free record ended. By the close of the decade the company refocused its attention on the flying side of the business, which was what John Bogie enjoyed the most, and was ready for a fresh start.

Becoming bilingual

While Laurentian had actively worked in Quebec since its founding in 1936, it had been, like most Canadian aviation companies, primarily unilingual. The employees were mostly English-speaking and the largely American clientele had been as well. When John Bogie, an American himself, took over the company in 1968, however, he decided to make the company's name bilingual. On June 14, 1968, John, who could speak and understand some French, officially changed the name to Laurentian Air Services

Limited–Services Aériens Laurentien Limitée. "It wasn't required," he said in an interview. "But we operated in Quebec and we thought that we should."

John Bogie also had a bilingual brochure created for Laurentian Ungava Outfitters to market its hunting and fishing services. On the cover, under a photo of a Cessna 180, the brochure announced: "Une aventure par air vers le Nouveau-Québec" – "Fly in to Adventure in the Ungava Wilderness." It invited people to enjoy "thrilling action in a true wilderness setting" and reminded would-be-tourists that non-residents of Quebec required a fishing or hunting guide by law.

Through these strategies, Laurentian was actively trying to attract more French-speaking clients to its hunting and fishing camps. It seemed to be working. In the late 1960s, Jean-Guy Whiteduck was flying northeast of Schefferville when he discovered his passengers were francophone. "I was flying in four hunters and they were all speaking French to each other," he remembers. "They didn't know I could understand them, and they kept going on about how there weren't any caribou and that they should go to another lake. I spoke to them in French, saying, 'What are you complaining about? There are tons of caribou here.' And I pointed to a hill that looked like it was moving because of all the caribou on it. They were surprised that I could speak French, and even more surprised to see the huge herd of caribou."

Gooney Birds over James Bay

At about the same time Laurentian made its name bilingual, it also changed its head office from Ottawa to Maniwaki, Quebec.[1] This provincial jump would be permanent, although the head office's location would change during the decade: in 1975 Laurentian took over the old Nordair offices in Dorval (near Montreal) and then in 1978 moved to Aylmer, just across the river from Ottawa.[2]

Having its offices in Quebec, Doug Pickering wrote in 1975, "allowed Laurentian to bid on Province of Quebec tenders, specifically the James Bay power project" – a massive hydroelectric development. In a time of rising Quebec nationalism, Hydro-Québec was seen as a success story, a way for Quebeckers to become *"maîtres chez nous"* (masters of our own house). As Paddy Gardiner wrote in a 1972 *Ottawa Citizen* article, "The $7 billion dollar James Bay Development program" was also "an ambitious attempt to provide a cheaper source of power for future needs while creating much-needed jobs for today and stimulating the lagging Quebec economy."[3] It was to be an immense undertaking.

Bush pilot Mac McIntyre flew out of Mataga-mi, Quebec, over 375 miles north of Ottawa, and the jumping-off point for much of the project. In 1999, he wrote an article for the *Journal of the Canadian Aviation Historical Society*, reflecting on one of the biggest projects of his career:

The engineers planned four power sites over a 265-mile stretch of the [La Grande] river, appropriately named LG-1, LG-2, LG-3, and LG-4. Eighty miles of dykes and a series of control structures and river diversions would give a water head of 1,250 feet and produce 10.2 million KW of power – the largest output on the continent, three times that of Churchill Falls – from a watershed twice the size of England. The largest of the sites to be built was LG-2, 73 miles from Fort George [today called Chisasibi] at the mouth of the river, and good for 5.3 million KW – almost three times the total 1971 Ontario Hydro production at Queenston…. The main dam is a mile-and-three-quarters long at the crest and 525 feet high in the river bed – as high as a 43-storey building.[4]

McIntyre flew for A. Fecteau Air Transport Ltd. – just one of many companies that submitted tenders for work after Premier Robert Bourassa's April 20, 1971, announcement. In the early

Laurentian's first Douglas DC-3, pictured here on wheel-skis, was purchased by the company in April 1972 for work on the James Bay hydroelectric development project. 'POY may be one of the oldest and most distinguished DC-3s still flying: manufactured in 1942, it started its wartime career with the RAF's 216th Squadron in India and was Admiral Lord Louis Mountbatten's staff airplane in the southeast Asian theatre, served with the French air force from 1957 to 1971, and is now operated by a Cuban firm, Aerotaxi Inc. (JB)

1970s, Laurentian joined Fecteau and Ottawa-based Viking Helicopters (among others) on the James Bay Project, although Laurentian worked primarily at the largest site, LG-2. There was certainly enough work to go around. As Paddy Gardiner wrote in 1972, "Hundreds of hours were flown with planes from the small seaplane base at Matagami, often with planes lining up in the lake waiting for space to dock and load." McIntyre saw this first-hand and recalled that "float pilots were putting in 200 to as much as 250 hours a month" in the early years of the project.

Aside from there being initially no roads, aircraft were indispensable as three months of the year the muskeg made it impossible to move heavy machinery overland. While eventually 1,000 miles of permanent road would link the various sites, McIntyre remembers that the road-building equipment could "only be moved when the ground was frozen. A machinery service man told me about one of the perils of working in

the muskeg after the thaw. The vibration from a bulldozer idling for a length of time could jiggle the machine down into the jelly until it was completely buried. Should this happen, the recovery job was indeed arduous." It was not surprising, then, that much of Laurentian's flying for the James Bay Project was done during the winter on skis.

In 1972 Jules Pilon started out flying one of two Cessna 180s, CF-BTK and CF-AJW, out of Schefferville to look at the ice near the James Bay sites and see if it would hold heavier aircraft: Beavers, Otters and Laurentian's newest addition, a Douglas DC-3.[5] The DC-3 – also affectionately known as the Gooney Bird, Dakota or Dak – had been a popular aircraft since its creation in the mid-1930s. As Henry Holden writes in his book *The Legacy of the DC-3*, this aircraft type "became standard equipment for almost all the world's airlines, remaining in front line service for many years."[6] Within a few decades

A view of the camp at Lac Brisay in 1973, one of the James Bay Project's many camps in northern Quebec. Thousands of workers were employed and air communications were vital for personnel and supplies. (JP)

of the Second World War, most North American airlines had replaced it with newer aircraft, but it was still being snatched up by northern operators for passenger and cargo transport. Author Larry Milberry notes that Austin Airways, one of Laurentian's contemporaries, bought its first DC-3 in 1956 specifically for winter work on the Mid-Canada Line.[7] The aircraft did very well on skis and its "legendary ruggedness" was critical in Canada's north.

Laurentian did not acquire its first DC-3s until 1971, when it began work on the James Bay Project. In this year, it purchased CF-POY from the French air force and CF-PAG from Proctor & Gamble, which had been using it as a company airplane. Initially, CF-POY was only licensed for cargo; by November 1972, however, it was properly equipped to carry passengers as well.[8] Laurentian continued to purchase or lease DC-3s during the 1970s and, as John Bogie recalls, these aircraft were used "to move the de-velopment workers around and haul freight out of Val-d'Or." Along with its other aircraft, Doug Pickering stated the company operated between 20 and 30 airplanes during this period. Jean-Guy Whiteduck remembers Laurentian running at least eight Otters, Beavers and DC-3s at LG-2 at any given time in those years.

Laurentian's chief pilot at the time, Tim Cole, notes that the "conditions were pretty spare during the James Bay Project. We lived in cabins or shacks for seven months at a time. Most pilots only did one tour and then moved on." Even so, there were always those willing to put up with rough conditions to fly, advance their careers, or both. In 1972, for example, two new DC-3 pilots, George Mirehouse and Stewart Brickenden, joined the company for the James Bay contract. Mirehouse, who became chief pilot, had been trained in the RCAF and had recently taken a refresher course with Millardair Ltd. ground school, getting 100 per cent on his exams as

The airport serving construction of LG-2, the largest dam of the James Bay Project, near today's village of Radisson, was a scene of constant activity in 1973. (Archives d'Hydro-Québec, fonds H1/Hydro-Québec 1963-)

Like hundreds of other DC-3s, CF-PAG was a wartime aircraft rebuilt by Montreal's Canadair. It started out with the USAAF Air Transport Command in June 1944, was sold as war surplus later that year, and was operated by several U.S. owners before going to Laurentian for work on the James Bay Project. This DC-3 has the small passenger door, in contrast to the large double door of the cargo version shown on page 157. (JB)

well as 15 hours flight training. Brickenden, Mirehouse's new co-pilot, had 3,000 hours on DC-3s and over 8,000 hours as pilot in command on multi-engine aircraft.[9] There was also a significant ground crew, incuding Roger Guay, who had obtained his DC-3 licence endorsement during his eight-year stint with Wheeler Airlines, and John Bogie's cousin Alan Kenny, who worked as a mechanic at LG-2.[10] In fact, at the James Bay Project's height in 1975, Doug Pickering wrote that Laurentian had approximately 150 employees at its various bases – many of them in James Bay.[11]

"The James Bay Project panic."

When Laurentian celebrated its 35th anniversary in 1971 it had an unblemished safety record. As John Bogie recalled during an interview, "I don't think Barnet had any accidents. Sure the pilots ran into mechanical issues every once in a while and would have to land in the bush, but no one was hurt and no aircraft were seriously damaged. Then the pilot would wait in the bush until an engineer came out with replacement parts. If it was a floatplane and it landed on a lake, sometimes the two would catch a couple of fish while they were at it!"

Paddy Gardiner worked for Laurentian on a freelance basis in the late 1960s, creating technical drawings for them, and parlaying his experience with the company, such as his August 1969 trip to Schefferville, into articles on aviation. After Laurentian he went to work as base manager for Johnny May Air Charters in Fort Chimo (Kuujjuaq). Here he is pictured circa 1979 with that company's Beaver C-GMAY after he and others pulled it out of the water to change it over from floats to wheel-skis. Interestingly, this aircraft was one of the U.S. Army Beavers B.M. Aviation overhauled in the early 1970s, and it ended up back at Laurentian for a tune-up and paint job circa 1989 (see page 140). (PG)

By the late 1960s, though, Laurentian had expanded its fleet and its personnel, and was, statistically speaking, more likely to have accidents. Eddy Lord had a couple of close calls in northern Quebec and off the Labrador coast, where things could get really dicey. "I've been lucky," Lord says. "I haven't had any major break-ups. But twice I lost an engine while flying and had to perform emergency landings." One of those times was during what Lord calls the "Panic of the James Bay Project." This description is apt as there were dozens of different companies working on contract and everyone was in a rush to meet strict deadlines. As Mac McIntyre wrote about his time flying out of Matagami during the "panic":

With no palletizing of cargos, the loading of lumber and plywood into aircraft was a slow process, and the whole operation became just a bit hectic at times. There was no DOT control. Even if the pilots could speak the same language – many did not – some of the radios could not get the same frequencies. So there was an understandable concern over the lack of communication and control. On top of this, inexperienced dockhands, if unsupervised, could create situations with obvious potential for disaster.[12]

In addition, many of the pilots were tired and overworked, logging upwards of 200 flying hours per month and often flying in difficult conditions.

During the early 1970s, Laurentian had several accidents, but no one was hurt. A few of these accidents occurred during work on the James Bay Project. As John Bogie notes, "Because the runways at LG-2 were so busy at the time, when an airplane crashed they would just bulldoze it out of the way. That happened with a couple of our planes." Jean-Guy Whiteduck recalls one accident with DC-3 CF-ECY that narrowly avoided a tragic ending:

I was checking out Jules Pilon on a ski-equipped Otter. There were really rough winter conditions – drifts of snow four or five feet high. We were doing our landings behind islands for some protection, but the landing gear wouldn't collapse under those conditions. We told Ted Bennett, the manager, that pilots wouldn't be able to see the drifts at night. But he said that they had to get the trip done.

The pilots came in on a DC-3 on skis around sunset (it got dark about 3 p.m.). They hit the first snow drift but went through it because they had enough speed. When they hit the second one, though, they were going slower and the aircraft broke right in two.

They had 15 drums of fuel on board and one of them fell on the pilot, injuring him. They were

Laurentian operated CF-ANA, the Beech E18S shown in the foreground, for a short time in 1976. The next year it sold 'ANA to Skycraft in Oshawa, Ontario, where it stayed until 1993 when it was exported to California. (JB)

Laurentian's DC-3 CF-ECY, showing damage to its wheel-skis and propellers after a tussle with snowdrifts in northern Quebec. Although 'ECY spent over 30 years flying with the U.S. Army Air Force, the Czechoslovakian airline CSA, the French air force and Astro Airlines of St-Jean, Quebec, it only lasted one year with Laurentian before being written off in 1975. (JP)

lucky no one was killed! The chief pilot later told me, "We should have listened to you." But Hydro Quebec was pushing for flights to land and if something went wrong it was always the pilots who got the blame. There weren't the same controls by Transport Canada in those days.

Even with these close calls, during Laurentian's first 37 years of operations it did not have a single fatality. Thinking back on those years, and especially on the James Bay Project, John Bogie remarked, "For all the flying we did, we were pretty lucky."[13]

"It all happened so fast."

On August 5, 1974, Laurentian's luck ran out. On that overcast Monday morning, one of Laurentian's DC-3s, C-FTAT, left La Tuque airport en route to Saint-Honoré, Quebec, a routine flight Laurentian undertook every two weeks for Canadian International Paper (CIP). Since March of that year, Laurentian had been under contract with CIP to transport its forestry workers to the Belle Plage logging camp, about a 45-minute flight from La Tuque, with a stop at Saint-Honoré to pick up additional workers. In a *Mauricie Journal* article from March 24, 1974, the workers expressed their delight at being flown in DC-3s rather than having to ride a

bus for four hours over bumpy roads.[14] On this particular flight, though, the DC-3 never made it to the logging camp. Instead, it crashed into the side of a mountain, killing all three crew members and two passengers.

One of the passengers who survived, Maurice Arbour, was a 55-year-old CIP employee from La Tuque. After the accident he spoke with reporters from several major newspapers and recounted the details.[15] "We left around 9 a.m. Monday morning," Arbour said. "It was overcast and the clouds were low. We flew over the clouds for about half an hour and then they told us that we were going lower to get under the clouds. Then the plane began to shake and two seconds later everything was topsy-turvy." When asked if he knew what had happened to cause the accident, Arbour hesitated: "There are no explanations – I don't know why it happened. It all happened so fast."

Apparently the pilots had misjudged their position, so that when the DC-3 descended from its normal position at 7,000 feet through the clouds, it flew into Mont Apica at 2,750 feet.[16] "We crashed into trees and we plowed about a quarter of a mile into the forest," recalled Arbour.

There was no fire, no explosion. I had my seatbelt on when we crashed, and everyone who was

wearing his or her seatbelt is still alive. My seat-
mate and I were sitting near the wings and that
part of the fuselage remained intact. I never lost
consciousness, but I had gasoline on my head and
face. Other than my seatmate and me, everyone
else was thrown around the cabin. I saw the pilots,
the stewardess, and another passenger laying dead
in the cabin.

I unbuckled myself and the others. I looked
for my suitcase because I had Valium and some
292s. After grouping the injured near the crash site
I gave them my pills to take away some of their
pain. I'd taken some first aid courses and it really
came in handy that day.

Arbour's experience as a woodsman was also
useful after the crash. He told reporters he had
worked in the woods since the age of 13 and so
he knew that he and the other passengers had
to set up a shelter and build a fire immediately.
Arbour and his seatmate, 19-year-old Louis
Paillé, kept the fire going through the night and

at 5:30 a.m. the two set out toward the signs
of civilization they had seen the previous day.
They walked for 11 hours before finally reaching
Route 160, where they were spotted by motorists.

When the DC-3 failed to arrive at Saint-
Honoré and its pilots were not heard from, a
general alert was sent out. The crash site was
several miles from a military installation, and
during Arbour and Paillé's absence military
searchers spotted the other four survivors. As the
military aircraft could not land because of the
terrain, a medical team was parachuted in from
3,000 feet. Using the searchers' coordinates and
details provided by Arbour and Paillé, by Tues-
day evening help finally arrived at the crash site.
Laurentian lost three talented employees in this
accident: pilot Claude Rousselle, co-pilot Walter
Ferguson and Sylvie Potvin, a flight attendant.
Two passengers died as a result of the crash.[17]
The aircraft was completely destroyed.

Exactly a year later, Laurentian had another
fatal airplane crash in northern Quebec. This

Laurentian Otter C-FCEE at the company's Squaw Lake base circa 1975. C-FCEE was a U.S. Army surplus Otter that
Laurentian bought in 1973. It is now being operated by Johnny May's Air Charter in Kuujjuaq. (JB)

Laurentian Beaver CF-BPA taking off from the Maniwaki seaplane base. A year after this photo was taken, this aircraft was involved in a fatal crash in Lac O'Keefe, Quebec. Pilot Laurie Robertson and three others were killed. (JP)

time the accident involved a Beaver, CF-BPA, which Laurentian had imported four years earlier from Aerial Agriculture in Australia.[18] On August 5, 1975, Laurie Robertson, a young Laurentian pilot, was flying two government conservation officers and another unidentified passenger when the aircraft went down in Lac O'Keefe, Quebec, just across the border from Labrador.[19] The Beaver had apparently been taking part in a forest fire patrol out of Wabush, Labrador, and, according to Jean-Guy Whiteduck, it looked as if the aircraft had stalled.[20] "They found it under 80 feet of water," he remembers. All four aboard the aircraft died from their injuries. They included Carl George and Gary Noseworthy – only 19 years old at the time of the crash – who worked as forest rangers for the Newfoundland Department of Natural Resources.[21]

The triangle weakens

After more than 35 years being crash-free, Laurentian hit an extended rough patch in the mid-1970s. While the DC-3 and Beaver accidents were the worst in terms of fatalities and aircraft write-offs, Laurentian had several other major accidents during those years. Jules Pilon

remembers that during the winter of 1974 in Roberval, Quebec, one of the aircraft operating out of Schefferville had the oleo of one of its wheel-skis come undone. "It was dusk when they landed," he recalls, "and the airplane careened when they went to land. The piston wouldn't go back in so one wheel was longer than the other. They finally landed with the wing one foot off the ground."

Jules himself was involved in an accident with Otter CF-APQ just before the major DC-3 crash in August 1974. "I was flying for an exploration company and was supposed to take them to a lake about 60 miles south of Schefferville," he says. "I was going in to land and misjudged my position, reducing power too early. Too tense to think clearly, it never occurred to me to put it up to full power again. Then I had to settle in the lake, but I didn't have enough room or airspeed to control the aircraft. I hit a sandbar or something and did considerable damage to the Otter."

What had happened to change Laurentian's impeccable safety record? Tim Cole, who was chief pilot in the early 1970s, has a theory. According to him, a successful aviation company is based on a triangle model. "A company has to have the right equipment, the right person-

Otter CF-VQD looking tipsy in Roberval, Quebec, in 1974 after the oleo of one of its wheel-skis came undone upon landing. (JP)

Otter CF-APQ after pilot Jules Pilon had a mishap in July 1974. He and the passengers managed to unload the aircraft and no one was hurt, but the Otter was heavily damaged. A dislodged float and bent propeller are clearly seen in this view. (JP)

nel and proper maintenance to be successful," he states. "During its first 35 years, Laurentian had all three points in this triangle nailed: the de Havilland aircraft were perfect for its needs; their maintenance and training were world-class; and the company had Doug Pickering, who

was an ideal general manager." Pilot Eddy Lord agrees: "Laurentian was one of the best at the time. I talked to some guys who were working for different companies and we were comparing notes. Laurentian was way ahead of them in terms of training, maintenance, and quality of the airplanes. Laurentian was number one at the time." By 1974, though, the triangle was weakening in Tim Cole's view: "It was a boom time in Canada for aviation and Laurentian couldn't get the exceptional personnel it had once had."

"A grand fellow"
In 1975, Laurentian also lost its long-time general manager, Doug Pickering, when he retired after 35 years with the company. While Doug stayed on as one of the company's directors for several more years, he was no longer the cornerstone of the Ottawa operation. Before he left, however, he cemented his reputation as a bush-flying legend with the younger pilots. Jean-Guy Whiteduck remembers doing some hangar flying with him: "In his last years at Laurentian Doug was doing dispatching out of Ottawa and we would get to talking. Doug used to tell me stories about flying the Governor of the Hudson's Bay Company around Quebec to the different outposts. He worked a lot in the region."

Doug still got up in the air from time to time as well. On one occasion in the late 1960s, he impressed writer Deane E. Bostick as well as Laurentian's other pilots when he jumped in the Grumman Goose on a fire-fighting mission while in his sixties.[22] The "boys," as he called the young pilots, were not sure this doting grandfather should go on such a dangerous mission. "Dangerous?" Bostick recalled Doug saying. "Hell, no. Not if the pilot knows what he is doing. And if he doesn't, he shouldn't be up there." Doug certainly knew what he was doing. After all, he had 47 years of bush flying under his belt and had never suffered an injury from a crash.

On this occasion the Forestry Service had reported a fire northeast of Ottawa and the normal ground crews were sent in. When the fire "crowned, rushing over the tree tops at a hundred miles an hour," the fire fighters were forced to flee the area." The next strategy was to muster as many aircraft as possible and water bomb the

area. While Bostick wrote with his customary hyperbole that many of Laurentian's aircraft – including the Cessna 305 "Bird Dog" and Goose – were fitted with water tanks and attacked the flames, Tim Cole laughs at this idea: "The Bird Dog and Goose were certainly not equipped for water bombing, and it wasn't until later that Laurentian outfitted Otter CF-VQD with a tank." Cole does note, however, that Gerry Taillefer and Paul Saunders may have been involved with two of the Beavers, and that Doug Pickering may have taken the Goose out for support work.

Doug was an accomplished bush flyer but by the late 1960s he knew both his and 'BXR's flying days were numbered. Jean-Guy Whiteduck remembers riding along with Doug to Hamilton at this time when 'BXR received a new paint job. On the way back, Whiteduck remembers, "he took it up for a few circuits and then landed on the river after about an hour. I told him he could teach me a few things with 10,000 hours on the Goose!"

Even outside Laurentian's offices or the Goose's cockpit, he knew how to get the job done. Laurentian pilot Brad Mackie was working in Ottawa one snowy winter:

I remember a young pilot struggling to plow the tarmac with an old military type monster jeep. Doug Pickering walked by and noticed the pilot wasn't getting anywhere: the wheels were slipping and the snow bank wasn't moving. So Doug jumped in the jeep, backed all the way across the tarmac, roared back and hit that snow bank so hard, the back wheels flew up in the air! The snow bank moved, Doug jumped out and said to the pilot, "There, that's how you do it."

During his nearly half century of flying, Doug amassed approximately 16,000 flying hours. Long after he left the cockpit – and Laurentian – he stayed connected to the flying community through the Canadian Aviation Historical Society and other organizations. Not surprisingly, this "grand fellow" (as one contemporary called him) continued to be "well-known and widely respected."[23]

"We couldn't compete with that."
As mentioned above, Doug Pickering stayed on as one of the directors of the company through the 1970s, along with F. Tanner, Gordon Maclaren, Joe Gorman and George Beveridge. Even with a dedicated board of directors, however, Laurentian was having trouble dealing with the volatile aviation industry, rising inflation and competition from new quarters. It had expanded rapidly during the James Bay Project and was faced with much more overhead.

In 1970, Laurentian had bases at Blue Sea Lake (Maniwaki), Lac-des-Loups, Schefferville and Little Wabush Lake in Wabush, Labrador.[24] It also operated out of La Tuque airport and Fort Chimo (Kuujuaq).[25] In May of that year, though, it began streamlining operations when it contacted the DOT indicating the company wanted to suspend its licence for the Maniwaki flying school "due to the poor economic outlook and slow down."[26] Then in June 1976, it asked

that its licence to conduct aerial photography and surveys out of Maniwaki be deleted as "there has been no demand for two years and only 138 hours have been flown between November 1975 and February 1976." Then in January 1979, Laurentian deleted its permission to fly non-scheduled specialty services from its Maniwaki, Lac-des-Loups and Schefferville operating certificates.[27] In addition, it deleted the aerial photography and survey portions of its operating licence for its Ottawa, Rockcliffe and Blue Sea Lake bases.

In 1979, Laurentian also decided to shut down one of its subsidiaries, Alliance Aviation. As mentioned in the previous chapter, Alliance had been created at the beginning of the decade to separate Laurentian's flying activities from its aircraft sales, maintenance and engine-overhaul services. As Alliance's listings in *Canadian Aviation* during the 1970s indicated, it specialized in single-engine and light twin-engine aircraft and Pratt & Whitney engines. One of its other selling points was its "non-destructive inspection service." John Kenny worked at Alliance Aviation from 1977 to 1979 in the engine shop. As he says, this non-destructive testing involved using Magnaflux and Zyglow for inspections. While the process may have been more gentle on the engines, it did not mean it was necessarily quiet. "We would run the engine in the test cell using a wooden club-type propeller," Kenny remembers. "It would take four to five hours, measuring fuel flow the whole time. The

After 35 years with the company, Doug Pickering (right) retired in 1975. Pictured at his retirement party (above) are founder and former president of Laurentian Barnet Maclaren and president John Bogie (standing). (DP)

This photo shows Laurentian's Grumman Goose, CF-BXR, with its final paint scheme before being sold to Trans-provincial Airlines in Prince Rupert, B.C., in 1974. The retractable wing floats are clearly visible. John Bogie remembers sending away for the retractable wing float kit from McKinnon Enterprises after 'BXR was heavily damaged in a wind storm in Ottawa in the late 1960s. "It was blown across the airport," he recalls, "and we had to rebuild a lot of it. We were able to re-use its original floats, though, along with the kit." (JB)

whole room would be shaking – the thing would just howl!"

Kenny had come to his cousin's business after quitting his bank job. "I was at the bank for six years and had four different postings in Ottawa," he says. "When I joined Laurentian in 1977 as an apprentice, I took a 50 per cent pay cut, but I had always been interested in engines and I needed a change." He still remembers when he and his brother fixed the cottage lawn mower when he was 12: "I took it apart and put it back together again. I was always tinkering with things and I got a good feeling growing up when I could fix anything from outboard engines to snowmobiles." He was also about 12 years old when John Bogie took him up

Double landing

As Tim Cole recalls, on October 7, 1973, a miraculous thing took place at Maniwaki Airport. Laurentian pilot Gilles Charlebois was flying two passengers in from Val-d'Or in the company's Cessna 337, CF-FGO. When he came in for a southbound landing, another pilot carrying one passenger in a Cessna 170, CF-FVD, landed on top of his aircraft. Amazingly, everyone walked away without injury. (TC)

for his first airplane ride in a Grumman Goose, CF-IFN, and he was bitten by the aviation bug. Working on aircraft and helicopter engines may not have been a very profitable experience for Kenny, but it was certainly an enjoyable one.

It was made especially so by the individuals he worked with. He still fondly remembers operations manager "Jungle" Jim Irvin, "240 Gordie" Bonham (so-called because he was one of the first of the crew to go 240 mph in an airplane), Paul White, Richard Row, Claude Hanson, Keith and Clark Maxsom, and "Doc" Harry Klaasen, who was Dutch and always worked in wooden clogs splattered with every imaginable colour of aircraft paint.

After Alliance's closure in 1979, many of these

men would be shifted to other bases, such as Schefferville, or would go to work elsewhere. As John Bogie stated during an interview, he really felt he had no choice in the matter: "The Canadian government started allowing American-inspected engines into the country. You see, in the U.S. any aircraft mechanic could overhaul an engine and you didn't have to have a special shop, whereas in Canada you had to do special test work. So it ended up being a lot cheaper in the States. Well, we couldn't compete with that so that's when I got rid of Alliance."

Lawrence Lalancette in northern Quebec during the winter of 1974. He and his brother flew Laurentian's DC-3s for several winters during the James Bay Project. (JP)

DC-3 C-FIAR, which began its career in 1944 with the U.S. Army Air Force, was owned by Laurentian from 1975 to 1978. The first photo shows the large double door that was standard on military C-47s (most DC-3s were originally C-47s, and some had smaller passenger doors installed during conversion). In the second view it undergoes engine work during a frigid northern Quebec winter. (JB)

OUTFITTING
DREAMS

Laurentian may have been streamlining its operations in southern Ontario and Quebec during the late 1970s, but business was picking up in the north. Aside from the James Bay Project, the company was expanding its hunting and fishing camps and outfitting services in the Ungava Bay region through its subsidiary Laurentian Ungava Outfitters. After Jack Hume got involved, it soon became a very successful operation and, with Jack's help, John Bogie decided to create a second outfitting company in the early 1980s: Delay River Outfitters.

"I love the north."

During the first decade of Laurentian Ungava Outfitters' existence, it had become clear frontier air tourism was a growth area and sportsmen were willing to go to the far reaches of the continent to seek out unspoiled salmon rivers and caribou grounds – places that were becoming increasingly rare. To attract these sportsmen – and increasingly sportswomen – John Bogie forged relationships with the owners of camps and outfitting operations, as well as created and advertised his own. He spent most of his time looking after the company's big picture in Ottawa, though, and relied upon his Schefferville staff to ensure smooth day-to-day operations at that base.

Ted Bennett, who had worked for Laurentian for two decades, was John's eyes and ears at

the company's most northerly base until he left in the the the late 1970s. Wendell Hume, who went on to become dispatcher, worked with Bennett in Schefferville after a short stint at Laurentian's Ottawa base. "I'm from Lachute, Quebec, and Colin McOuat helped get me a job with Laurentian in the early 1970s," Wendell said in an interview. "I started as traffic manager in Ottawa. I had my pilot's licence, but I promised Jim Irvin, operations manager in Ottawa, I would stay on the ground. In the summer of 1972, he sent me to Schefferville, which I loved – I love the north. I worked with Ted there and got to know all the outfitters." This included some inside knowledge about Laurentian's clients:

We used to look after all the outfitters in the bush: we'd take their food orders, make phone calls for them, that sort of thing. Dave Defoe, one of the outfitters there, used to call up on the high frequency radio – there was only radio communications at that time up there. Dave had a ham radio and I learned that anytime I heard a gurgled radio signal, it was likely him. Ted told me, "If you can't understand the radio it'll be Dave and you gotta turn the radio to A.M." I remember that summer the first thing Dave ordered was a case of whiskey. Ted would always say to him: "Send out the money, Dave. Send out the money."

Wendell also learned about working with Laurentian's pilots at Schefferville at Bennett's side. He remembers Bennett getting annoyed

Schefferville dispatcher Wendell Hume with Laurentian Otter CF-LAB in the Torngat Mountains of Labrador circa 1978. (WH)

Laurentian pilot Andy Keller (left), Laurentian's Schefferville radio operator Martine Hume (woman in centre) with her sisters, and Wendell Hume in front of Otter CF-CEE before flying north to Schefferville. (WH)

with one pilot in particular in 1972. Serge Malle, a young pilot from Germany, was flying one of the DHC-3 Otters. "Serge would make five or six trips a day in the Otter and would not follow Ted's instructions for start-up," Wendell recalls. "You're supposed to use the primer, but Serge would just pump the throttle a few times. Ted kept yelling at him that he would start an engine fire doing that."

"Still," Wendell notes, "Serge knew how to get himself out of a tight jam and was a great pilot."

Quite a few of the pilots were young guys who enjoyed the local night life. "Sometimes they would come out of the disco at 2 or 3 a.m. and then have to climb into a cockpit a couple

Operations manager Jim Irvin (left) and director of maintenance Iain Bogie putting Otter C-GLAA on amphibious floats in Schefferville in the late 1980s. Laurentian bought 'GLAA in 1974 from the U.S. Army Stockton Depot in California and operated it until 1996. (JB)

(Left) Laurentian pilot Merv Langil motoring away from Otter CF-APR in the early 1970s. (WH) (Right) Pat Patterson had been working for the Iron Ore Co. of Canada when he learned Laurentian was hiring pilots. He started on the Cessna 180 before moving up to a Beech 99, becoming chief pilot. (IB)

An unknown mechanic in Schefferville gets what Laurentian employees called "the night shift" repairing one of the Otters' cowlings. (IB)

of hours later – they'd be pretty sad looking," he recalls. "Some of them would also take advantage of bad weather to have a party, visit a girlfriend, or just have a day off." One eager pilot did not fit this mould. Harry Schafer, who became a captain for Air Canada, was always looking to fly: "He was such a gung-ho lad! When he was a kid he had his own little airplane in Schefferville. I never forced a pilot to go flying – I would tell them, 'Go and have a look and if you don't like the conditions, come back.' Well one day a bunch of the other pilots had decided not to fly but Harry went ahead. When he landed at Squaw Lake afterward, did they ever give him a hard time." Roger Gagnon was another Laurentian pilot in Schefferville that did not fit the stereotype. "He was an old bush pilot from Air Fecteau," Wendell says. "He would always come back – what we called a 'real truck driver' of a pilot."

Wendell certainly understood why some of

the younger pilots felt the need to blow off some steam from time to time – or have a day off:

It was unbelievable the hours we worked – we wouldn't get away with it today! The flying was coordinated so tightly: we'd have all these land-ing lights coming in at night – five or six planes arriving all at once before "official darkness." All the pilots had to do their own paperwork in those days and then Martine and I would check it over for mistakes. We didn't get finished work until 9 p.m. most nights and then I would get up at 3 or 3:30 a.m. to get the planes fuelled up and loaded so the pilots could grab their breakfast and be out by dawn.

Craig Bogie, pictured at left in 1973 with one of the U.S. Army Beaver overhauls on its way to Lac Seul Airways, also grew up helping out around the company. At right is Iain Bogie, director of maintenance in Schefferville. (IB)

He and his wife, Martine, did not get much of a chance to socialize, even though they received many invitations. "The outfitters appreciated our work and we made a lot of friends up there," Wendell says. They got to know Martine, especially, as the bilingual woman on the Laurentian radio during the summer months, and appreciated her skill in taking messages, getting weather reports and receiving orders from the outfitters. In the early 1970s, for example, the outfitters would call in with a food order and "Martine would have to transcribe the whole order," Wendell remembers. "Then someone would go to the Hudson's Bay Company and place the order. The HBC would then bring it down to us – we had a warehouse full of groceries and freezers." Eventually many outfitters set up trailers in Schefferville to store their food, but until then they were dependent on Martine, Wendell and the rest of Laurentian's northern staff.

"The last great unspoiled salmon river"

Laurentian provided flying and outfitting services to camps as far north as Fort Chimo (Kuu-jjuaq), about 230 miles away. "Stan Karbowski's camp was as far north as we would fly for the outfitting companies," Wendell Hume recalls. "But Laurentian flew to the Eaton Canyon Club, Tuktu, and Phil Larivière's camp – Wedge Hills – among others. We were one of the first flying services up there, but even when Airgava moved in, a lot of the early outfitters stuck with John Bogie because he'd helped them out by flying them around looking for campsites and salmon rivers. They told me they thought he was a really great guy for doing that." While these outfitters provided some competition for Laurentian's own hunting and fishing camps, the passenger traffic they generated more than compensated.

During Wendell's first few years in Schefferville, Laurentian Ungava Outfitters still catered mostly to fishermen like long-time customer Marc Terziev who wanted to fish the tributaries of the Koksoak River. One of the places the company set up in the early 1970s was the Maricourt camp on the Delay River. During the summer of 1972, John's teenaged son, Iain, his nephew Charles, and one of Iain's friends, Ralph

McOuat, worked alongside senior guide Keith Moore at the camp. Pilot Ted Bennett had found the location earlier, and John Bogie decided to develop it during the summer of 1972 , getting Iain, Ralph, and Charlie to take down the old K. River Lodge buildings and use the lumber to construct the Maricourt camp. They also spent much of the summer fishing the whole of the Delay River, scouting out other good locations.

The Delay River was the "brand-new Quebec river" writers James C. Jones and Len Barnes raved about in the May 1975 issue of *Motor News*. They had been assured by a veteran fishermen that "the elusive fish," the Atlantic salmon, averaging 15 pounds could be "caught readily from outboard boats trolling through holes."[1] To see for themselves, Jones and Barnes joined a group of automobile executives on a fishing trip with Laurentian Ungava Outfitters during the summer of 1974. They set out from Quebec City for Schefferville aboard a Quebecair 727. After a chance encounter with Marc Terziev at the airport, the group flew the 200 miles to Ungava Outfitters' newest camp, the Maricourt camp, in Laurentian's Grumman Goose and an Otter. The authors were captivated by their northern experience:

If it turns you on, as it does us, to realize you are hundreds of miles from a road or other humans, your only path to civilization is an airplane which lands on floats, exotic animals like caribou and wolves in the vicinity, you'll like the trip no matter the fishing luck. We remember after dinner one night building a fire atop the permafrost and sitting outdoors sipping brandy-laced coffee as the northern lights began to pulsate above, lighting up the whole sky, silhouetting the scrubby spruces topping a distant hill.

While the group enjoyed certain aspects of "roughing it," they apparently had expectations – at $1,200 for a five-day all-inclusive package – of more luxurious accommodations and gourmet food instead of "canned soup and sandwiches for lunch, an occasional piece of beef, and slabs of salmon and lake trout poorly prepared" by their Innu guides. The authors graciously recognized, however, that the company was still working out the kinks "as this was the first year of camp." This group was in fact among Laurentian Ungava Outfitters' first customers at the Maricourt camp, along with a couple from New Jersey and a "well-known millionaire sportsman-business tycoon [who] was accompanied by a beautiful blonde model." They were also among the first non-natives to visit the river, as Jones and Barnes wrote: "Only in the last few years has it been explored, and few maps even show it."

Lee Wulff, a well known sports fisherman, was among those trying to uncover the secrets of the Delay. As he wrote in a 1976 *Sports Afield* article, he and a friend, Gene Hill, were exploring the river, trying to find out more about its Atlantic salmon runs.[2] They stayed at the Maricourt camp, having flown in aboard a Laurentian Beaver. The camp, Wulff wrote, "looks stark against the bush background, blocky buildings covered with aluminum sheeting … piles of red and blue gasoline drums on the bank, airplane fuel for the lifeline to civilization." He noted several boats and canoes had been flown in but that they were not in use yet, as "the guides for the season had not come in. We were pretty much on our own," Wulff wrote, which was "really the way an old bush pilot and wilderness angler would prefer it, anyway." After

Two Laurentian Otters at the Schefferville seaplane base circa 1981. (IB)

fishing along the Delay he concluded that it "may be the last great unspoiled salmon river of this continent, and, therefore, of the world." In the years that followed, fishermen and biologists alike would become increasingly intrigued by the Atlantic salmon of the Koksoak and its tributaries – and Laurentian was more than happy to accommodate them.[3]

A Hume family affair

It was not just salmon enthusiasts flying north, however; Laurentian Ungava Outfitters had a steady stream of Quebec-Labrador caribou hunters each year as well. Quebec citizens could hunt independently of an outfitter, Iain Bogie remembers: "They would call in and pick a spot and Laurentian would put a pin on its map so as not to book other people there. Then a pilot would pick up the hunters at the dock and fly them out to the spot." There were also a lot of hunters who would fly themselves to Schefferville. "All Quebeckers, if they had a hunting permit, could hunt up by Schefferville," Iain Bogie notes. "We sold a lot of av gas to hunters who came up in private planes."

In 1977, with the expansion into new camps and increased bookings, Wendell Hume found he was too busy to manage both the Scheffer-

ville base and Ungava Outfitters. At this precise time, his brother, Jack, was laid off from his job as a machinist in an ammunition plant in southern Quebec. Jack had been taking a month off each fall since 1972 to work as a guide for Ungava Outfitters. "I did a lot of hunting and had taken a taxidermy course," he says. "Ungava Outfitters ran into some trouble with its guides – they didn't know how to properly cape caribou heads. So when the hunters got home, the taxidermists didn't have a properly caped head to work with for a wall mount. Laurentian started getting complaints and Wendell hired me for that month each year basically to show the guides how to cape heads." When Jack lost his job, he searched out John Bogie: "I had heard he was looking for a new manager for Ungava Outfitters. I told him, 'I'd like to be your new manager and I'm looking to go into the outfitting business permanently. I know I can handle the camps and the guides, but I don't know if I can fill up your planes. Give me one year and if you're not happy, I'll resign.'"

John gave Jack Hume the job, but the new manager of Ungava Outfitters knew he had a tough road ahead. "I had a hard time at first," Jack recalls:

I had no recent references or pictures to show at the January sportsmen's shows. People would ask, "Who hunted with you last year?" and I'd try to explain how the previous manager hadn't left any of that information. I did pretty well in the end, though – I managed to book about 65 hunters the first year – the same as the previous manager had done – and with nothing to work with. John Bogie was quite pleased, of course, because he was making money from both the outfitting and the airplane businesses.

One of these 1978 bookings was John Power and his group of hunters, which was fortunate as Power went on to write a glowing article for *Legion* magazine. His descriptions of Laurentian Ungava Outfitters' Lac Dihourse camp stimulated the imagination of readers: the exciting two-hour flight in an Otter from Schefferville; the tent camp site that accommodated a dozen sportsmen per four-day hunt; and the "scores" of caribou they saw as the animals began their annual migration. Even his statement that "caribou is the tastiest fare in nature's pantry" must have aroused curiosity.[4]

Five years later, there was no question of Jack Hume resigning. He had doubled his bookings annually, until he reached an average of 750 hunters per year. This was largely due to increased publicity as more American publications featured articles about hunting Quebec-Labrador caribou. Jack attended conventions in the United States, such as the Safari Club International convention in Las Vegas in 1983, where he signed up California-based outdoor writer Craig Boddington among others.[5] Then there were those who heard of the hunting opportuni-

ties through word of mouth. After his friend had gushed about his experiences with Laurentian Ungava Outfitters, Gordon Christiansen immediately booked with Jack Hume.[6] In late August 1983, he drove the 825 miles from his home in Palmer, Maryland, to Drummondville, Quebec, in his pick-up truck, spending the night in a restaurant parking lot before starting for Sept-Îles at first light. He spent another night in his truck at Sept-Îles airport before flying to Schefferville, and then onwards to the Lac Dihourse Camp in a Beaver with a freighter canoe strapped to the floats. His trip met his expectations. Even though he had missed a migration of 30,000 caribou that had passed by the camp two weeks earlier, he still proudly noted that "my caribou meat and horns ... just barely got through the door" of the Beaver on the trip back.

Avid hunter and author John Wootters wrote an article for *Petersen's Hunting 1983 Guide* that would also have made trophy hunters salivate: "The bulls grow such antlers in this region that the Boone and Crockett record book makes a distinction between the ordinary Barren Ground caribou and these, which it sets apart under the term 'Quebec-Labrador caribou.'"[7] A hunter would have a good chance of spotting a trophy rack – there were an estimated 400,000 animals in the Ungava herd alone – and could revel in the knowledge that he was among the first wave of hunters to discover this land and these herds. As Wootters noted, the region had just recently been opened up to hunters because of float-plane operations like Laurentian. Before then, there was simply "no way to get at it."[8]

A hunter would also be well-situated at

The entrance to Laurentian Ungava Outfitters' Maricourt camp on the Delay River circa 1975. (JB)

the Lac Dihourse camp. As H. Lea Lawrence wrote in 1983, Laurentian Ungava Outfitters had located the camp "right in the migration path of three caribou herds."[9] Still, bagging a trophy bull was not guaranteed, Lawrence noted: "Sparse cover on the tundra presents barren ground caribou hunters with mental and physical challenges. Successful hunters must be able to execute well-planned stalks, anticipate the bull's path of travel, and shoot accurately at long ranges." Furthermore, the larger bulls brought up the "rear near the end of September" – which was also nearing the end of the hunting season – and so many trophy hunters would take the last booking of the season. This was a gamble, though, as caribou migrations could be delayed by warm weather and the "untold billions of mosquitos and black flies that emerge whenever the temperature rises much above freezing."[10] When that occurred, the caribou would simply wait in a more northerly location or on higher ground. Other times, unseasonably cold weather could interfere with the best-laid plans: in late September 1983, for example, a group of hunters had to be flown out by helicopter as the lakes had frozen over.[11]

Jack Hume, manager of Laurentian Ungava Outfitters (left) poses with former shooting editor of *Outdoor Life* magazine, Jim Carmichael. (JH)

While some hunters wanted an easy hunt and a guaranteed trophy, for many the gamble was part of the excitement. Many hunters embraced Jack Hume's insistence on "strictly fair-chase hunting" and the age-old idea of man versus nature. As Wootters noted, running along the tundra in heavy clothes with a rifle over your shoulder seemed "to be a regular part of caribou hunting in Quebec" and visitors should expect to brave tough conditions in Quebec's sub-arctic. "Some of these lakes are big," he wrote. "The rivers are swift, and the merciless wind never ceases; you quickly become aware of the fragility of the canoe." Especially as if you were to fall into the frigid water, he warned, "the average survival time in it is less than ten minutes."

It is beautiful and majestic in its own way, as all totally wild places are, and it is also cruel and unforgiving. A man is not permitted very many mistakes in this subarctic wilderness, and the statistics prove it. During my visit and the month previous, three caribou hunters had lost their lives in the area through momentary carelessness, and three more were presumed dead, their bodies unrecovered.

During Wootters' time at the Lac Dihourse camp, "a big wind storm came up one day and one of the groups of hunters did not come back to camp." Those at camp wondered if they were "still alive and, if so, how they were faring with no shelter, no food, no firewood, and no hope of rescue until the wind died. A party of guides left about 4:00 the next morning, after the wind had abated slightly, and found them safe and cheerful after their ordeal. Men, canoes, rifles and a pair of beautiful caribou heads literally were sheathed in ice, but they made it."

Like the ones that rescued the party of hunters, the guides Jack Hume hired for Laurentian Ungava Outfitters' camps were top-notch. Jack

John Bogie poses above with one of Laurentian Ungava Outfitters' best guides, Barnabe Raphael, and a Quebec-Labrador caribou that his octogenarian friend Dr. Charlie Schwartz had just killed with a single shot. Below, John shows off the catch of the day at the Delay River Fishing camp. (JB)

assigned Wootters a guide named Henry Blacksmith who, along with the six other guides, was from the Mashteuiatsh reserve (formerly known as Pointe-Bleue) near Lac Saint-Jean, Quebec. People in this community, Wootters wrote, were "famous hunters and guides. Henry has eyes that would make a farsighted eagle hang its head in shame…. He speaks three languages, including English, but he's not likely to wear out his stock of words very soon." Bowhunting enthusiast H. Lea Lawrence was similarly impressed with guide André Charlis' "exceptionally keen eyesight." He also witnessed his talent at field dressing: "André, so skilled and fast with a knife that Jack assured us our assistance would only interfere, had the task halfway completed before we were finished admiring the trophy."[12] Jack had tremendous faith in André and other men from Mashteuiatsh, as he made clear to Lawrence: "They are certainly the most dependable and skilled guides I've ever encountered" and were responsible for the fact that the Lac Dihourse camp produced "several record book heads each year."[13]

Laurentian had improved the Lac Dihourse camp in the five years it had been open. For one, it now had cabins instead of tents. As Craig Boddington excitedly noted "each cabin had bunks and a stove, and, miracle of miracles, there were hot showers!"[14] The Maricourt camp was also "full facility" by the mid-1980s, as H. Lea Lawrence reported, but Laurentian had opened new tent camps for caribou hunting, like Audipur – 125 miles south of the Lac Dihourse camp – which still had "more rustic accommodations."[15] In 1983, customers paid an average of $1,600 to $3,000 for a week-long hunting trip, including return flights between Schefferville and the camp. Hunters would then pay an additional $255 for a caribou licence for two tags, and $26.50 if they wanted to add a black bear and small game licence.

In 1984, Jack Hume decided that although "John Bogie was one of the best men I've ever worked with," it was time to move on. His ambition had always been to have his own outfitting business and he was starting to get restless. "At that time in Quebec, you had to buy an existing outfitter – you couldn't get a new licence, " Jack explains. "So I approached John Bogie: 'You've got two licences. If I could get hunting added to your fishing licences at the Delay Salmon camp, would you sell me Laurentian Ungava Outfitters?' And John replied, 'I've been lobbying for about ten years for precisely that – but you can give it a try'." Jack had some contacts from his frequent trips to meet with provincial officials at Quebec City and, as he says, "I made one phone call to the guy in charge – who I got along with real well – and got the hunting added. A half hour later, a copy of the licence was sitting on the fax machine."

After setting up a meeting with John Bogie in Ottawa, however, it became clear to Jack that his boss did not want to lose his services or the outfitting licence right away. Jack patiently waited for two years until January 1, 1986, when John signed Laurentian Ungava Outfitters over to him.[16] Part of the deal was that John would finance Laurentian Ungava Outfitters for five years, during which time Jack had to fly exclusively with Laurentian. "In three years I had booked enough hunters to pay off my debts to John and had my own company," Jack notes.

"Caribou Capital of the World."

During his last two years with Laurentian, Jack Hume helped John Bogie expand the Delay River camp to include both hunting and fishing, eventually creating another subsidiary, Delay River Outfitters (DRO), known in French as Les Pourvoyeurs de la rivière De-

lay. As Jack recalls, there were approximately two bowhunting and eight rifle camps under this licence, as well as salmon fishing camps. To help publicize this venture, Jack got in touch with one of North America's premier hunters, Bob Foulkrod, whom he had met at a convention in Harrisburg, Pennsylvania. Foulkrod was interested in caribou hunting with DRO so Jack arranged for him to hunt with writer and outdoors enthusiast H. Lea Lawrence. This turned out to be an inspired partnership that benefited Laurentian in the years to come and led to an enduring friendship between the two men.

Foulkrod and Lawrence spent 16 days travelling from camp to camp: they began at the Maricourt camp and then flew north 60 miles to the aptly-named North camp. They had flown in aboard a Laurentian Beaver and stayed in "a tiny log cabin on the river bank," with a forest of black spruce, tamarack and overflowing blueberry bushes behind them. As Lawrence wrote in 1986, they had chosen this camp because "there was word that the caribou migration was underway in the vicinity."[17] As he goes on to note, "The word had been correct, and in three days we'd seen more caribou than either of us had seen in three years of hunting in Quebec." During that leg of the trip, Foulkrod captured the new Quebec-Labrador caribou Pope & Young title after he bagged a prize bull with his bow and arrows.

They did not spend their whole trip at the North Camp, however, because part of their mission was to explore new territory for DRO. According to Lawrence, "the caribou migrations had become somewhat erratic and deviated from some of their traditional courses," likely due to dramatic

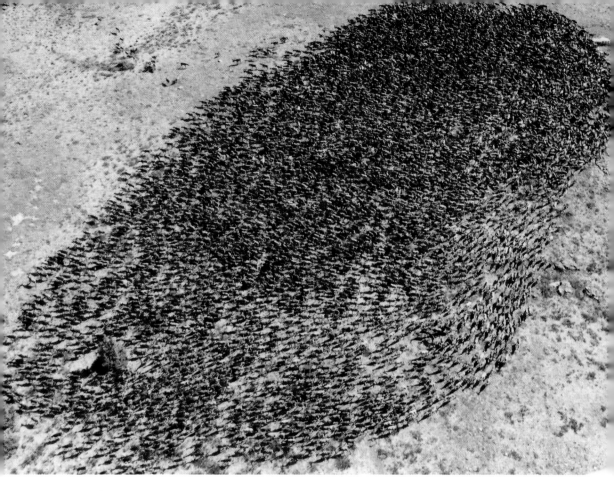

Caribou on the move. (JB)

increases in herd size, which led to overgraz-
ing along their usual routes.[18] "Old camps that
have always had high kill levels have dropped off
to nearly zero in some cases, so survival in the
outfitting business has meant exploration and
establishment of new camps." John Bogie was
well aware of this and was anxious that Foulkrod
and Lawrence find "places where new outpost
camps could be located." Their next stop was Indian Lake, about 250 miles northwest of Schefferville, where a "government geologic station"
had been abandoned several years earlier. As was
the regional custom, the government had left
everything behind, including "a tent-frame cabin
and an abundance of scrap wood and metal." As
DRO had been using the site as an occasional

outpost camp, "it required only minor clean-up
and rearranging to be usable."

In late August 1986, Lawrence and Foulkrod
went even further afield in search of camp locations, flying three and a half hours from Schefferville to a remote point in Labrador's Torngat
Mountains. The men travelled in a DHC-2
Beaver piloted by Jean-Yves Lafontaine, and, as
Lawrence wrote in 1987, the flight was a little
nerve-racking:

*The plane was winding its way up a canyon that
we weren't sure continued all the way through the
mountain range. If it didn't and we were boxed
in, it meant a return trip down the tortuous route.
That is, if the ceiling didn't lower even further and*

Richard Hume: All fished out

Jack would often bring his teenaged son, Richard, along to Laurentian Ungava Outfitters' camps in the summertime to help him set things up. During the summer of 1983, they set out for one of the fishing camps at Lake Champdore, about 80 miles north of Schefferville, to repair the dock and bear-damaged camp before a group of anglers arrived. The morning they were due to leave, they woke up early "and packed all of our supplies, including building materials and enough food to hold us for a week or longer" onto Otter CF-CEE with the help of pilot Roger Gagnon. As Richard recalls:

"Although fixing the camp and repairing a dock in frigid water wasn't something either of us were ever looking forward to, I can speak for both of us when I say that we couldn't wait to get to Lake Champdore and some of the best trout fishing you can dream of. To our dismay just as Roger pulled up in the Otter, Wendell came out and told us the weather wasn't holding up and that we would have to wait for better weather before departing.

"It wasn't long and the winds picked up and the rain started to pour down. I remember standing at the door of Laurentian's warehouse thinking it would never stop raining when Wendell came in and told me to get the food out of the Otter and put it back in the cold room. I had all but given up on getting in to the camp when a few hours later the rain came to a halt all of a sudden and Wendell and Roger came running out to the dock and yelled out to me and my father to get to the plane quickly as Roger was going to give it a try before it got too late.

"You would have to know Roger Gagnon in order to understand what kind of rush my father and I were in at this point. Roger was yelling, 'Let's go – we don't have much time,' and Roger was the kind of guy who spoke once and you had better listen or you might stay behind! He once had me jump out of the Otter into freezing cold water up over my chest as he was trying to sail the plane onto a rock-covered shore line. I certainly wouldn't dare hesitate when he gave me an order.

"Anyhow off we went. Upon arriving we unloaded the Otter and as there was only about an hour until sunset, Roger didn't hang around but took off back to Schefferville immediately. It wasn't until he was on the step and just about out of the water that my father looked over to me

and asked if I had reloaded the food into the plane. I said, 'Nope. Did you?'

"Well, we had no radio communication with the base and Roger was long gone. We were looking at a week without any food, a bear-wrecked camp that was in far worse shape than we had expected, a dock to repair that had been pushed ashore by the ice, and enough mosquitoes to drive a person insane. We sat around feeling sorry for ourselves for a bit, but then got to work repairing one of the damaged buildings enough to use as a shelter.

"When I woke up the next morning, my father was lighting a fire and had a little grin on his face. It turned out that he had found a half-filled box of corn bread. That first batch of corn bread was terrible – it was hard as rock, a little burned and pretty much tasteless. As bad as the corn bread was, as the week went on and the only other food we had was the trout we caught, we started guarding our corn bread rations.

Jack Hume (on aircraft) with his son Richard (Dick) Hume prepare Jack Hume Adventures' Cessna 185, C-GQDB, a few years after they took over Laurentian Ungava Outfitters from John Bogie. (JH)

"We survived the week and were very happy when Roger returned to pick us up. When we arrived in Schefferville, though, we were not impressed with the dinner menu: trout! We had eaten unseasoned pan-fried trout for breakfast, lunch and supper for over a week and felt the universe was definitely playing a trick on us. Needless to say, I asked for a bologna sandwich, and it was the best one I've ever had. I'll tell you, in the past 26 years of helping my dad and running an outfitting business I have never forgotten another food order."

Laurentian acquired its first DHC-6 Twin Otter, C-GDQY, in 1976 and sold it two years later to Labrador Airways. In the second view it is at La Tuque and below it calls at one of Tuktu's outfitting camps, still wearing its Bakhtar Afghan Airlines colours. The versatile Twin Otter was equally useful for scheduled services and for flying into remote camps. (JB)

Laurentian bought this aircraft, a Cessna 337 Skymaster, in 1978 in "as is" condition from Confederation College in Thunder Bay, Ontario. The college's mechanical engineering students had been practising on it and it had not been flown since 1975. Even so, as Iain Bogie recalls, it was useful in Schefferville throughout the 1980s: "When we were flying a Twin Otter packed full of hunters and tourists, we would put all the excess baggage in the 337 and fly it behind the Twin Otter." In this photo, its "push-pull" configuration is quite visible: instead of having engines on each wing, one is mounted on its nose and the other is at the rear of the fuselage. (JB)

close things off entirely…. There had been a few small snow squalls, but they had been scattered and hadn't posed any visibility problems …. [but] the conditions had gone from fair to forbidding very rapidly. Not that it had been a surprise, because from the time we had been able to see the Torngat Mountains, we had known that the clouds shrouding them were going to pose a problem. [19]

While there was a stream flowing through the canyon below them, Lawrence commented that it "wouldn't have accommodated even a 17-foot canoe," so there was no hope that Lafontaine would be able to land the Beaver on it in an emergency.

Luckily they, along with DRO's top guide, Barnaby Raphael, made it to their destination in one piece. Lawrence then had the opportunity to survey his surroundings: "There were deep, narrow fjords with precipitous walls and icebergs dotting the Labrador Sea, countless glaciers and gin-clear glacial lakes, and absolutely no indication that human beings had ever visited the land below us." This landscape, which held "no appeal for the ordinary traveller," Lawrence stated, was

heaven for hunters as it was "the summer home of great numbers of caribou, which migrate to the area to escape the pestilence of blackflies and mosquitoes." He and Foulkrod had even greater reason to be excited: they were the first nonresidents to be granted a licence to hunt caribou in Labrador. Their expectations were quickly met when the group spotted caribou before they even landed: "Two bull caribou were standing at the water's edge, and they didn't bolt when the Beaver's pontoons touched down. Instead, they stood and watched as the plane taxied to the spot on shore we had picked as a possible campsite." Once they stopped, Bob got out and stalked the caribou, shooting one. Then Lafontaine taxied the Beaver downstream, where they loaded the carcass and brought it back to the campsite.

The caribou were not the only large mammals in the vicinity, Lawrence noted, and hunters had to beware of polar and black bears: "The serious problem is that polar bears consider everything food, including people. And if such an attack were to occur, a scoped rifle beside a sleeping bag in a tent isn't of much use." As Lawrence related, Lafontaine tried hard to impress upon the group the importance of vigilance:

Jean-Yves had heightened our consciousness of these chilling facts by telling us of a trio of college students on a scientific project whom he'd flown into this area a couple of years before. He had returned to the base, and several days later when he came back in with supplies, he found them in a state of shock and hysteria. The first day, a polar bear had raided their camp and made a shambles of it. Fortunately, they hadn't been present when this had happened, although they had seen the bear. And if this wasn't enough, after they had moved the camp away from the lakeshore farther up on the bank, a black bear came through the next night and devastated what they had left. As Jean-Yves took them out, they were vowing never to return. He said one of the party was so badly shaken that he could barely talk.

The Three Musketeers and the Stolen Beer (as told by Richard Hume)

Another summer, when Richard was about 15 years old, he was sent to the Lac Dihourse camp with 19-year-old Craig Bogie and his friend Bruce "Boots" Hineman, to tear down the original kitchen building so that a new one could be built. Craig and Bruce had been working as dockhands that summer, but it was decided they could be spared for the project and Jack sent his son along to help.

Laurentian pilot Bob McKenzie flew them in, and Jack helped them unload the food and a radio off the plane while sternly warning them "not to take out the three-wheel ATV joy riding and, most importantly, not to drink the beer he had stashed in his cabin. My father decided to take extra precautions and wrapped a big chain around the ATV and attached it with a padlock before leaving. I was a bit surprised that he trusted us with his beer but it wasn't my place to say anything!"

Richard continues, "It hadn't been an hour when Craig and Boots gave up working on the kitchen and decided to put me to work cutting the chain off the bike with a hack saw they had found in the tool shed. At first I refused to be the one to cut the chain, but when you're young and there are two bigger guys teamed up against you, arguing doesn't seem like the best idea. So, off came the chain and off went Craig on his joyride. Then it was Boots's turn. As soon as Boots came back off I went and this continued for a while until we finally decided to get back to work. That very same night Craig and Boots also decided they would look around for Dad's beer and once again I tried to stop them but only succeeded in getting locked outside as the wolves began to howl. I was frightened to death and stayed by their cabin door until they finally let me in about an hour later.

"We actually managed to get the kitchen torn down and everything was looking pretty good when we heard the roar of the Otter as it flew over us. We started feeling a little panicky as we watched my father get off the Otter – it would only be a few minutes until he would see the chain was cut off the bike and, worse yet, that all his beer was gone. I knew we were in serious trouble. My father is a fair man but you don't want to upset him!

"We walked up to the kitchen and he congratulated us on a job well done and went on to offer each of us a beer. At this point we were all pretty much scared for our lives; none of us had the nerve to tell him about the beer so we just followed him to his cabin. I can't begin to describe the look on his face (and I won't repeat the words he used) when he discovered what we'd done. We all apologized. Then, as we made our way back towards the kitchen, he stopped to look at the ATV and noticed the chain had been cut.

"Once again nobody spoke up and we all took the blame.

"Craig and Boots were supposed to stay and help rebuild the kitchen, but after all this my father decided it might be best if they went back to Schefferville. Of course Craig and Boots loved the idea – until Dad made his final demand: that they give us their bug jackets in exchange for leaving Lac Dihourse early and in payment for the beer they drank. Back in those days nobody had even heard of bug jackets but Craig and Boots owned them and they worked great (in fact, we sell those same bug jackets at my company today). So off went the jackets and off went my good friends Craig and Boots."

Three Otters returning from the same work area do a fly-by of the base at Squaw Lake. As John Bogie remarks, "Some pilots always fly with the landing light on so others will see them. On floats you never landed at night so you did not worry if the light burned out." Two of the machines here are former Norwegian Otters still in their green paint and the other wears Laurentian markings. (JB)

Soon, the two hunters were actually seeking out bears – at least black ones. As Lawrence wrote in several articles during the late 1980s, when the caribou were not moving, or simply when an opportunity presented itself, a black bear could be a welcome target to pursue.[20] After a four-day stakeout at the Lac Audipur archery camp in 1987, Lawrence and Foulkrod had not seen a single caribou worth shooting. While eating breakfast on the fifth day, Lawrence spotted a black bear and spent the next day trying to outsmart it. In the end, he bagged his bear and was very pleased with the trip – even without getting a caribou.

By this time John Bogie had hired Bob Foulkrod as DRO's U.S. marketing manager. Jack Hume's earlier work and Foulkrod's contacts meant that hunts from the main camps along the Delay River – Maricourt and North Camp – were now booked at least a year in advance.[21] It is not surprising, given outdoor writers like Don Kirk were now proclaiming Schefferville the "Caribou Capital of the World," and DRO "one

of northern Quebec's most outstanding caribou guide services."[22] The cost of a fly-in hunting trip up north, he argued, was "only a little more than a quality Rocky Mountain elk hunt," and the price of caribou hunting licences (with two tags) had dropped from C$255 in 1983 to C$110 in 1986 – or about US$80 with the exchange rate. If that were not enough to convince hunters, Kirk reported that DRO had a success rate of almost 100 per cent, and four out of five caribou racks made a record book entry.

Even with increased competition from other outfitters and camps in the region, Laurentian Ungava Outfitters and later Delay River Outfitters became very successful operations in the 1980s. John Bogie had taken his uncle Barnet Maclaren's original idea of flying sportsmen one step further by creating his own fly-in fishing and hunting spots, which meant he was making money on multiple fronts. In 1988, it appeared as if Laurentian could maintain this magic formula indefinitely.

LAURENTIAN'S LAST FLIGHT

In the 1980s, Laurentian created another successful subsidiary, Air Schefferville. This new company, which John Bogie formed in 1981, provided all the flying for Delay River Outfitters Inc. (DRO) and became the umbrella company under which DRO operated. John's son, Iain, who had become maintenance supervisor at Schefferville in 1979, was on-site to help create the new company.

Iain had been captivated by aviation since childhood and became involved in his father's company at an early age. As mentioned before, as a teenager Iain spent a summer locating new fishing camps along the Delay River. He also worked as a dock boy, loading planes for Laurentian in the early 1970s before getting his Airframe and Powerplant (A&P) licence in the United States and his Aircraft Maintenance Engineer (AME) licence in Canada. "I really got into working for Laurentian around 1976," Iain remembers. "After I got my licences, my dad put me to work in Ottawa." When John shut down Alliance Aviation in 1979, he sent Iain up to Schefferville to be director of maintenance for Laurentian. As Iain says, this was not an unwelcome move: "I liked it up there. My wife and I were young, and we managed to save for a good down payment when we later moved to Ottawa. It was interesting work, too. I was busy and there were always new people coming in – pilots, workers and so on. The winters could be hard, but in May it was great for skidooing."

In 1981, when he and his father started up Air Schefferville, Quebecair pulled its Boeing 737-200 from scheduled service to the northern town as it "found the volume of passengers and freight was insufficient" outside the caribou hunting season "to warrant a jet service five days a week.[1] Quebecair continued its jet service to nearby Wabush, however, and Air Schefferville agreed to operate as the larger company's feeder airline for this location.[2] From Wabush, passengers could fly with Quebecair to Sept-Îles or on to major cities like Montreal.[3]

John Bogie used a number of the aircraft for this work, but the company's DHC-6 Twin Otters proved to be ideal. As he recalls, "We mainly used them for the sched service but they offered a lot of flexibility because they could also get into our hunting and fishing camps on floats or tundra tires, while the DC-3s couldn't." According to Fred Hotson, de Havilland Canada's engineers had "always visualized an Otter with two engines" and northern bush operators liked the DHC-3 Otter but wanted a second engine for safety, and "more payload to stay competitive."[4] DHC started manufacturing the Series 100 Twin Otter in 1966 and it immediately caught the interest of buyers around the world, even as far away as Afghanistan. In fact, Laurentian's first one, C-GDQY, which it purchased in 1976, had also been the first of the five Twin Otters Afghanistan's Sultan Ghazi ordered between 1966 and 1969.

In 1982, when the Iron Ore Company shut down mining operations completely at Schefferville, a mass exodus took place. By the following year, the population of the town had fallen far below early-1960s figures of approximately 4,000 people to 1,050. Wendell Hume, who was still working for Laurentian as a dispatcher for Air Schefferville, remembers that "after the Iron Ore Co. left town, it started looking pretty run down. There were all these abandoned buildings and no landscaping anymore – they used to import top soil and plant grass around the houses. Then it became hard to get anything – fresh vegetables, etc." Still, he and his wife, Martine, who did clerical work and operated the radio for Air Schefferville, stayed on.

Even with the departure of the Iron Ore Company, Iain notes, "We were always busy." During the winter months,

A Beech Queen Air, C-FIAQ, Air Schefferville purchased from Labrador Airways, still with that company's markings, is pictured at Schefferville airport circa 1983. (IB)

Come August, when the official caribou hunting season began, Air Schefferville continued to fly groups to Delay River Outfitters and other camps. The company would be busy with maintenance on its own aircraft as well as privately owned planes. One of the things pilots learned quickly in Schefferville was how strong the winds could be. "When you tie up a plane to a dock," Iain explains. "You never park it with the tail to the wind. Well, one guy did this once with a little Cessna and we got some heavy

There were lots of First Nations passengers. Around May or so we would usually bring out a few groups of native hunters for the caribou hunt. The hunters would go and herd the caribou onto the ice and shoot them, letting them freeze into the snow to preserve them until we came back up with the plane. They wouldn't cut them up and pack them into boxes and sometimes the bodies were pretty fresh. You can't believe the blood in the belly of the planes that carried the caribou back. We'd have to do a thorough cleaning afterwards – not only for our other passengers, but because the salt in the blood would make the plane corrode like crazy.

Two First Nations hunters take a break after loading their caribou into an Air Schefferville Otter. (IB)

An unexpected engine change. Iain Bogie took these photos in the summer of 1978 when he and engineer Bob Tunis had to change the engine on Otter CF-VQD out in the bush. As Iain recalls, "Something failed – a blower or supercharger. We made an engine hoist out of poles and got it sorted out." (IB)

winds. The aircraft was half-sunk the next morning. The guy wanted us to help him get it out of the water but we couldn't. They had to bring a crane in to lift it out."

Iain often had helpers on hand, such as apprentices Ed Lucos and Geoff Campbell, whom he fondly remembers as the best workers he had ever had.[5] Usually, Iain notes, "There were only two people doing maintenance on all the planes. It was a job that lasted seven days a week, and sometimes we would work through the night to get a plane fixed up. We were constantly doing maintenance." It was hard work that often took place away from the base. "One time," Iain recalls, "an Otter blew an engine in the bush and a helicopter had to fly a new one in. I changed the engine out there in the bush – and boy was that a pain. The bugs were awful!"

Another time, which Iain and the crew dubbed the "four-wheel-drive Beaver" incident, a pilot landed across a lake but did not have enough room to complete his landing, ending up on shore where the leading edge of one of the floats struck a tree. Iain remembers he and pilot Pat Patterson went to assess the damage: "We decided it was flyable and since the weather was good and the water was calm we were able to fly it back to base even with the damaged floats."

Iain also notes that the company aircraft suffered a lot of ski damage in spring, when the ice and snow conditions were trickiest:

A photo of the "four-wheel-drive Beaver" incident circa 1988. This shot shows that the far float has a big crease where it buckled on impact, and also illustrates one style of canoe rack Laurentian used on its Beavers. (IB)

We had a lot of trouble with skis folding back and jamming into the tails of aircraft. Once a pilot landed an Otter and the ski broke when he landed, cutting into the tail. I had to go out there and fix it, but the plane that brought me in landed two miles away where the ice was better. I had to walk all the way to the Otter carrying my toolkit and then work on it out there – putting on a new tail wheel – before walking back.

Carrying out maintenance at the Schefferville base was not necessarily any more comfortable – especially in winter. As Iain noted during an interview, "In 1978 or 1979 the Quebec DOT made us build a hangar at Schefferville. This really made Dad mad – boy was he fuming. So we built the cheapest hangar we could up there. I tell you, when it was -40 or -50 Celsius in the winter time that hangar didn't do anything to keep the cold out." In fact, inflatable balloon tents were often more practical: "We could set up heaters in them and as long as it wasn't too windy, you could be in there working in short sleeves while it was -40 outside!"

In 1985, after struggling financially for several years, Quebecair sold its assets to Canadian Pacific Airlines. Air Schefferville continued to operate the scheduled feeder service to Wabush, first with Twin Otters, and later using Beech Queen Airs for a short period.[6] "We sold one of our Beech Queen Airs to someone down in Florida," Iain remembers. "Its piston engines didn't work too well in the northern Quebec winters." By the late 1980s, Laurentian was using its 15-passenger Beech 99s for this twice-daily run and was renting counter space at the Wabush airport. As John Bogie wrote, at this time "Wabush contributed about 25 per cent of our total traffic" and the company was looking to increase this number.

Jeff Campbell (left) and Ed Lucos, maintenance engineer apprentices working on Otter C-FCEE. Behind them is a DC-3 engine tent made to be inflated and heated by a Herman Nelson heater for working outdoors in cold northern winters. (IB)

The last years of Delay River Outfitters

In 1989 Laurentian – like Quebecair, Airgava and so many other companies during this period – ran into its own financial crisis. This was largely due to a cash shortage when the company started up Air Laurentian, a scheduled service between Hamilton and Ottawa. As John Bogie notes, "Canadian Airlines shut down that route and so we decided to try it with smaller aircraft like Beech 99s and King Airs. A short while later, CP Air also shut down its Buttonville [north of Toronto] to Ottawa route, and we decided to try that as well. Competition from other carriers didn't make it worthwhile, but at that point it was too late to shut down as the route was tied to our Air Schefferville licence and you have to give 90 days notice to shut down a sched service. We didn't want to lose our licence, so we shut down the route but had to operate until the 90 days were over.

It was at this point that Wendell and Martine Hume decided to leave the company and go to work for Wendell's brother, Jack, at Jack Hume

Otter C-GLAA on a calm Labrador day circa 1993. John Bogie, Colin McCouat and pilot Roger Gagnon are in the raft. The men were flying around the region looking for prime arctic char fishing spots for future DRO camps. (JB)

Adventures. Bob Foulkrod, however, was still the U.S. marketing agent for DRO, and his old hunting buddy H. Lea Lawrence helped to keep it in the public eye with an article in *Game Country: The Journal of Big Game Hunting.* In it, he describes his flight from Schefferville to the North Camp in one of Air Schefferville's Otters, and the changes to the camp that had occurred over his four years of hunting caribou there: "Since my initial visit, I had seen it transformed from a single, one-room cabin and no amenities to a comfortable operation with hot and cold running water, an indoor toilet and shower, generator power, and eight buildings and tents. Still an 'outpost,'

perhaps, but in a more sophisticated sense."[7]

Bowhunters like Lawrence were particularly appreciative of Foulkrod's caribou archery camps. Wildlife photographer and hunter Leonard Lee Rue III wrote in 1989 that the Delay River camp was "a bowhunter's idea of paradise," even with frequent rainy weather and black flies that "so savaged" his friend's face and ears "that they were swollen and had the surface texture of … ground round."[8] As he noted, however, with the proper insect repellent and rain gear, a hunter could comfortably engage in the most thrilling stalk of his life. Outdoor writer Dan Brockman was at the North Camp at the same

One of Air Schefferville's Beech 99's, C-FEJL, at Schefferville airport loading passengers for its scheduled operation circa 1991. The company only had this paint scheme with the caribou on the tail for a short period. In the second photo, C-FEJL sports Canadian Airlines colours circa 1996. Air Schefferville provided feeder service to Sept-Îles for the latter company in the 1990s. (JB)

Air Laurentian operated Beech 99 C-FAWX for its southern scheduled service between Ottawa and Hamilton beginning in 1989. As Iain Bogie recalls, "Passengers loved this aircraft – it had these big windows so they got a great view of the Toronto harbour when we flew over it. Also, one of the pilots was an ex-Air Canada captain called Frank, and he would give them a running commentary during the flight, just like a tour guide! People always wanted to know if Frank would be flying them and were disappointed if he wasn't." The Beech 99 helped create modern commuter aviation in the early years of deregulation and is still making money for small carriers in Canada and the U.S.A. (JB)

time as Rue, lured by its "outstanding" hunting record and "amazing" promotional videos. He flew into camp in one of Air Schefferville's Beavers, joining a group of ten hunters, mostly Americans from Wisconsin, Oklahoma and Massachussets. His assessment of the "prime archery caribou camp in northern Quebec" was positive: "The scenery unique and beautiful, the camp comfortable, the food ample and good, the equipment in good shape, and as an added bonus, everyone in camp got along well together.[9] Outdoor writer G. Fred Asbell gave a similarly favourable review in 1990:

Delay River Outfitters runs one of the classiest camps I've ever seen.... The camp is as modern as my home in Colorado. There are generator-powered electric lights, showers – indoors, with hot water from a hot water heater – flush toilets, a kitchen with two really attractive lady cooks, refrigerators, ovens and microwaves.... And those two lady cooks put meals together for us that were better than the last big dinner we had in Montreal. I can't imagine more courteous, more competent people existing in any camp.[10]

NFL running back Walter "Sweetness" Payton bags a caribou while hunting with renowned trophy hunter and Delay River Outfitter's U.S. marketing manager Bob Foulkrod (in white hat), circa 1990. (JB)

While Foulkrod and the DRO staff could do their best to ensure their clients' comfort and enjoyment, they had a harder time getting the caribou to cooperate. As Brockman wrote, "Bob Foulkrod got us together after dinner and apologized for the slow hunting and complimented us on maintaining our enthusiasm through the less than favourable hunting conditions. Bob believed that unseasonably warm weather and multitudes of black flies had kept the caribou up on the open ridges above the water.[11] Monty Browning, who worked as an occasional guide and taxidermist for Delay River Outfitters, also noted during his August 1990 hunt that the caribou were "stalled out on the high ridges to escape the flies in the warmer, low-lying areas" around the Dunphy Lake camp.[12] As he wrote in *Traditional Bowhunter*, "There, stretched before us, were thousands of tracks where caribou had been. But not a caribou in sight." Browning also thought the "explosive increase in the number of Quebec-Labrador caribou" could be to blame. Some estimates had the northern herds numbering nearly one million animals, which he argued led to too much pressure on their food supplies and forced the "once tremendous herds" into "smaller, wider ranging groups of animals."

This meant that the caribou herds' movements remained largely unpredictable; as in previous years, the best way to maintain DRO's reputation and record was to create new camps. As writer Don Kirk noted in 1990, this is precisely what Foulkrod and top guide Barnaby Raphael did.[13] They "located this new camp to coincide with shifting caribou migration routes. Following an exhaustive search they found and settled on this crossing, where together prior to the hunting season they hewed out the camp from scratch." The camp was simple – it only had a wood-framed tent – but "it was located on a prime, yet never hunted, caribou crossing at the junction of two major rivers."

Some hunters were content to be ferried in

Laurentian leased this Series 300 Twin Otter, C-GPJA, from C&S Enterprises Ltd. when Airgava ceased operations in 1981. John Bogie noted in an interview, "I still wish I'd bought it: it was being offered at a great price and the 300s were so much better than the 100s." (JB)

Airgava's former Twin Otter C-GPJA that Air Schefferville leased from C&S Enterprises Ltd. The company operated the aircraft until September 22, 1982, after which it was bought by a firm in the U.S. Here it can be seen with its Air Schefferville markings. (JB)

Air Schefferville's Twin Otter C-FGQL at Schefferville in the late 1980s. The company sold the aircraft to Jacques Levesque in Sept-Îles in 1990. (JB)

freighter canoes to this and other crossings to watch for bulls, but when caribou movements stopped, many ardent bowhunters like Browning preferred to go in search of their quarry. "From camp it was a tough ten hour round trip" to the "tundra covered mesa" where Browning and his two Colorado hunting buddies tagged seven bulls.[14] "While trudging over mountain after mountain in search of caribou may not be every hunter's idea of having a fun time," Browning wrote. "For the serious bowhunter, it is maybe the extra challenge needed to make a hunt memorable. The most valuable trophies are those that are hard earned."

The next year, Browning had an easier time of hunting, but it was no less thrilling.[15] The Delay River camp, he noted, "was overrun with big white maned bulls," and "was without

a doubt the easiest camp I have ever had the pleasure of hunting." It also afforded a more comfortable hunt: "Because the main travel route of the caribou practically trekked through the camp, hunters had the freedom of hunting all day or strolling in for lunch or to warm up and dry rain-soaked clothes during days of foul weather." Furthermore, the location provided many ambush points and "the caribou could be easily spotted long before their arrival and racks scrutinized for trophy quality."

Schefferville was still the "Caribou Capital of the World" in the early 1990s, and writers like Asbell reported seeing "People in hunting uniforms everywhere. The airport is full, the hotel and the restaurant are full."[16] Bob Foulkrod's ability to find new camps and woo customers, and the superior guides he hired, meant

Richard "Sasquatch" St-Laurent

One of Air Schefferville's most colourful pilots must have been Richard St-Laurent, nicknamed "Sasquatch" by his friends, Iain Bogie explains, because he was "a great big man with a huge beard." This pilot was "the first guy to fly over 5,000 hours on an Otter in one year," Iain says. "We popped a bottle of champagne and celebrated!"

Richard may have been a good pilot in some ways – "he always brought the aircraft home" dispatcher

Wendell Hume says – but passengers did not always appreciate having him at the controls. "He'd eat garlic all the time," Wendell remembers. "He'd keep it under the seat and snack on it during flights. We got so many complaints from the smell in the cabin we finally had to threaten to let him go if he didn't stop eating garlic." St-Laurent managed to keep this interesting addiction in check and ended up flying for Air Schefferville for several float seasons.

Richard St-Laurent with Otter C-FCEE (left) and in scuba diving gear with fellow pilot Ned McGee. (IB)

From left: Craig Bogie, two potential investors, John Bogie and Iain Bogie with Air Schefferville Otter C-FCEE in July 1994. (JB)

that DRO continued to be a successful hunting operation even when faced with increased competition. The North American Hunting Club hosted life members from West Virginia, Missouri and Indiana at the Maricourt Camp for two weeks in 1993.[17] And that same year, George Steiner won a caribou hunting trip at the Annual Bowhunters of Connecticut banquet.[18] He, along with a group of American hunters, flew north with high expectations, but "bad weather continued to wreak havoc with his hunting plans." Even after a turbulent ride in an Air Schefferville Beaver where three group members were airsick, and a delay of several days due to the weather, Steiner said that Delay River Outfitters "was a first class operation with super accommodations and he would recommend hunting with them to anyone."

Shutting down

In the mid-1990s, Laurentian hit another rough spot and the hunting and fishing business John and Iain Bogie and their talented staff had created was shut down. John had stepped down as president and owner in 1992, handing the reins over to his son, Iain, but remained involved as

chairman of the board. They both felt they could no longer compete with all the new outfitters and flying companies entering the field. In particular, several First Nations entrepreneurs from the Schefferville area began taking advantage of Indian and Northern Affairs–Department of Industry Aboriginal Business programs, which provided grants and subsidies that allowed them to charge less for the same services.[19] As John said during an interview, "At one point an aboriginal group from Lac-Saint-Jean wanted to buy me out in the early 1990s and I should have sold to them. But the aboriginal people at Schefferville talked me out of it. They said, 'No no, don't sell to that crowd, we'll buy you out eventually.' But they never did."

John and Iain also faced competition from non-natives, especially on Air Laurentian's southern routes. "I don't know how the start-ups flying from Ottawa to Toronto for $99 did it," John says, "especially with the cost of fuel rising at the time." As Iain recalls, in 1995 it was clear "the north was supporting the south. The scheduled service out of Buttonville almost bankrupted the company, and so we closed down Air Laurentian and split up the company." He and his father sold off the company's last Beech 99 and King Air that year, which it had been using for the feeder service to Sept-Îles for Canadian Airlines as well as Air Canada, another of its partners.[20] Air Schefferville continued, however, to fly its Schefferville-Wabush-Sept-Îles scheduled service several times a day.[21]

The summer before, Iain, who had moved back to Ottawa several years earlier, began making plans with H. R. "Biff" Wheeler, president of Placements Preservation in Saint-Jovite – and the nephew of Tom Wheeler, former owner of Wheeler Airlines – to operate a new airport in that town.[22] Iain wrote to Roger McCarthy, VP and GM of the Mont-Tremblant ski resort, to remind him of the main points of their meeting the previous week: he and Wheeler intended to "upgrade the airport at Lac Ouimet [owned by Wheeler's company] at nearby Saint-Jovite and provide charter and scheduled air service to the Tremblant resort area with commuter and larger turbo-prob aircraft." The airport they envisioned would be "all-weather, night and day, with instrument approach facilities and a length of 4,000 feet that will accommodate most private aircraft."

From left: Likely co-pilot Fabian Maraviglia, Pete Arpin, Iain Bogie and Real McKenzie with Beech 99 C-FEJL circa 1996. (JB)

As Iain explained in the letter, Laurentian Air Services "today is mainly a holding company for aviation investments." The major holding, of course, was Air Schefferville, which still operated approximately 19 aircraft. He wanted to begin operations that fall "with a small commuter prop-jet aircraft" to offer daily flights from Saint-Jovite to Ottawa and Montreal, with Friday and Sunday flights to Toronto. As traffic increased, the company could "add larger prop-jets to cover further distances for groups direct to Tremblant out of such places as New York's Teterboro, Morristown and White Plains

executive airports. [Then] in the future, [could add] other executive airports in Philadelphia, Washington, Raleigh-Durham, Pittsburgh, Cleveland, Detroit." He emphasized Laurentian's continuing contacts with Canadian Airlines in northern Quebec and the fact that his company was listed in the American Airlines' reservation system, which would facilitate connecting U.S. passengers and allow them to use airline points for travel.

In another communication, Wheeler wrote that "preliminary discussions with the mayors of the parish and village of Saint-Jovite and representatives of the MRC des Laurentides have been most favorable." Even though he noted that many felt "this type of service would greatly benefit the area, " the project fell through when Wheeler and Transport Canada's timetables did not match up. In the end, Iain recalls,"Biff had some other offers for his plots of land and he cancelled the project."

At the same time as the Saint-Jovite airport scheme fell through, Iain and John shut down the Schefferville base entirely. It was 1998 and the two realized the company was in its most serious financial crisis yet. As John recalls:

That August I couldn't figure out why we didn't have a lot of cash on hand, because that was always our busy season. I brought in a relative who was a chartered accountant to look at the books. He told me, "John you're in trouble. You're broke." It turned out our accountant hadn't been able to handle all the transactions and he had just been stuffing invoices in the drawer, and not entering them into the computer like he was supposed to. He left town – I think he was just incapable of handling the responsibility – and I had to shut everything down. I sold or leased the planes we had left.

That year, Laurentian and Air Schefferville entered bankruptcy. The company was officially dissolved in 2004.

AFTERWORD

I t has been over a decade since Laurentian and Air Schefferville shut its doors, but it has not faded from the memories of those who made it a successful – and often pioneering – aviation company.

John Bogie, for example, who was a U.S. Navy aviation ordinance man in the 1940s, flew bigwigs for mining magnate M.J. Boylen, and is a founding member and honorary director of COPA, still lists his time with Laurentian as one of his greatest achievements.

Founder Barnet Maclaren would probably say the same thing were he alive today. This shy and unassuming man passed away in Ottawa in 1992 at the age of 94 after having been the president of the Maclaren Power and Paper Company and Laurentian, as well as helping to finance Spartan Air Services and several Ottawa-area high tech firms. Not one to court publicity, he quietly went about his business and as one Laurentian employee said, "You'd never have guessed he was one of the wealthiest men in town."

Barnet's accomplishments are an important part of Canadian history, however, and in August 2009, John Bogie will honour just one of his uncle's acts of generosity by having a plaque placed on the Experimental Aviation Association's Memorial Wall at Oshkosh, Wisconsin. The plaque, entitled "The Savior of Cessna," commemorates Barnet's meeting with Dwane Wallace in Ottawa back in 1939, and reflects Barnet's support of North American aviation.

When discussing the plaque and Laurentian during an interview John said, "I had hoped Laurentian would continue through the next generation, but aviation is a fickle business sometimes and I can't help but be happy looking back on all the company accomplished over its 62-year history." His son, Iain, agrees with this statement and looks back fondly on being raised within the company and eventually becoming Air Schefferville's president. While shutting down operations was definitely a disappointment for both men, they have continued to be heavily involved in aviation. Iain went on

During their travels, John and Iain Bogie often run into former Laurentian colleagues and employees, unsurprising given there are dozens of them still running in various aviation circles. In April 2008 while on a trip to Vancouver, for example, John met former Laurentian chief pilot Tim Cole, who took him up in his 7AC Aeronca Champion. Here John is pictured (right) with Cole (left) and John McGregor (centre) in front of McGregor's Cessna L-19 Bird Dog. (TC)

to work for Caravan Air Service in Ottawa for several years before being hired by Environment Canada's Emergency Science Division to direct maintenance on its specially-equipped Douglas DC-3 and Convair 580 aircraft. John, though fully retired at the age of 82, attends as many COPA meetings and conventions as he can, sometimes with his aviation-minded granddaughter, Kassandra, in tow.

The men and women who worked for Laurentian and its subsidiaries also remember the company that gave many of them their start in aviation, launching them on long careers with Transport Canada, Air Canada, and a multitude of other organizations and businesses. Even those whose eventual day jobs did not involve flying or fixing engines had their love of all things aviation nurtured by Laurentian.

John Bogie (far right) remains an honorary director of COPA. In this 2008 photo he is pictured with the other COPA directors. Front row, left to right: Doug Ronan, Frank Hofmann, Marc Charron, Bill Beaton. Rear row: Brian Chappell, Paul Hayes, Ernie McLean, Michel Moreau, Terry Wilshire, Earl Kickley, Jerry Roehr, Harold Fry, Ken Armstrong. (Kevin Psutka)

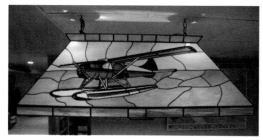

Peter (Lou) Goodwin, who flew for Laurentian from 1966 to 1976, immortalized "his" Beaver, CF-GCW, with the help of pilot and stained glass artist Ralf Bauch. (LG)

John Kenny never flew for his cousin's company, working in the engine overhaul shop instead, but he has made up for lost time. Here he is pictured with the Beaver he now owns, C-FFZM, "September Pops." It can regularly be seen doing circuits of McGregor Lake in southwestern Quebec.

APPENDIX 1:
AIRCRAFT OPERATED
BY LAURENTIAN AIR SERVICES

Using a variety of sources I have attempted to construct as complete a list as possible of the aircraft Laurentian and its subsidiaries leased and owned. It has been a challenging task, however, and there may be an aircraft missing; if you have any information on additional aircraft, please contact me through my website <www.laurentianstory.com>. Also, for full histories of each Beaver and wonderful images of this quintessential bushplane, please visit Neil Aird's website <www.dhc-2.com>. Karl E. Hayes has done similar research with Otters and has compiled a 900-page pdf file available on CD, which he updates periodically. You will find information on his CD and how to order one in the Aviation History Resources section of my website, <www.laurentianstory.com>.

Registration	Aircraft Type	Serial	Acquired	Disposed	Notes
	Avro Avian				Several sources suggest Laurentian owned or operated one in its early years, but I have not been able to find any registration information. Confusion may have arisen because Barnet Maclaren used the Ottawa Flying Club's Avian from time to time.
CF-ADB	DC-3	33540	c.1975	c.1979	Laurentian leased it from Air-Dale Ltd. for several years in the 1970s for the James Bay Project. The aircraft still belonged to Air-Dale Ltd. in 1991 when it was scrapped.
CF-AJW	Cessna 180H	18052136	c.1970		A 1970 model owned by Laurentian and operated in the 1970s, it was flown by several Canadian companies until 1994, when it was exported to the U.S. It is now registered as N2171Z to an individual in Anchorage.
CF-ALG	General 102A Aristocrat	10	1938	1938	Dry-leased in April 1938 for $4 per hour and operated during the summer months. It came to Canada in February 1930 and had several owners in the Maritimes before being sold to Fleet in August 1937 and then to Walter Deisher. He disposed of it in 1940 and not much is known about it after a record of it being sold to a buyer in Alberta in September 1942.
CF-ANA	Beech E18S	BA-333	1976	1976	This aircraft came to Canada in 1970 serving first with Port Colbourne Flying Service, and then two years later with White River. Laurentian operated it next in 1976 and the following year it went to Skycraft Air Transport Inc. of Oshawa, Ont. In 1993 it was exported to a private owner in California, where it remains registered as N5867.
CF-APC	Cessna 180	32158	c.1970		According to Brad Mackie, this 1956 model was leased from an individual at Blue Sea Lake, just south of Maniwaki, on a regular basis to satisfy temporary requirements in the early 1970s. Since 1988 it has been registered to Pelican Services Ltd. in Creighton, Sask., as C-FAPC.

Registration	Aircraft Type	Serial	Acquired	Disposed	Notes
CF-APP	Otter	138	1971	1973	Widerøe Flyveselskap & Polarfly Air Services of Norway received it in 1956 and registered it as LN-BDD. Laurentian purchased it in 1971 and put it to work in 1972, leasing it to Labrador Airways the following year. It was lost on May 5, 1973, at Port Burwell, Nunavut, when the pilot taxied it onto unstable ice. Although the passengers and pilot were fine, it sank to the bottom and was never salvaged.
CF-APQ	Otter	201	1971	1977	Widerøe received it in 1957 and registered it as LN-BIB. The oldest of the three Otters Laurentian purchased from the Norwegian company, it had 12,240 hours on the airframe by 1971. On August 2, 1974, it was involved in an accident at Esker, Nfld., but was repaired and sold to Direquair in 1977. It was last registered as N205RC to Rapids Camp Lodge in Alaska.
CF-APR	Otter	31	1971	1977	This Otter was originally delivered to the Royal Norwegian Air Force in 1954, but Widerøe purchased it from them in 1967 and registered it as LN-LMM. Laurentian purchased it from Widerøe in 1971, operating it for six years before selling it to Bearskin Lake Air Services Ltd. in Big Trout Lake, Ont. Since 1988 it has been registered to Ignace Airways Ltd. of Ignace, Ont.
CF-AVB	De Havilland 80A Pussmoth	DHC224	1934	1939	Barnet Maclaren bought this aircraft in July 1934 and sold it to Walter Deisher in 1936. The following year, Deisher sold the aircraft to Laurentian before leaving for Fleet Aircraft. It remained in storage until it was sold 1939. According to Terry Judge, this was because "in June 1937 all Puss Moth aircraft in Canada were grounded until further notice after a number of fatal accidents due to flight into turbulent weather."
CF-AYP	Standard Cabin Waco YKS-6	4458	1936	1948	Barnet Maclaren purchased this aircraft from Jack Saunderson at Fleet Aircraft. After operating it for 12 years, he sold it to P. Lewin, who was still operating it in 1957 with T. Carr when it broke through the ice landing on Burchell Lake, Ont.
CF-AYR	Otter	436	1970	1980	This aircraft was manufactured in 1962 and put to work by the UN in January 1963 in the Congo as UN serial 307, as one of four Otters the UN bought and shipped there. It arrived in Leopoldville in June 1963 and was sent directly to Yemen, where it was required for a UN support mission until December. Then it was ferried to El Arish in Egypt, where it went into storage at 115 ATU and was put up for sale. It was registered to several companies before joining Geoterrex Ltd. in May 1970 (which registered it as CF-AYR) as a replacement for Otter CF-SKX, which had crashed during a test flight with its new survey equipment. Geoterrex owned it until 1980, and Laurentian operated and maintained it during this period. According to one website, it is currently for sale in Minnesota for $700,000.
CF-BDO	Custom Cabin Waco ZQC6-7	4592	1937	1951	Laurentian purchased CF-BDO directly from the Waco Aircraft Co. In 1951 it went to E. McEachern in the U.S. and was registered as N1130.
CF-BPA	Beaver	1612	1971	1975	This was one of the Beavers Laurentian imported from Aerial Agriculture in Australia, which had it registered as VH-IDX. On August 5, 1975 it was involved in a fatal crash at Lac O'Keefe, Que. The registration was cancelled in 1977.

Registration	Aircraft Type	Serial	Acquired	Disposed	Notes
CF-BTK	Cessna 180H	18052243	1972	1979	Laurentian bought it new in 1972 and operated it for seven years before selling the aircraft to Temair Inc. of Temiscaming, Que.
CF-BXR	Grumman G21-A Goose	1059	1945	1974	Manufactured in 1939, it was originally registered to Lehman Bros. in New York as NC2788. That company sold it to the American military, who then sold it to the RCAF in June 1942 (which had it as tail no. 797). In 1974, Laurentian sold it to Transprovincial Airlines in Prince Rupert, B.C., where it sank on October 8, 1979. The company recovered it and it remained in B.C. until 1990, when it was bought by Devcon Construction in Tualatin, Ore.
CF-CUW	Cessna 337 Skymaster	337-0009	1978	1990	Laurentian bought it as-is from Confederation College in Thunder Bay, Ont., where it was being used for mechanical engineering students to practice on (and had not been flown in three years). In 1978, Laurentian transferred it to Air Schefferville, and then registered it to Delay River Outfitters in 1987 as C-FCUW. Laurentian cancelled the registration in May 1989 and sold it to Eagle Aviation in Pine Falls, Man., on April 24, 1990. It has been owned by Blue Water Aviation Services Ltd. in Pine Falls since 1996.
CF-CWX	Cessna 172L	17259487	c.1970	1972	Laurentian operated this aircraft primarily on fire patrols out of Maniwaki.
CF-CZO	Otter	71	1975	1975	Laurentian leased this Otter during the summer of 1975 while it was owned by Ontario Northern Airways Ltd. of Jellicoe, Ont. It is currently registered to Osnaburgh Airways based at Pickle Lake, Ont.
CF-DAC	Cessna T-50 Crane		1945		Laurentian purchased the Cessna T-50 trainer from the Canadian War Assets Corporation. Fate unknown.
CF-DJI	Beaver	27	1949		Laurentian purchased this aircraft from DHC in 1949 with the intention of operating it for Atlas Aviation Ltd. One source says that Spartan Air Services pilots then flew 'DJI in the early 1950s. The next known operator was White River Air Services, which sold it to Austin Airways in 1963. In 1970 Boreal Airways registered it, but shortly thereafter it burned in Moosonee, Ont., and was destroyed.
CF-DQY	Fleet Canuck	77	1948		Laurentian operated it in the late 1940s on floats. In June 2006, Terry Tykolis owned and operated it in the Niagara, Ont., region.
CF-DXN	Beech C18S		1961	1963	This aircraft was imported into Canada in 1948 and in 1955 was registered to Algoma Steel of Sault Ste. Marie. Laurentian operated it out of Ottawa for charters and multi-engine instrument instruction, as well as for flying Anaconda American brass executives.
CF-ECY	DC-3	9264	1974	1975	This aircraft was manufactured in 1943 and first served with the USAAF. Then it went to a Czechoslovakian airline as OK-WDE, and on to the French air force from 1960 to 1971. In 1973 it was registered to Astro Airlines at St-Jean, Que., who sold it to Laurentian the following year. On September 25, 1975, it was involved in an accident on Lac Guyer, Que., and was damaged beyond repair.

Registration	Aircraft Type	Serial	Acquired	Disposed	Notes
CF-EGC	Beaver	1546	1972	1981	Before going to Laurentian, this aircraft was registered as VH-IDP to Hawker DH Australia. In 1981 Laurentian sold it to Calumet Air Services Ltd. in Fort Coulonge, Que., in as-is condition along with a long-range belly tank, canoe rack, engine tent and other equipment.
CF-EGE	Beaver	1539	1972	1978	Laurentian purchased this aircraft from Aerial Agriculture Ltd. in Australia, where it had been registered as VH-IDK. When Laurentian began operating it, it registered it CF-EGE. Since 1978 it has been flown by Quebec, B.C. and Ontario companies. It is currently owned by Viking Air in Sidney, B.C.
CF-EYN	Beaver	508	1953	c.1972	Laurentian bought this aircraft for the Brinco contract in 1953 after an inexperienced pilot damaged one of the other Beavers. Laurentian operated it for a number of years, at least until the early 1970s. On July 18, 1975, it had an engine failure on take-off at Togiak, Alaska, while registered to Kodiak Western Alaska Airlines Inc (N28365). There were no fatalities and it is still being actively flown from a base at Port McNeill on Vancouver Island.
CF-EYT	Beaver	487	1953	1973	Delivered to Laurentian April 24, 1953, and operated for 20 years before being sold to Air Kipawa and then Anaconda American Brass. It was written off in September 1981 and cancelled from the register in December 1982. Fate unknown.
CF-EYU	Beaver	491	1953		Delivered to Laurentian May 1, 1953, and was possibly the Beaver that had to be replaced on the Brinco contract. In 2006 it was registered to Sheyenne Air LLC in Argusville, N.Dak., as N4081F.
CF-FAC	Aero Commander 680		c.1963	c.1971	Laurentian operated it for a period in the 1960s to fly Anaconda American Brass executives and employees. As of January 4, 1971, the records show Laurentian was no longer operating it. Its last known owner was Futura Airlines in Vancouver, B.C. The registration was cancelled in December 1989.
CF-FGO	Cessna 337 Skymaster	337 01212	c.1973		Tim Cole notes that Laurentian pilot Gilles Charlebois was flying this aircraft in 1973 when it was involved in a non-fatal crash with a Cessna 170 at Maniwaki airport. It was apparently fixed, as it was being operated by Orillia Air Services Ltd. until 1985 when it was removed from the Canadian Civil Aircraft Registry. Fate unknown.
CF-FHB	Beaver	1	c.1970		Laurentian leased this aircraft, the first Beaver, from B&B Aviation in Edmonton, Alta., for a brief period before it went to Canada's Aviation Museum in Ottawa to be preserved for future generations.
CF-FHP	Beaver	57	c.1968		First delivered in July 1949 to Senator F.W. Pririe, Laurentian operated this aircraft during the 1960s before selling it to Irving Oil Transport. In 1971 Austin Airways bought it and it has been registered to Home Air Ltd. in Homepayne, Ont., since 1978.
CF-FHR	Beaver	46	1949	1973	Laurentian took delivery of this Beaver in 1949, operating it for 24 years before selling it to Northwestern Airways in Noranda, Que., along with floats, wheel-skis and a VHF radio in 1973. It is still being flown by White River Air Services in northern Ontario.

Registration	Aircraft Type	Serial	Acquired	Disposed	Notes
CF-FPQ	Cessna 170A	19050	c.1952		Laurentian used this 1949 model for its operations out of Lac des Oblats at Maniwaki, Que., in the early 1950s. It was deleted from the register in 1989.
CF-GCW	Beaver	198	1952	1973	Delivered to Laurentian April 24, 1952, and used on Mid-Canada Line work in Great Whale and Winisk. Two decades later the company sold it to Larivière Air Services Ltd, Schefferville, Que. It is currently registered to a private owner in Anchorage as N918SL.
CF-GIB	Beaver	6	1948	c.1970	Laurentian took delivery of this Beaver in May 1948. Company records indicate it then sold the aircraft to Joe Bertrand at Fort Coulonge, Que. in the early 1970s and that it remained with the company after former Laurentian employee Bob Burns bought it and renamed it Calumet Air Service in 1972. It was then registered to Expeditair Inc. in Alma, Que., in 1989. It Is still active, being flown by Aviation Bastican Inc. in St. Raymond, Que., registered as C-FGIB.
CF-GKZ	DC-3	9395		1975	Ex-N1348 with Midwest Aviation. Registered to Bradley Air Services 1975-90. Scrapped.
CF-HGV	Beaver	581	c.1969		Laurentian operated this aircraft for a short period before selling it to Wilderness Airlines in Dawson Creek, B.C. It is currently registered to Talkeetna Air Taxi Inc. in Alaska as N561TA.
CF-HLY	Cessna 180	30917		c.1972	Former employee Bob Burns, who had just started Calumet Air Service, bought it from Laurentian circa 1972. It was removed from CCAR in 1997.
CF-HOE	Beaver	630	1964	c.1978	Laurentian purchased this aircraft in 1964, operating it for over a decade before it went to a Swedish company, Tammert Aero AB, in 1980. It is currently registered to Southern Seaplane Inc.
CF-HPQ	Cessna 180	31198	1955		Laurentian purchased this 1954 model new. It was removed from CCAR in 2004.
CF-IAR	DC-3	20877	1975	1978	Ex-USAAF 8-44 until an accident in 1956. After being repaired it went to the French air force until 1971. It returned to Canada for operations with Air Fecteau in 1973 and two years later Laurentian purchased it for work in northern Quebec on the CIP and James Bay contracts. While registered to Nunasi Central Airlines in 1988, it was destroyed in an accident.
CF-IFN	Grumman Goose	1187	c.1964		Laurentian kept a lease out on mining magnate M.J. Boylen's Goose, CF-IFN. in the early-to-mid 1960s in case anything should happen to its Goose CF-BXR. The company also did all of 'IFN's maintenance work while Boylen owned it and two of Laurentian's employees, John Bogie and Reg Phillips, spent quite a few hours in its cockpit while working for him.
CF-IGM	Otter	75	1956	1956	Delivered to Rio Canadian Exploration Ltd. in 1955 which used it for geophysical survey with its subsidiary Gresham Exploration Inc. In May 1956, Laurentian pilot Don Routhier flew this "flying prospector," as Karl Hayes calls it, out of Rouyn, Que., for Gresham. In 1979, registered to Norcanair, it was in a relatively minor accident that resulted in severe damage to the aircraft and was eventually parted out.
CF-ITH	DC-3	20228	c.1975		Registered to Terra Surveys of Ottawa until 1990. Leased from Kenting Aviation. Derelict.

Registration	Aircraft Type	Serial	Acquired	Disposed	Notes
CF-IUU	Beaver	945	c.1960		In 1956 it was delivered to Hollinger Mines/Labrador Mining and Exploration, which hired Laurentian to operate it for several years. Since 1982 it has been registered to Sudbury Aviation Ltd. in Sudbury, Ont.
CF-JFH	Otter	155	1962	1966	Delivered to Shell Avion of Shell Canada Ltd. in Edmonton in 1956. Laurentian purchased the aircraft from them in 1962 and flew it for four years, using it on a contract to resupply the USAF radar station at St. Anthony, Nfld. In 1966 Laurentian sold it to Wray Adair Douglas of Inuvik. He leased it to Northward Aviation Ltd. of Edmonton, which had an accident two months after receiving 'JFH on July 13, 1966. The pilot, crewman and two passengers were fine but the Otter was irreparably damaged.
CF-ZVQ	Beaver	1063	1982	1984	Laurentian purchased this aircraft in 1982 from Direquair of Chibougamau, Que., transferring it to Air Schefferville the next year. In 1984 it sold the Beaver to L.R. Busk in Anchorage, who registered it to the Bonanza Christian Retreat as N5359J. In 1995 Neil Aird noted that it seemed to be in a state of disrepair. Fate unknown.
CF-KAZ	DC-3	19345	c.1975	c.1980	Leased from Trans-Provincial for a period in the 1970s. Was registered to Ilford-Riverton Airways in Winnipeg until July 1982 and then Bearskin Lake Air Service in Sioux Lookout, Ont., until December 1982. It was removed from CCAR in 1985 while owned by Soundair of Mississauga, Ont.
CF-KJQ	Piper PA-23 Aztec Apache	23 1216	c.1970	c.1978	Laurentian likely purchased this aircraft in 1970 for fire patrols out of Maniwaki. It was removed from CCAR in 1986.
CF-LHQ	Piper PA-18A 150 Super Cub	18 7051	c.1967		Laurentian operated this aircraft for a period in the late 1960s, listing it for use at its Maniwaki flying school. It was removed from CCAR in 2005.
CF-MIR	Super Canso	8166	1964	1965	This aircraft was built in 1944 as a model 28-5A PBY-5A Catalina and delivered to the U.S. Navy as Bu. 46633. It was withdrawn from service in 1952 and registered as N10023 to Trade Ayer Inc. in New Jersey in 1956, and as CF-MIR to Miron & Frères Ltd in Canterville, Que., from 1957 to '61. It was this last company that had it converted to a model 28-5ACF Super Canso 1000 by Noorduyn Aircraft in Montreal in 1960. Laurentian bought it in September 1964, but sold it a year later to Survair in Ottawa, which operated it until 1967. Afterwards it completed survey operations for various companies in Europe, Ireland and South Africa, ending up at Super Catalina Restoration in the UK in 1999. Current status unknown.
CF-MPX	Otter	280	1979	1982	This aircraft was manufactured in 1959 and purchased by the RCMP, which operated it until 1979. In September of that year the Crown Assets Disposal Corporation put it up for sale and Laurentian bid on it. After flying it for three years, Laurentian sold it to Hyack Air Ltd. in New Westminster, B.C. It is now operated by Air Saguenay in Chicoutimi, registered as C-FMPX.

Registration	Aircraft Type	Serial	Acquired	Disposed	Notes
CF-MUA	Piper PA-23-160 Apache	23 1400	c.1968		Pilot Tim Cole remembers flying this 1958 model on charter work with Laurentian from the late-1960s to mid-1970s: "MUA is the one that we did all the work with. I flew it in the winter time on 'executive charter'. I particularly remember flights to Sudbury at -40. I would be in a skidoo suit and my passenger would be in toe rubbers and a fall coat. I would lift them out gently at the other end so that they wouldn't break as the heater usually quit in the first five minutes!" Currently registered to a private owner in Goose Bay, Nfld.
CF-OII	Beech 18 Expeditor		c.1960		Laurentian's first Beech 18, it had a cargo door modification and was operated on floats. It was later used by Ignace Airways in northwestern Ontario and ended in a scrap yard in Kenora in the 1990s. It is still there and is being overgrown by vegetation.
CF-OSJ	Cessna 172 I	17256637	c.1968		Laurentian listed it with the Schefferville flying school in 1968. It is currently registered as C-FOSJ with the Collège d'enseignement général et professionnel Édouard-Montpetit in St-Hubert, Que.
CF-PAG	DC-3	20444	1971	c.1980	Ex-USAAF Air Transport Command in June 1944. Sold as war surplus to Winged Cargo of Philadelphia that same year, it was imported Canada in October 1971 by Proctor & Gamble, which registered it as CF-QZU. The next month Laurentian bought it and operated it until 1980, when it went back to the U.S. Last noted in 2003 lying dormant in Edinburg, Texas.
CF-POX	DC-3	20875	c.1972	c.1980	One of the DC-3s Laurentian purchased from France, it has been converted to a Basler BT-67 Turbo-67 and is now registered to the Colombian national police as PNC-0213.
CF-POY	DC-3	10028	1971	c.1980	This was the first DC-3 Laurentian bought from France, where it had served with the French air force since 1957. Before that, it was with the RAF 216 Sqn in India and was Admiral Lord Louis Montbatten's staff airplane in the southeast Asian theatre. Laurentian purchased it in June 1971 and operated it during that decade. In 1998 it was deleted from CCAR, going to Aerotaxi of Havana as CU-T1192. On March 19, 2003, it was hijacked at Key West International Airport by men wielding kitchen knives, tape and the airplane's emergency hatchet. They demanded to be flown to Miami. Florida Air National Guard F-15 fighter jets and a Black Hawk helicopter escorted it to Key West where it landed at 20:06. No fatalities among the 29 occupants. Current status unknown.
CF-PUZ	Piper PA-18A 150 Super Cub	18 8147	c.1967		This 1964 model was used by Laurentian for forest fire patrolling at its southern bases and at the Maniwaki flying school. Since 1999 it has been registered to a private owner in Montreal.
CF-PWI	DC-3	4880	c.1973	c.1980	One of the DC-3s Laurentian purchased from France. Fate unknown.
CF-RDA	Turbo Beaver	1578TB7	c.1969	c.1970	Laurentian briefly leased this Turbo-Beaver from Rodair, who had had it registered since 1965. It is currently at Beaver Aircraft LLC in Missoula, Mont., as N812LT.

Registration	Aircraft Type	Serial	Acquired	Disposed	Notes
CF-RRE	Beech 18 Expeditor		c.1964	c.1969	Laurentian purchased this aircraft from the RCAF, which had operated it from 1951 to 1964. The company flew it on floats but after selling it to St. Félicien Air Service in St- Félicien, Que., it was fitted with Bristol 5100 wheel-skis, one of only eight Beech 18s with this 800-lb kit installed. CF-RRE was lost in a crash in September 1973 when it still was with St. Félicien.
CF-RRG	Cessna 172F	17252196	c.1970		Laurentian leased this aircraft in the early 1970s from Del Thompson, a former Laurentian pilot and captain for Air Canada. It was primarily used on fire patrol at the company's Maniwaki base. It is currently registered to several private co-owners in Sault Ste-Marie.
CF-RRJ	Cessna 172	17252019	c.1970		Laurentian operated this 1964 model for fire patrols at Maniwaki in the early 1970s. It is currently registered to Exploits Valley Air Services Ltd. in Gander, Nfld.
CF-RSW	Beech 18 Expeditor	1505	c.1969		This aircraft was registered to Inland Air Transport of St. Laurent, Que., in 1964. Laurentian operated it for a short period c.1969, when it was captured on film in Schefferville without a Laurentian paint job but with the company's name on the fuselage. In 1976 it was owned by Nipawin Air Services of Nipawin, Sask.
CF-SKX	Otter	1	1970	1970	This was the original Otter prototype, registered as CF-DYK-X in 1951, and transferred to the RCAF the following year, although, as Karl Hayes notes, it remained based at Downsview on "indefinite loan" and was used for test work. In 1968, two years after it had been re-registered as CF-SKX, this Otter was sold "as is, where is" to Lambair of The Pas, Man., in 1969. Apparently there were difficulties getting it returned to a standard Otter configuration at this time because it had been experimented on so much. On September 5, 1969, however, it received a Certificate of Airworthiness. The next year Geoterrex Ltd. of Ottawa purchased it, arranging for Laurentian to operate and maintain the aircraft on its behalf. On May 1, 1970, it crashed during test flying and was destroyed, killing the pilot, who was not a Laurentian employee.
CF-SZJ	Cessna 172 G	17253875	c.1968		Laurentian operated it at Lac des Loups for a brief period circa 1968. It is currently registered to a private owner in Trenton, Ont.
CF-TUR	Beaver	1529	1976	1978	Laurentian leased this aircraft in 1976 and 1978 from Rodair Inc. As pilot Peter Goodwin recalls, "We weren't sure we'd get the engine for the season in 1976 – it kept steaming out. Within a few weeks we flew it down to Ottawa for a 24-hour engine change. We nicknamed it 'The mighty TURD'." It is currently registered to Air Mont-Laurier in Ste-Véronique, Que.
CF-UKM	Cessna 180H	18051616	c.1970		Laurentian operated this 1966 model in 1970 and 1971. It was exported to the U.S. in 1997.
CF-UQI	Cessna 150 F	15064211	c.1968		Laurentian used this 1966 model for its Schefferville flying school in 1968. It is currently registered to a private owner in Oshawa, Ont.

Registration	Aircraft Type	Serial	Acquired	Disposed	Notes
CF-URQ	Beech C55 Baron		c.1966	c.1971	This aircraft was owned by Anaconda American Brass and operated by Laurentian for a number of years on both corporate and charter operations. It flew all over eastern Canada and the USA.
CF-VBQ	Cessna 172 H	17255233	c.1968		Laurentian used this 1966 model in Schefferville and Lac des Loups in 1968. It is currently registered to a private owner in Saint-Romuald, Que.
CF-VQD	Otter	466	1967	1977	The last Otter built by DHC, it was delivered to Laurentian June 16, 1967. The company sold it to Sabourin Lake Airways (Sabair) of Cochenour, Ont., a decade later. It was the second Otter to be converted with the Walter turbine engine (by Eagle Aviation) and is now being operated by Adventure Air in Pine Falls, Man.
CF-VXB	Cessna 180H	18051852	c.1967		Laurentian operated it in 1967, and it may have been one of the aircraft from its Cessna dealership that it used temporarily. Since the early 1980s it has been registered to Alberta-based companies and was recently spotted in that province.
CF-XBX	Cessna 305	22709	c.1970		Laurentian initially used this aircraft mostly for fire spotting during patrols at Maniwaki, but in 1972 it was fitted with wing-tip pods for surveying. It was exported to the U.S. in 1984.
CF-YEK	Cessna 172K	17257890	1971	1971	This 1969 model was a Laurentian Cessna dealership aircraft that it used for part of a season before selling it on. It is currently registered to a private owner in Elliot Lake, Ont.
CF-YOI	Beaver	1052	1969	1972	Laurentian purchased this Beaver from Aerial Agriculture Ltd. in Australia, where it had been registered VH-AAV. Three years later it sold the airplane to Columbia Airlines in Prince George, B.C. In 1983, while owned by Vanderhoof Flying Services Ltd, in B.C., the aircraft was booby-trapped, killing the owner and destroying the aircraft. The murder is still unsolved.
C-FAUS	DHC-6 Series 100 Twin Otter	34	c.1978		Laurentian leased this aircraft to Labrador Airways and then sold it to them circa 1980. On October 11, 1984, while registered to LabAir it crashed into the side of Mealy Mountain, Nfld., killing all four aboard.
C-FAWX	Beech 99	U64	1992	1992	Briefly registered to Delay River Outfitters Inc. in 1992 before going to Ontario Aircraft Sales and Leasing Inc., which quickly sold it on to La Ronge Aviation Services Ltd. In 1997 it was exported to the U.S.
C-FCBU	Beech 99	U-159	1988	1988	Delay River Outfitters owned this aircraft from July to December 1988, before selling it to Sabourin Lake Airways Ltd. in Cochenour, Ont. It cancelled the registration in 1991.

Registration	Aircraft Type	Serial	Acquired	Disposed	Notes
C-FBEU	Otter	119	1975 1981	1976 1982	Ex-U.S. Army 55-3273. In 1972, Air Craftsmen Ltd. in New Brunswick purchased the aircraft, restoring it to a civilian configuration and selling it to Laurentian in May 1975. The next year, Laurentian sold it to Survair Ltd., where it was involved in a serious accident on April 22, 1977 on take-off from Leaf Bay, Que. Luckily no one was injured. Air Inuit Ltd. of Fort Chimo (Kuujjuaq) purchased it in 1979 after a lengthy rebuild. The next February it crashed again after stalling but was repaired and leased to several other operators. On September 7, 1982, Air Schefferville registered it for the caribou hunting season, returning it to Air Inuit on November 25. In 2005 it was exported to the U.S.
CF-CEE	Otter	282	1972	1999	EX-U.S. Army 57-6134. Laurentian bought it at the Atlanta Army Depot and flew it to Ottawa for conversion to civilian configuration. The company initially registered it CF-CEE but later re-registered it C-FCEE. In 1981 it was transferred to Air Schefferville and remained with the company for 18 years. In 1998, it leased 'FCEE to Huron Air & Outfitters of Armstrong-McKenzie Lake, Ont., for the summer; it returned briefly before being sold to a leasing company in Sault Ste-Marie along with C-GLAA. Since 1999 it has been on lease to Johnny May's Air Charter in Kuujjuaq, Que.
C-FCGL	Beech King Air 200	BB190	1992	1992	Registered to Delay River Outfitters Inc. from January to July 1992, before going to Central Mountain Air Ltd. in Smithers, B.C. The registration was cancelled in CCAR in 2006.
C-FCGT	Beech King Air 200	BB-159	1993	1995	Registered to Delay River Outfitters Inc. for two years before being sold to Wasaya Airways Ltd. in Thunder Bay. It is currently registered to Keewatin Air Ltd. in Winnipeg.
C-FCGV	Beech King Air 200	CC264	1991	1992	Delay River Outfitters Inc. operated this aircraft for a year before it was exported to Colombia in 1992.
C-FCGW	Beech King Air 200	BB-207	1992	1995	Laurentian purchased this aircraft from Air Ontario Inc. in London, Ont., operating it for three years before selling it Air Nunavut Ltd. in Iqaluit, which continues to fly it.
C-FEJL	Beech 99	U-75	1991	1996	Laurentian purchased this aircraft in 1991, registering it to Delay River Outfitters Inc. In 1996 it sold it a numbered corporation created by Air Schefferville, which leased it out until 1999. Since then, it has been operated by Bradley Air Services Ltd. in Carp, Ont.
C-FCGM	Beech King Air 200	BB-217	1993	1995	Delay River Outfitters Inc. operated this aircraft for two years before selling it to Air Ontario Inc. in London, Ont. Since 1999, North Cariboo Flying Service Ltd. of Fort St. John, B.C., has owned it.
C-FGQL	DHC-6 Series 200 Twin Otter	182	1984	1990	Air Schefferville operated this aircraft June-December 1984, having leased it from La Ronge Aviation Services Ltd., La Ronge, Sask. It leased it from La Ronge again in 1985, returning it in November. In April 1986, it purchased 'FGQL and registered it with Delay River Outfitters until October 1990, when the company sold it to Jacques Levesque of Sept-Îles. It was removed from CCAR in July 2006.

Registration	Aircraft Type	Serial	Acquired	Disposed	Notes
C-FIAQ	Beech 65-B80 Queen Air	LD 328	1983	1985	Laurentian purchased this aircraft from Labrador Airways Ltd. of Goose Bay, Nfld., in September 1983, operating it on Air Schefferville's scheduled service to Wabush, Labrador. In April 1985, it was sold to buyers in Florida.
C-FQHC	DHC-6 Series 100 Twin Otter	21	c.1981	1983	Air Schefferville sold the aircraft to Kenn Borek Air Ltd. of Calgary in November 1983. In November 1995, it was exported to the Maldives.
C-FQND	Otter	233	1993	1994	Ex-U.S. Army 57-6114. After being "civilianized" it was operated by several American companies until 1993 when Delay River Outfitters, trading as Air Schefferville, purchased it. The following year it was sold on to Waweig Lake Outfitters Ltd. of Thunder Bay and was soon converted to a Vazar turbine Otter. It is currently flying for Waweig Air.
C-FTAT	DC-3	11850	c.1972	1974	Laurentian purchased this aircraft for work on the Canadian International Paper contract out of La Tuque, Que. It was involved in a fatal crash into Mt. Apica, Quebec, on August 5, 1974. The aircraft was destroyed.
C-FUHX	Cessna 180H	18051699	1985	1995	Air Schefferville/Delay River Outfitters operated this aircraft from 1985 until it was exported to the U.S. in May 1995.
C-FYPP	DHC-6 Series 200 Twin Otter	223	1982	1982	Air Schefferville briefly owned this aircraft from May to July 1982, selling it on to Chaperal Charters of Dorval, Que., It was exported to the U.S. in 1996.
C-GCQK	Otter	141	1975	1976	Ex-U.S. Army 55-3290. One of eight surplus Otters Ferrer Aviation Inc of Miami bid on in 1971 at the Coleman Barracks in Mannheim, Germany. This aircraft was ferried to England and then to Shannon, Ireland where it was fitted with ferry tanks for the long flight across the Atlantic (with stops in Iceland, Greenland and Newfoundland). It was converted to civilian configuration by St. Louis Aviation Inc. of Montreal and sold to Ilford Riverton Airways in Winnipeg in 1974. The next year Laurentian leased it, returning it to Ilford in 1976. Since then it has been operated throughout Canada and is currently being flown by Jespersen Aircraft Services Inc. of Bettles, Alaska, registered as N560TR.
C-GCST	Beech 65-B80 Queen Air	LD 418	198?	1985	Iain Bogie and his wife, Marianne, bought the aircraft and leased it to Air Schefferville, which operated it until October 16, 1985. The following May, Watson's Algoma Vacations Ltd. of Wawa, Ont., owned it, flying it until 1992 when it was removed from CCAR.
C-GDQY	DHC-6 Series 100 Twin Otter	77	1976	1978	The first Twin Otter Laurentian purchased, it went first to Bakhtar Afghan Airlines, Afghanistan, as YA-GAS and returned to Canada in January 1976 with St. Andrews Airways, Man. Laurentian bought it August 1976 and sold it in June 1978 to Labrador Airways, Goose Bay, which still owns it.
C-GEPC	Cessna A185F	18503649	1995	1996	Laurentian purchased it from a private owner in Gatineau, Que., in 1995, registering it to Delay River Outfitters Inc. In 1996 Air Schefferville placed it in its numbered corporation until 1998 when it was sold to a private owner in Maniwaki. It is still being flown, currently registered to a private owner in St-Jean-Chrysostome, Que.

Registration	Aircraft Type	Serial	Acquired	Disposed	Notes
C-GLAA	Otter	226	1974	1999	Ex-U.S. Army 57-6108. Laurentian purchased it at the Sharpe Army Depot in Stockton, Cal., for $18,200. In 1981, it was transferred to Air Schefferville, where it had two small accidents: once in May 1989 when the rear ski and wheel were damaged during the take off roll, and another in October 1991 when it struck a moored aircraft in high winds. In 1999, it was sold to a leasing company based in Sault Ste-Marie along with C-FCEE. Since then it has been converted with the Garrett TPE 331 engine by Texas Turbines Inc. and had large scenic windows installed. It is now being operated by Ultima Thule Outfitters as N226UT in Chitina, Alaska.
C-GLAB	Otter	348	1974	1992	Ex-U.S. Army 59-2210. Laurentian purchased this Otter at the Sharpe Army Depot in Stockton, Cal., along with three others in January 1974. In 1981 it was transferred to Air Schefferville and was operated until 1992, when it was sold to Aviation Québec Labrador Ltée of Sept-Îles, Que. It is currently owned by Wildernes Air Ltd. and being converted to a Vazar turbine Otter.
C-GPJA	DHC-6 Series 300 Twin Otter	505	1981	1982	Laurentian leased this aircraft from C&S Enterprises Ltd. on behalf of Airgava Ltd., which had ceased trading in 1981 due to financial difficulties. Laurentian operated it until September 22, 1982. The following year, it was exported to the U.S. and registered N606GH.
C-GUJU	Beaver	1639	1979	1991	This aircraft was originally purchased by the South Arabian government. Laurentian bought it in July 1979 after it was imported to Canada, transferring it to Air Schefferville in 1981. In 1991, the company sold the Beaver to Desraps Aviation Inc. in Natashquan, Que., which continues to operate it.
C-GUJV	Beaver	1643	1979	1990	This Beaver had also been originally delivered to the South Arabian government. Laurentian imported it to Canada in 1979 and operated it until 1990, when the company sold it to Contact Charters in Fort McMurray, Alta. It is currently registered to Air Mikisew Ltd. in that city.

APPENDIX 2:
AIRCRAFT BOUGHT AND SOLD
BY LAURENTIAN AND B.M. AVIATION

Serial	Registration	Aircraft Type	Bought/Sold	Notes
144	VR-RBV 9M-ALV VH-AAS CF-BPC C-FBPC	Beaver	Bought in 1971 Sold in 1972	Laurentian imported VH-AAS from Aerial Agriculture in East Sydney, Australia and registered it as CF-BPC. In 1972 it sold 'BPC to Cargair Ltd. in St-Zenon, Que. Over the next two decades it was owned by several Quebec and Ontario operators. In 1992 Wabakimi Air. Ltd. in Armstrong, Ont., registered it C-FBPC and continues to fly it.
178	N52409 HP-375 N1018A	Beaver	Sold in 1978	Company records indicate Laurentian sold this aircraft to Kenmore Air Harbor Inc., Kenmore, Wash., in 1978. Since 2000, it has been operated by S&S Aircraft Leasing in Ketchikan, Alaska.
314	C-GCDX N413JP	Otter	Bought and sold in 1974	Ex-58-1700 U.S. Army. Afterward, it went to the Sharpe Army Depot in Stockton, Cal., until it was purchased by Laurentian in 1974 with three other Otters. It was not in flyable condition, and was immediately sold on to Ag Air Company of Latah, Wash., which collected the Otters in Stockton and trucked them to Washington. Ag Air restored it and sold it to Nipawin Air Services Ltd. of Nipawin, Sask., which registered it as C-GCDX. Nipawin had been flying it for four years when it crashed at Otter Lake, Sask.. in May 1978. After it was repaired, it was sold to Bearskin Lake Air Services of Big Trout Lake, Ont., in 1980. It is currently flying with Bald Mountain Air Service in Homer, Alaska, with tail number N413JP.
316	N521BK C-FSGD	Otter	Bought and sold in 1974	Ex-U.S. Army 58-1704. Purchased from the Sharpe Army Depot in Stockton, Cal., but was not in flyable condition and so was immediately sold on to Ag Air Company of Latah, Wash. After several owners in the U.S. and Canada it has been operated by Transwest Air Ltd. since 2001, based at La Ronge, Sask.
377		Beaver		Ex-U.S. Army 51-16832. Fate unknown.
646	CF-TCW	Beaver	Sold in 1973	Laurentian imported this aircraft from Aerial Agriculture Ltd. in Australia. Alliance Aviation (subsidiary of Laurentian) sold it to Norcanair in Prince Albert, Sask., and since 1993 it has been operated by Harbour Air in Richmond, B.C.
682	C-GQHT	Beaver	Bought in 1976 Sold in 1979	Ex-53-3725 U.S. Army. B.M. Aviation sold it "as is" – just the airframe – to Lauzon Aviation Ltd. in Algoma Hills, Ont. According to Laurentian's records, it did not have wings, an engine, and was missing many parts as well as its records. In 2004, while registered to Pickerel Arm Camps in Sioux Lookout, Ont., it crashed. Fate unknown.
745		Beaver		Delivered Dec. 19, 1954, to Aerovias Rojas S.A. and registered as XA-LEB. Serial number appears in Alliance Aviation records. Fate unknown.

Serial	Registration	Aircraft Type	Bought/Sold	Notes
1001	CF-ZKJ	Beaver	Bought and sold in 1971	Laurentian registered it as CF-ZKJ in May 1971 before selling it to Air Ste-Agathe. Later it was registered to Cargair Ltée as C-FZKJ and Air Brochu-Brochu Industries beginning in 1982. The registration was cancelled in 1987. Current status unknown.
1128		Beaver		Ex-U.S. Air Force 56-0395. Appears in Alliance Aviation records. Fate unknown.
1130	G-GAQJ	Beaver	Bought in 1975	Ex-U.S. Army 56-4411. B.M. Aviation imported it in 1975 and sold it to Red Lake Airways in Red Lake, Ont., which still operates it.
1246		Beaver	Sold in 1976	Ex-U.S. Air Force 57-6151. B.M. Aviation sold it to Nipawin Air Services Ltd in Nipawin, Sask., for $28,200 in 1976. Fate unknown.
1285		Beaver	Bought in 1975 Sold in 1978	Ex-58-2053 U.S. Army. Imported to Canada in 1975 and registered in Chibougamau, Que., in 1976 as C-GUBB. Possible that B.M. Aviation purchased it, as records show the company then sold it to Alliance Aviation in 1977, which then sold it to Direquair Ltée in 1978. Since then several Quebec bush operators have owned it, and it has been operated in Newfoundland, Washington and British Columbia, where it is registered as C-FWCA with Vancouver Island Air Ltd. in Campbell River.
1362	C-GAQX	Beaver	Bought in 1975 Sold in 1982	Ex-58-2029 U.S. Army. Registered to the Texas State Technical Institute in Jan. 1972 as N6476. Then it was sold to an individual in Hayward, Cal., and re-registered as N88919. B.M. Aviation imported it in 1975 and sold it to Staron Flight in 1982. It was destroyed in 1993.
1381	N1018U	Beaver	Sold in 1978	Ex-58-2049 U.S. Army. B.M. Aviation sold it to Kenmore Air Harbor Inc., Wash., in 1978. It was also operated by Pumpkin Air circa 1983. Since 2001 it has once again been registered to Kenmore.
1434	VH-IDF CF-BPB	Beaver	Bought in 1971 Sold in 1972	Laurentian sold this aircraft on behalf of Aerial Agriculture in East Sydney, Australia to Ste-Anne-du-Lac Air Servces in Ste-Anne-du-Lac, Que., in 1972 with the registration CF-BPB.
1465	C-GUIG	Beaver	Sold in 1977	First delivered in 1961 as N144Q to de Havilland, New York. B.M. Aviation sold it to Kenmore Air Harbor, Wash., in 1977, and the company operated it until 1985. It crashed in 1995 and 2002 with different operators but was repaired both times. Since 2004 it has been registered to Talkeetna Air Taxi Inc., Talkeetna, Alaska.
1575	CF-CCJ	Beaver	Bought in 1972 Sold in 1984	This aircraft was registered to Aerial Agriculture of Australia as VH-KWF when Laurentian purchased it. In 1984 the company sold it to Pierre Brossard Ltée and it has been registered as C-FCCJ with Pierre Ferderber in Val-d'Or since 1985.
1657	C-GUJW	Beaver	Bought in 1976 Sold in 1979	The South Arabian government owned this aircraft until B.M. Aviation imported it to Canada in 1976. The company then sold it to Contact Airways Ltd. in Fort MacMurray, Alta. Included in the sale were floats, a canoe rack, wheels-skis and a new paint job. According to a *Canadian Aviation* article, it was considered to be the lowest-time Mk. 1 Beaver at the time, with only 164 hours total. It is currently registered to Voyage Air Ltd. and is still in Fort McMurray.

64 Beavers Bought at U.S. Army Auction, Coleman Barracks, Mannheim-Sandofen, Germany

Date of Auction: February 14, 1973
Bill of Sale: April 1, 1973

Serial	Registration	Date Sold	Comments
256	N1018B N166BM	Dec. 19, 1978	51-16796 U.S. Army. #1072. L-20 No. 73. Command A-2. B.M. Aviation sold the fuselage to Kenmore Air Harbor Inc., Kenmore, Wash., which registered it as N1018B. Since 1981, it has been registered to Bill Martin Fish Alaska, Inc. in Anchorage as N166BM.
257	C-GVHT		51-16797 U.S. Army. #1073. L-20 No. 74. Command A-2. Registered to Steinwand's Transport Ltd. in Rae, NWT, on Jul. 11, 1985. In 1987 went to Wahkash Contracting Ltd. in Campbell River, B.C., On Aug. 13, 2001, while still registered to Wahkash, it crashed at Mackenzie Lake, B.C., and has been in storage since.
262	N1018C N698TK	Dec. 19, 1978	51-16798 U.S. Army. #1077. L-20 No. 78. Command A-2. B.M. Aviation sold the fuselage to Kenmore Air Harbor Inc. which registered it as N1018C. Registered to Tikchik Narrows Lodge Inc. in Anchorage, Alaska, as N698TK since 1980.
268	SE-FUH N2140X C-FMDB	Jul. 3, 1975.	51-16800 U.S. Army. #1082. L-20 No. 83. Command A-2. Registered as SE-FUH to Turistflyg i Aejeplog AB in Sweden. Exported to U.S. on Aug. 8, 1989 and registered as N2140X, then imported back to Canada and registered as C-FMDB in 1993 to Nestor Falls Bait and Tackle Ltd. in Nestor Falls, Ont. It is still registered to that company.
269	N37741 N3129S C-GMSX N49443	Apr. 9, 1974	52-16801 U.S. Army. #1063. L-20 No. 84. Command A-2. B.M. Aviation sold it to A. Dean Carrell in Anchorage, Alaska, in "as is condition … as received from U.S. Army before ITRAN inspection," according to records. It was last registered to Hyack Air Ltd. in British Columbia as C-GMSX in 1982. Fate unknown.
274	C-GHCT C-GSIH N323RS	Apr. 5, 1974	51-16803 U.S. Army. #1088. L-20 No. 089. Command A-2. B.M. Aviation sold it in as-is condition to Trans-Provincial Airlines in Terrace, B.C., who registered it as C-GHCT in Aug. 1974. On Nov. 1, 1981, while owned by Tradewinds Aviation Ltd. of B.C., it was involved in a wreck during the filming of *Mother Lode* (directed by Charlton Heston) in Vancouver, and the crash sequence was incorporated into the movie. Since 2000, it has been registered to Legend Airways of Morrison, Col.
293	N1018D	Dec. 19, 1978	51-16810 U.S. Army. #1106. L-20 No. 107. Command A-2. B.M. Aviation sold it to Kenmore Air Harbor Inc. in Kenmore, Wash. It has been operated by several Alaskan companies since, and was most recently registered to Willow Air in Wasliia, Alaska, in 2006.
372	C-GAEF	Jul. 30, 1974	51-16830 U.S. Army. #1178. L-20 No. 179. Command A-2. Sold to Air Alma in Alma, Que., circa 1980. It has been registered to Air Saguenay in Lac Sébastien, Que., since 1993.
393	C-GUJY	Mar. 7, 1977	51-16841 U.S. Army. #1197. L-20 No. 198. Command A-2. B.M. Aviation sold it to Sioux Narrows Airways Ltd. in Winnipeg, where it is still registered.
398	C-GUWC	1979	51-16843. B.M. Aviation sold it to Direquair Ltée, which registered it as C-GUWC circa 1979. It crashed on Jan. 13, 1982, and the registration was cancelled Jun. 1 after it was reportedly destroyed by fire. Fate unknown.
399	C-GNZO	Dec. 19, 1977	51-16844 U.S. Army. #1203. L-20 No. 204. Command A-2. B.M. Aviation sold it to Orillia Air Services in Orillia, Ont., in as-is condition. Has been registered to Waweig Lake Outfitters Ltd. in Thunder Bay, Ont., since 1994.
400	C-GUGQ	Mar. 3, 1979	51-16845 U.S. Army. #1204 L-20. No. 205. Command A-2. B.M. Aviation registered it in Jun. 1976 and sold it to Air Roberval Ltée in Roberval, Que. It has been registered to Propair Inc. in Rouyn-Noranda, Que., since 2001.

Serial	Registration	Date Sold	Comments
610	C-GSZA	Sept. 30, 1976	53-2813 U.S. Army. #1356. L-20 No. 357. Command A-4. B.M. Aviation sold it to Orillia Air Services Ltd. in Orillia, Ont., in as-is condition. While registered to Kabee-lo Airways Ltd. in Ear Falls, Ont., the left wing struck trees bordering Confederation Lake on Jun. 22, 1979. It was also involved in an accident on Jul. 13, 1991, where it water-looped and sank upon landing. It was recovered, however, and is currently registered to Pavillon du lac Berthelot Inc. in Senneterre, Que.
611	C-GUXW	Mar. 19, 1977	53-2814 U.S. Army. #1357. L-20 No. 358. Command A-4. Alliance Aviation sold it to Harvey Christiansen in Saskatchewan. It was then registered to Nipawin Air Service in Nipawin, Sask., in Jul. 1977. It continued to be operated in Saskatchewan until Aug. 2, 2003, when it was in an accident on an unnamed lake about 5 miles southeast of the Pelican Narrows airport in Saskatchewan. The owner and pilot, Christiansen, was killed but his two passengers survived. The aircraft is being stored in Nipawin for an eventual rebuild.
616	CF-DLV C-FDLV N911W	Sept. 1973	53-2818 U.S. Army. #1361. L-20 No. 362. Command A-4. B.M. Aviation did not register it before it sold the aircraft to Joseph Veverka of Cochrane Air Services Ltd. in Cochrane, Ont. Mr. Veverka traded in his Cessna 180C, CF-MEO, toward this aircraft, and operated it until 1985. It is currently registered to Roderick M. Grant in Dillingham, Alaska, as N911W.
631	C-GVQE	Dec., 19, 1978	53-2829 U.S. Army. #1372. L-20 No. 373. Command A-4. B.M. Aviation sold it to Jean H. Lonergan of Laval, Que., with wheels and floats. Mr. Lonergan traded in a Cessna 180.5, C-FFTV, toward the Beaver, which he flew until 1983. Since 1994, it has been registered to Safari Nordik Inc. based at Kuujjuaq.
703	C-GAEB	Oct. 1974	53-7895 U.S. Army. #1436. L-20 No. 437. Command A-4. B.M. Aviation sold it to Athabaska Airways of Prince Albert, Sask., in Dec. 1974. Since 2001, Transwest Air of Saskatchewan has operated it.
705	CF-DVK C-FDVK	Aug. 1, 1973	53-7897 U.S. Army. #1438. L-20 No. 439. Command A-4. B.M. Aviation sold it to Labrador Air Safari on Aug. 1, 1973, but within a year it was registered to Golfe Air Québec Ltée in Hauterive, Que. In 1977, it was back to Labrador Air Safari, to which it was registered on Jul. 4, 1985, when it was involved in a crash at Baie Comeau, Que. Fate unknown.
708	C-GUDK	Oct. 14, 1975	53-7900 U.S. Army. #1441. L-20 No. 442. Command A-4. B.M. Aviation sold it to Highfield Corporation Ltd. in Calgary, delivering the aircraft on Dec. 5, 1975. Within two years it was being operated in B.C. and is currently registered to Liard Air Inc. in Fort Nelson.
710	N1018G N62SJ N1018F(2)	Dec. 19, 1978	53-7902 U.S. Army. #1443. L-20 No. 444. Command A-4. B.M. Aviation sold it to Kenmore Air Harbor Inc. in Kenmore, Wash., which registered it as N1018G and sold it north to Alaska Coastal Construction in 1981. On Sept. 2, 1995, it hit a rock off of Blakely Island, Wash., and was severely damaged. Neil Aird noted it back at Kenmore Air Harbor and was informed it would not be rebuilt. But the next year it was back flying for Kenmore, registered as N1018F(2).
711	C-GACK	Feb. 1974	53-7903 U.S. Army. #1444. L-20 No. 445. Command A-4. Registered to B.M. Avia-tion in Mar. 1974 as C-GACK. According to the company's records, the wings were dismounted and stored at flight operations. Its movements for the following two decades remain shrouded in mystery until it surfaces in Sechelt, B.C. in 1993. It is currently registered to Corilair Charters Ltd. in Campbell River, B.C.
715	C-GUMF N700WB C-GMWB	1976	53-7907 U.S. Army. #1448. L-20 No. 449. Command A-4. B.M. Aviation registered it as C-GUMF in 1976. Nothing is known of this aircraft until Apr. 1988, when it was registered to Claude Michaud in Ste-Marceline, Que. While it left for the U.S. for several years, it is back in Canada, being operated by Ten-Ee-Ah Estates Ltd. in Lac la Hache, B.C.

Serial	Registration	Date Sold	Comments
716	C-GUDZ	1976	53-7908 U.S. Army. #1449. L-20 No. 450. Command A-4. B.M. Aviation sold it to Sabourin Lake Airways Ltd., with which it crashed on Aug. 1, 1981 at Big Hook Lake, Ont., resulting in one death. The accident was possibly caused by a wing separation. The aircraft was destroyed.
724	C-GAEE N754LA N54LA	1982	53-7915 U.S. Army. #1456. L-20 No. 457. Command A-4. B.M. Aviation agreed to sell the aircraft to Taku Air Transport in Atlin, B.C., in Apr. 1979 but the deal did not appear to go through, and it was sold to Richard G. Bond in B.C. in 1982. On Jul. 19, 1996, it was destroyed in a fatal crash in Alaska while registered to Kenneth and Craig Loken.
730	C-GADE	Jun. 5, 1974	53-7919 U.S. Army. #1460. L-20 No. 461. Command A-4. B.M. Aviation sold it to James Bay Outfitters in Cochrane, Ont. Since Jul. 2008 it has been registered to Kississing Lake Lodge Ltd., in Steinbach, Man.
732	N1018H CF-DTW	Dec. 19, 1978	53-7921 U.S. Army. #1462. L-20 No. 463. Command A-4. B.M. Aviation sold it to Kenmore Air Harbor Inc. in Kenmore, Wash. which registered it as N1018H in Mar. 1979. While registered to Kenmore, it was hit by another Beaver, N127WA, at a dock in Metlakatla, Alaska, but escaped relatively unscathed. Since 2000, it has been registered to Northern Rockies Air Charter Ltd. in Watson Lake, Yukon.
733	C-GVHS	1979	53-7922 U.S. Army. #1463. L-20 No. 464. Command A-4. Alliance Aviation took the struts off this aircraft and put them on s/n 1096 before selling the latter to Aviation Maintenance Ltd. B.M. Aviation then sold it to Hooker Air Services in late 1979. A decade later it was registered to Allen Airways Ltd. of Sioux Lookout, Ont., where it was flown and then stored until 2007. It was then exported to Wipaire Inc., Minn., for rebuild and eventual turbine conversion.
735	C-GUIG N5CM C-GSRS N123EF	Apr. 1977	53-7924 U.S. Army. #1465. L-20 No. 466. Command A-4. B.M. Aviation sold it to R.G. Bond of Atlin, B.C., who registered it as C-GUIG in Jun. 1977. On Mar. 21, 1979, it struck the snow surface of a glacier 8 miles northwest of Mount Hanley, B.C., and then crashed in 1993 while registered to Jabbee Air Services Ltd. in Moose Factory, Ont. It is still active, however, and registered as N123EF in Anchorage, Alaska.
736	C-FDUW	Jul. 10, 1973	53-7925 U.S. Army. #1466. L-20 No. 467. Command A-4. B.M. Aviation sold it to Lac Seul Airways Ltd. in Winnipeg. Since 1999, it has been operated out of Atlin, B.C., most recently by Apex Air Charters Ltd.
737	C-GAEU N91AK	Sept. 16, 1974	53-7926 U.S. Army. #1467. L-20 No. 468. Command A-4. B.M. Aviation sold it to Lindberg's Hunt and Fish Air Service in Cochrane, Ont. It is now registered to Wings of Alaska Airways in Jun.au.
740	C-GAEA N1954J	Jun. 18, 1974	53-7929 U.S. Army. #1470. L-20 No. 471. Command A-4. B.M. Aviation registered it in 1974. It was operated by West Coast Air Service in 1978 and remained with B.C. operators until the mid-1980s. It is now in Bettles, Alaska, registered to J. Jespersen as N1854J.
743	C-GWEY	c.1978	53-7931 U.S. Army. #1472. L-20 No. 473. Command A-4. Registered to W.K.K. Aviation in St-Laurent, Que., in 1978. Since 1999, it has been registered to Geary's Sportsman's Lodge Ltd. in Red Lake, Ont.
746	C-GDHM N746DB N67LU N41PS C-FEBB	Jul. 15, 1977	53-7932 U.S. Army. #1473. B.M. Aviation registered it in Jul. 1977 as C-GDHM and sold it to Brazeau Oil Distributors Ltd. in Fort Smith, NWT, fully loaded with hydraulic wheel-skis, a ventral fin, splash rails, a canoe rack, a winter shutter kit and a whole avionics package. In 1978, it was registered to Fort Smith Air Services Ltd. and remained with that company until 1982, when it was exported to the U.S. It has been back in Canada since 2000, registered as C-FEBB to H.N. Hybrid Nurseries Ltd. in Pitt Meadows, B.C.

Serial	Registration	Date Sold	Comments
747	C-GUBD	Aug 20, 1976	53-7933 U.S. Army. #1474. L-20 No. 475. Command A-4. B.M. Aviation sold it to Wentzell's Flying Service in Corner Brook, Nfld. It remained with local operators until it crashed Jan. 10, 1986, near Border Beacon. The aircraft was reported destroyed. Fate unknown.
748	C-GAZJ	Apr. 24, 1975	53-7934 U.S. Army. #1475. L-20 No. 476. Command A-4. B.M. Aviation sold it to the Northern Quebec Inuit Association before going to Johnny May's Air Charter Ltd. in Kuujjuaq, Que. Since 2003, it has been registered to Aviation 2000 Inc. in La Tuque, Que.
754	N1018M N91WF N8LU N1018N(2) N878PS N601MS N629TE	Dec. 19, 1978	53-7939 U.S. Army. #1480. L-20 No. 481. Command A-4. B.M. Aviation sold it to Kenmore Air Harbor Inc., Kenmore, Wash., as part of a batch sale of 12 Beavers when it shut down in 1978. It has been registered to a number of companies in Alaska and Washington. Since 2007, it has been operated by What's the Point LLC in Bellevue, Wash.
841	C-GAXE		54-1698 U.S. Army. #1541. L-20 No. 542. Command A-6. B.M. Aviation imported it in Mar. 1973, and may have sold it directly to Hyack Air Ltd. in Pitt Meadows, B.C. in May 1982. It has remained in B.C. since, and was most recently operated by Avnorth Aviation Ltd. in Nimpo Lake. The registration was cancelled in 2000, however, and it has been in storage since.
891	C-GVGL	Dec. 14, 1977	54-1736 U.S. Army. #1579. L-20 No. 580. Command A-6. B.M. Aviation sold it to Kyro Albany River Airways Ltd. in Jellicoe, Ont. Walter J. Shulmoski of Wabowden, Man., has owned it since 1985.
892	CF-DSG C-FDSG	Oct. 3, 1973	54-1737 U.S. Army. #1580. L-20 No. 581. Command A-6. B.M. Aviation sold it to Wilderness Airlines in Williams Lake, B.C., delivering it on Dec. 19, 1973. It is now registered to Pacific Coastal Airlines Ltd. in Richmond, B.C.
1095	C-GUME N47SM N9RW	1977	56-0382 U.S. Army. #1684. L-20 No. 683. Command A-11. B.M. Aviation sold it to Sabourin Lake Airways in 1977. It remained with Canadian operators until 2001, when it was exported to Alaska. It is currently registered to T-Corp. in Anchorage.
1096	C-GQKS	Mar. 24, 1977	56-4399 U.S. Army. #1685. L-20. No. 686. Command A-12. B.M. Aviation sold it "as-is where-is" to Aviation Maintenance Ltd. in Sault Ste. Marie, Ont. Note in the records says: "Struts for this A/C not available. Using struts off A/C #64 serial No. 733." Since 2003, it has been registered to T.C. Leasing in La Ronge, Sask.
1098	C-GUIH VP-FAT	1976	56-0383 U.S. Army. #1686. B.M. Aviation briefly registered it as C-GUIH. Once the Falkland Islands government purchased it, the company changed the registration to VP-FAT. It was demolished by British bombardments on Jun. 11, 1982, during the Falkland Islands War.
1100	C-GAEG N995WA	Jun. 4, 1975	56-0384 U.S. Army. #1687. L-20 No. 688. Command A-11. It was registered to B.M. Aviation in May 1975 and nothing noted about it until Austin Airways registered it in 1980. It was exported to the U.S. circa 1995 and crashed in 2007 in Alaska while registered to Promech Inc. Destroyed.
1101	5A-DBH (1) C-GUOY	Sept. 13, 1976	56-4400 U.S. Army. #1688. L-20 No. 689. Command A-12. B.M. Aviation sold it to L.C. Abbey in Cloverdale, B.C., along with serial no. 1103. The note in the records says, "Mr. Abbey and Mr. Williams to decide between themselves which aircraft each will take." Most recently, it has been registered to the Fibermax Timber Corp. in Victoria, B.C., and was featured on the cover of Sean Rossiter's book *The Immortal Beaver*.

Serial	Registration	Date Sold	Comments
1103	C-GUOZ	Sept. 13, 1976	56-0385 U.S. Army. #1689. L-20 No. 690. Command A-12. B.M. Aviation sold it to L.C. Abbey in Cloverdale, B.C. along with serial no. 1101. The note in the records says, "Mr. Abbey and Mr. Williams to decide between themselves which aircraft each will take." This aircraft ended up with Kimsquit Air Ltd. in Prince George, B.C., and after going to other B.C.-based companies over the years, has returned to that company.
1108	CF-JRO	Dec. 17, 1973	56-0387 U.S. Army. #1693. L-20 No. 694. Command A-11. B.M. Aviation sold it to Ranger Oil in Calgary, which operated it until 1992. LAS also did the check-out on Ranger Oil's chief pilot, Donald MacLeod. It is now operated by Ranger Air Charter in Whitehorse, Yukon.
1109	C-GDYT	Sept. 30, 1976	56-4403 U.S. Army. #1694. B.M. Aviation sold it to Orillia Air Services Ltd. in Orillia, Ont., in "as-is where-is" condition for $16,000. Orillia registered it as C-GDYT in May 1977. Since 1989, it has been operated by Kabeelo Airways Ltd. at Ear Falls, Ont.
1123	C-GMAY	Feb 20, 1974	56-0393 U.S. Army. #1705. L-20 No. 706. Command A-11. B.M. Aviation sold it to Fastener Corporation of Franklin Park, Ill., on Feb. 20, 1974. It has been registered to Johnny May's Air Charter since 1975 and has been operating under the name "Pengo Pallee" since Dec. 1989.
1124	C-GUBS	Apr. 6, 1976	56-4409 U.S. Army. #1706. L-20 No. 707. Command A-12. B.M. Aviation sold it to Norm Hegland of Sabourin Lake Airways. From there it went to several operators in Saskatchewan and Newfoundland before ending up with Canadian Airways Ltd. in Chapleau, Ont. in 1997.
1127	N1018N (1) N340KA	Dec. 19, 1978	56-4410 U.S. Army. #1708. L-20 No. 709. Command A-12. B.M. Aviation sold it to Kenmore Air Harbor Inc. in Kenmore, Wash., which registered it as N1018N. From 1993 to 2004, Alaskan operators flew the aircraft. In 2006, after Fly Fish Air Inc. in Shoreline, Wash., registered it, the aircraft crashed into the water off Vancouver Island's Port Alberni area. Before the aircraft sank, the passengers and pilot were able to escape and none were injured. The aircraft was substantially damaged, though, and Neil Aird believes it is being parted out.
1132	C-GUJX	Apr. 18, 1978	56-4412 U.S. Army. #1712. L-20 No. 713. Command A-12. B.M. Aviation registered it as C-GUJX in Jun. 1976 before selling it to Air Citadel Inc. in Lorette, Que., along with long-range tanks, floats, a canoe rack, etc. It is now being operated by Lawrence Bay Airways LTd. in La Ronge, Sask.
1133	N1018P	1979	56-0397 U.S. Army. #1713. L-20 No. 714. Command A-11. B.M. Aviation sold it to Kenmore Air Harbor Inc. in Kenmore, Wash. Since Sept. 1982, the aircraft has been registered to Norman G. Hayden in Kent, Wash.
1151	C-GHCS N67680 N9558Q	Apr. 5, 1974	56-0406 U.S. Army. #1731. L-20 No. 732. Command A-11. B.M. Aviation sold it in as-is condition to Trans-Provincial Airlines Ltd. in Prince Rupert, B.C., which in turn registered it as C-GHCS in Jun. 1974. Operated by firms in B.C., the Northwest Territories and Washington for over three decades before being involved in a fatal accident on May 17, 2008, while registered to Lake Chelan Air Service in Chelan, Wash. The aircraft flipped upon landing, killing two passengers and injuring another two. The aircraft was recovered and was noted for sale on Ebay in Nov. 2008.
1153	C-GADD	Jan. 16, 1976	56-0407 U.S. Army. #1733. L-20 No. 734. Command A-11. B.M. Aviation sold it to Westminster Air Ltd. in North Vancouver, B.C. Since 1989, it has been operated by Neisk'a Air Ltd. in Timmins, Ont.
1154	C-FDSB		56-4423 U.S. Army. #1734. L-20 No. 735. Command A-12. B.M. Aviation registered this aircraft in Dec. 1973 as C-FDSB. The next available information has it registered to Ledair Ltd. in Les Cèdres, Que., on Feb. 7, 1992. Since 1994, it has been operated by E.J. Aviation Ltd. in Newfoundland.

Serial	Registration	Date Sold	Comments
1169	C-GAJU	Apr. 29, 1975	56-0415 U.S. Army. #1749. L-20 No. 750. Command A-11. B.M. Aviation registered the aircraft in Dec. 1974 and sold it to Canadian Voyageur. It is currently registered to Pine Air Inc. in Sioux Lookout, Ont.
1171	C-GUJZ N100HF C-GTMC	May 31, 1979	56-0416 U.S. Army. #1751. L-20 No. 752. Command A-12. B.M. Aviation registered it as C-GUJZ and sold it to Air Nat Ltée in Natasguan, Que. On Jun. 11, 1988 it sank on a take-off run while registered to Granite Air Inc. It was restored in Surrey, B.C., in May 1995 and purchased by Maketea Productions Inc. in Burbank, Cal. In 1998 it returned to Canada: Seair Seaplanes Ltd. in Richmond, B.C., reigstered it C-GTMC.
1230	N1018T N6786 (2) N1544	Dec. 19, 1978	57-6144 U.S. Army. #1802. L-20 No. 803. Command A-14. 8th Infantry Division. B.M. Aviation sold it to Kenmore Air Harbor which registered it as N1018T in Mar. 1979. Andrew Airways Inc. in Kodiak, Alaska, has owned it since 2000.
1233	C-GUHH VP-FAV	1976	57-6145 U.S. Army. #1805. L-20 No. 806. Command A-14. B.M. Aviation registered it briefly as C-GUHH in 1976 before selling it to the Falkland Islands Government air service. It was next to VP-FAT during the bombardments in 1982 but was reportedly still serviceable several months later. In 1989 the fuselage was spotted in the quarry at the FIGAS airport.
1245	C-GZJJ	1977	57-2577 U.S. Army. #1814. L-20 No. 815. Command A-13. B.M. Aviation sold it to Nipawin Air Services in 1977. In Jul. 1983 it was destroyed by fire while registered to High Noon Holdings Ltd. in Calgary. Fate unknown.
1329	CF-GMK C-FGMK	Aug 8, 1973	58-2003 U.S. Army. #1883. L-20 No. 884. Command A-16. B.M. Aviation sold it to Ontario Northern Airways in Jellicoe, Ont. Since 1982 it has been registered to Wilderness Air in Vermillion Bay, Ont.
1358	C-GSKY DQ-GEE	Mar. 28, 1974	58-2027 U.S. Army. #1907. L-20 No. 908. Command A-16. B.M. Aviation registered the aircraft C-GSKY in Jul. 1974 and delivered it to Skymaster Aviation Ltd. in Buttonville, Ont., on Jul. 26, 1974. It was then registered to Wilderness Airline Ltd. in Richmond, B.C., in 1975. On May 24, 1982, while registered to Wilderness Airline, it crashed near Port Hardy, B.C., but was recovered. Since 2002, it has been registered to Pacific Island Seaplanes in Fiji.
1359	C-GUFZ N67687 (2)	1978	58-2028 USAF. #1908. L-20 No. 909. Command A-16. B.M. Aviation registered it in 1978, selling it to Canadian Voyageur in that year. Since 1989 it has been registered to Clyde E. Carlson in Seattle, Wash., as N67687 (2).
1364	C-GTBC	Dec. 3, 1976	58-2032 U.S. Army. #1912 L-20 No. 913. Command A-16. B.M. Aviation sold it as is to Thunderbird Enterprises Ltd. in Pelican Narrows, Sask. It is currently registered to Pelican Narrows Air Services Ltd. in that location.

ENDNOTES

Preface

1. Dick Pickering, "The Life of a Bush Pilot: Douglas S. (Doug) Pickering," *Journal of the Canadian Aviation Historical Society* (Fall 2001).
2. Deane E. Bostick, "Bush Pilot," *Cavalier*, August 1974.

Chapter 1: A New Company for a New Age

1. "Laurentian Air Services Limited, Ottawa," *Canadian Aviation*, August 1936, 6.
2. At the end of 1936 there were only 450 licensed aircraft in Canada: 60 were owned by governments, 73 by individuals, 76 by flying clubs, and 241 by commercial operators. Furthermore, there were only 1,000 licensed pilots in the country. Charles A. Ashley, *A Study of Trans-Canada Airlines: The First Twenty-Five Years* (Toronto: Macmillan, 1963), 3-4.
3. "L'Aviation à la portée de tous," *La Presse* (Montreal), July 22, 1919, and "Ottawa has Air Service all its own," *Ottawa Evening Journal*, July 21, 1919. Thank you to George Fuller for bringing these sources to my attention and sharing his notes. Thanks also to Terry Judge, who provided important details on Deisher's early involvement in Ottawa's aviation scene, discovering that he quickly resigned as president of the OFC amid allegations of unfair flying practices. Judge uncovered some discrepancies about Deisher's flying activities in Transport Canada records and later accounts, noting that more research into this Ottawa aviation pioneer's life is needed.
4. "Airdrome notes," *Aviation and Aircraft Journal*, September 1921.
5. Dick Pickering, "The Life of a Bush Pilot: Douglas S. (Doug) Pickering," *Journal of the CAHS* (Fall 2001), 100. Information on the Maclaren family and company taken from the following sources: James W. Thomson, *Lumbering on the Rivière du Lièvre: a saga of Maclaren's* [sic] *and Buckingham* ([Ottawa?, 1973?]), 77-87; Pierre-Louis Lapointe, *La Vallée assiégée: Buckingham et la Basse-Lièvre sous les MacLaren, 1895-1945*, (Boisbriand, Que.: Diffusion Prologue, 2006), 32 and 42-3.
6. Wayne C. McNeal, "General Aviation in Canada" (master's thesis, University of British Columbia, 1969), 25-7.
7. "Flying Clubs' Activity Reviewed," *Canadian Aviation*, March 1936, 13-15.
8. "Notes and News From the Clubs," *Canadian Aviation*, February 1936, 22.
9. "Chatting with the Editor," *Canadian Aviation*, January 1936, 1.
10. "On the Need for Teamwork," *Canadian Aviation*, January 1936, 3.
11. K.M Molson, *Pioneering in Canadian Air Transport* (Winnipeg: J. Richardson, 1974), 188 and McNeal, "General Aviation in Canada," 50.
12. "A New Era Dawning," *Canadian Aviation*, November 1936, 3.
13. Susan Goldenberg, *Troubled Skies: Crisis, Competition and Control in Canada's Airline Industry* (Whitby, Ont.: McGraw-Hill Ryerson, 1994), 4.
14. This quotation and the next are from "News and Views of the Month," *Canadian Aviation*, December 1936, 3.
15. The information in this paragraph is taken from: Dick Pickering, "The Life of a Bush Pilot," 98-100.
16. Gatineau Fish and Game Club to its members, August 10, 1936. Private collection. Barnet may have gotten some family support in publicizing his company to the Club's members. His father, Alexander, and his uncle, Albert, were both founding members of the Club in 1894.
17. Bob Ross, "Laurentian Air Services: In 35 years, 500 million charter miles," *Ottawa Journal*, October 2 1971.
18. Ross, "Laurentian Air Services."
19. Ross, "Laurentian Air Services."
20. "Notes and News From the Clubs," *Canadian Aviation*, October 1936, 20-1.
21. "Laurentian Air Services," *Canadian Aviation*, March 1937, 36.
22. Honeywell, Wilson & McDougall, Barristers and Solicitors, to Powell, Aylen & MacLaren, Barristers, April 22, 1937. Private collection.
23. Doug Pickering, "Resume: Laurentian Air Services Limited," November 25, 1975.
24. "Notes and News From the Clubs," *Canadian Aviation*, August 1936, 20-1.
25. "Notes and News From the Clubs," *Canadian Aviation*, May 1936, 28.
26. "Notes and News From the Clubs," *Canadian Aviation*, February 1936, 22.
27. "Aerial History in the Making," *Canadian Aviation*, April 1937, 3.
28. McNeal, "General Aviation in Canada," 42-44.
29. "What of Our Airports?" *Canadian Aviation*, October 1936, 3.
30. The information and quoted material in the two preceding paragraphs was taken from: T.M McGrath, *History of Canadian Airports* (Canada: Lugus Publishing, 1992), 165.
31. McNeal, "General Aviation in Canada," 31.
32. McGrath, *History of Canadian Airports*, 165.
33. Paddy Gardiner, "Trials and tribulations of the Ottawa Valley pioneers," *Canadian Aviation*, August 1968, 11;

and Ross, "Laurentian Air Services."

34. Barnet Maclaren to C.D. Howe, February 15, 1938. Private collection.

35. Barnet Maclaren to G.W. McNaughton, April 13, 1937. Private collection.

36. Barnet Maclaren, "Notes on Negotiations Leading to Acquisition of 'Uplands Airport' by Laurentian Air Services Ltd." Private collection.

37. J.A. Wilson to Ottawa Flying Club, April 26, 1937. Private collection.

38. "The Trans-Canada Airway Progress Report," *Canadian Aviation*, March 1937, 6-9.

39. Barnet Maclaren to J.A. Wilson, May 18, 1937. Private collection.

40. Barnet Maclaren to C.D. Howe, July 28, 1937. Private collection.

41. Yates to Barnet Maclaren, July 30, 1937. Private collection.

42. J.P. Crerar to Barnet Maclaren, September 21, 1937. Private collection.

43. Barnet Maclaren to J.P. Crerar, September 24, 1937. Private collection.

44. "Airports," *Canadian Aviation*, December 1937, 22.

45. Barnet Maclaren to C.D. Howe, February 15, 1938. Private collection.

46. Barnet Maclaren to Walter Deisher, March 2, 1938. Private collection.

47. Department of Transport, "Lease to Laurentian Air Services," May 11, 1938. Private collection.

48. "Airport Developments," *Canadian Aviation*, July 1938, 28.

49. "The Ottawa Airport Opening," *Canadian Aviation*, September 1938, 8.

50. "Laurentian Air Services," *Canadian Aviation*, March 1937, 36.

51. While I would like to give DND the benefit of the doubt, it is possible that they did know about Laurentian. Several *Canadian Aviation* editorials in 1938 centred on the government's duty to provide contracts for commercial operators instead of the RCAF: "The need for co-operation," *Canadian Aviation,* October 1938, 6.

52. Barnet Maclaren to Lieut. Commander C.P. Edwards, May 25, 1937, RG 12 vol. 2249, Library and Archives Canada (hereafter cited as LAC).

53. R.K. Smith to C.P. Edwards, May 26, 1937, RG 12 vol. 2249, LAC.

54. Brown to deputy minister of Department of Transport, June 3, 1937. RG 12 vol. 2249, LAC.

55. Laurentian may also have had to buy the second Waco at the time because, as Terry Judge notes: "After a number of fatal accidents due to flight into turbulent weather, in June 1937 all Puss Moth aircraft in Canada were grounded until further notice. Deisher was furious, pointing out that other countries had not taken this step and that they couldn't earn money with the aircraft grounded. New certificates were issued as Private, with the proviso

that they could be used commercially for freight only. Apparently this didn't help Laurentian, which wanted its aircraft for passenger transport, and so the Puss Moth was put in the back of the hangar and was not flown again until it was sold in May 1939. The file does show, however, that the engine was turned over regularly.

56. Ross, "Laurentian Air Services."

57. "Commercial Air Services in Review," *Canadian Aviation*, March 1938, 34.

58. Barnet Maclaren to Piper at Imperial Oil, June 5, 1937. Private collection. Laurentian and Imperial Oil created "an extensive gasoline storage and dispensing installation" in 1938 that used "modern computing meters" according to the author of "Laurentian Air Services Help Speed the Victory," *The Salesmotor*, 8.

59. Agreement between Fleet Aircraft and Laurentian Air Services, June 13, 1938. Private collection. Business may have seemed like it was booming, but, as Barnet's nephew John Bogie remarked during an interview, with Barnet and Bill only flying a few hundred hours each, "You don't make much money doing that much flying." Nevertheless, Barnet and his cousin Gordon kept a close eye on operation costs, paying property taxes promptly to save 2.5 per cent, making sure they had a firm contract with Robert Taylor, who built the new Laurentian hangar in 1938, and carefully setting rates for hangar accommodation and airfield storage.

60. *Canadian Aviation*, June 1938, 38.

61. "Our New Customer – The Air Tourist," *Canadian Aviation*, August 1939, 4.

62. Barnet Maclaren to J.A. Wilson, April 14, 1939, RG 12 vol. 2249, LAC.

63. "The Case of the Commercial Operators," *Canadian Aviation*, March 1939, 9. In 1938 Laurentian reported the following statistics: 495 hours flown, 9,404 pounds of freight, 1807 passengers carried, 2 pilots employed and two planes in operation.

64. Barnet Maclaren to C.D. Howe, July 5, 1939 and J.A. Wilson to Barnet Maclaren, October 6, 1939. Private collection.

65. J.A. Wilson to Barnet Maclaren, November 26, 1938. Private collection.

Chapter 2: Warner Bros. and the War Effort

1. "War: Canada's Position in the Air," *Canadian Aviation*, September 1939, 4.

2. Robert B. Parke, "Wallace," *Flying: 50th Anniversary Issue,* September 1977, 257.

3. Robert Bothwell and William Kilbourn, *C.D. Howe: A Biography* (Toronto: McClelland and Stewart, 1979), 113.

4. Quoted material taken from the Nanton Lancaster Society Air Museum's website: <http://www.lancaster-museum.ca/crane.html>. In a *Canadian Aviation* article, "Canadian Order put Cessna on its feet," the author wrote: "the company might have folded had it not been

for the sale of the Cessna T-50 Crane to the RCAF in 1939." Additional background information taken from the Canada Aviation Museum's website: <http://www.aviation.technomuses.ca/collections/artifacts/aircraft/CessnaCrane.shtml>.

5. Doug Pickering's recollection 30 years later was that Laurentian operated two Puss Moths but records indicate there was only one at this time. Doug Pickering, "Resume: Laurentian Air Services."

6. "Twenty-five years in aviation: the Success Story of Laurentian Air Services Limited," *Canadian Flight: the Pilot's Magazine,* June/July 1961.

7. Jack C. Charleson, "Rambles of a Pioneer Pilot: A Half Century of Hangar Flying By One Who Was There, Part II," *Journal of the CAHS* (Spring 1985): 6. I would like to thank former journal editor Bill Wheeler for bringing this article to my attention and providing me with a copy.

8. "Twenty-Five Years in Aviation:," *Canadian Flight,* June/July 1961; and Ross, "Laurentian Air Services."

9. While Jean-Paul Fournier, who was inducted into the Quebec Air and Space Hall of Fame in 2003, was the "first Canadian airman to qualify himself solo on a helicopter," Jack Charleson was the first Canadian to receive his civil helicopter licence. U.S. Coast Guard Aviation Society, <http://uscgaviationhistory.aoptero.com/history02.html > and Fondation Aérovision Québec, Inc, <http://www.aerovision.org/doku.php?id=en:jean_paul_fournier>. Charleson discusses his introduction to the helicopter in his article, "Rambles of a Pioneer Pilot, Part II," 10-11.

10. Robert Rennert, *A City Takes Flight: the Story of Ottawa International Airport* (Montréal : R. Rennert, 2000), 14.

11. Charleson, "Rambles of a Pioneer Pilot, Part II," 5.

12. Charleson, "Rambles of a Pioneer Pilot, Part II," 8.

13. Ross, "Laurentian Air Services."

14. Pierre-Louis Lapointe, *La Vallée assiégée,* 43.

15. The information in this paragraph is taken from Dick Pickering, "The Life of a Bush Pilot," 98-100.

16. Doug Pickering, "Flying the Delta," *SKY-ADS,* 66.

17. Ross, "Laurentian Air Services." R.H. Jones to Doug Pickering, December 21, 1942 and Doug Pickering's Logbook #3. Private collection.

18. Doug Pickering Logbook #3. Private collection.

19. Dick Pickering, "The Life of a Bush Pilot," 101. According to Dick, his father and Jack Charleson flew approximately "300 aircraft on test or ferry operations."

20. C.T. Travers to Doug Pickering, March 29, 1941, RG 12 vol. 2249, LAC and Doug Pickering's logbook #3. Private collection.

21. Two previous quotes taken from: "Ottawans See Big Searchlight 'Cover' Aircraft," *Ottawa Citizen,* March 31, 1941.

22. C.S. Abbott, Memorandum, April 3, 1941, RG 12 vol. 2249, LAC; Doug Pickering's Logbook #3. Private collection; and "Three dead, six injured in wreck on C.P.R.

Line at Inkerman, ON," *The Ottawa Citizen,* April 1, 1941.

23. Controller of Civil Aviation to W.H. Rea, telegram, July 21, 1944, RG 12 vol. 2249, LAC.

24. "Pleasure Flying and Aircraft Banned," *Canadian Aviation,* October 1942, 107.

25. "Civilian Air Services are Hard Pressed," *Canadian Aviation,* December 1942, 162.

26. Controller of Civil Aviation to W.H. Rea, telegram, July 21, 1944, RG 12 vol. 2249, LAC.

27. Dick Pickering, "The Life of a Bush Pilot," 102. According to Doug's logbook, he also managed to sneak away for some fishing at Lac Repos on May 8, 1942 likely with one of his colleagues at Laurentian.

28. John Bogie, interview with author in Ottawa, October 6, 2007.

29. For example, George went with Barnet on a rescue mission to Sept-Îles, Quebec, on July 6, 1944, after they received word that two mining prospectors had gone missing. John Bogie, interview with author in Ottawa, October 6, 2007. Doug Pickering also flew to Sept-Îles on that mission in Laurentian's Waco CF-AYP.

30. Doug Pickering, "Resume: Laurentian Air Services," and Ross, "Laurentian Air Services."

31. The quoted material in this paragraph taken from: "Laurentian Air Services Help Speed the Victory," *The Salesmotor,* 8-9.

32. Contract between the Department of Munitions and Supply and Laurentian Air Services, July 1, 1943, RG 28 vol. 355, LAC.

33. For example, on December 30, 1943 G.E. Wallingford, Chief Aeronautical Engineer for the Department of Transport, requested that George Beveridge inspect and do maintenance on the DOT's Beechcraft D17S (CF-BJD) at Ottawa Airport. G.E. Wallingford to George Beveridge, December 30, 1943, RG 12 vol. 2249, LAC.

34. "Laurentian Air Services Help Speed the Victory," *The Salesmotor,* 8.

35. This and the following quotation are from: "We Think," *Canadian Aviation,* October/November 1939, 6.

36. "What's in the Air?" *Canadian Aviation,* January 1941, 15.

37. The information and quotations in this paragraph are from Rudy Mauro, "The Making of Captains of the Clouds: A Half-Century's Perspective on the First Canadian Air Epic," *Journal of the CAHS* (Summer 1991): 41-2.

38. Mauro, "The Making of Captains of the Clouds," 42.

39. Bruce W. Orriss, *When Hollywood Ruled the Skies: the Aviation Film Classics of World War II* (n.p., Aero Assoc., 1985), 42.

40. Orriss, *When Hollywood Ruled the Skies,* 43.

41. Mauro, "The Making of Captains of the Clouds," 44.

42. "Agreement Between Warner Bros. Pictures, Inc. and Canadian Commercial Air Operators," July 15,1941. Private collection. Laurentian was paid $40 per flying hour and was given a minimum daily payment of two hours

flying, including ferrying the airplane to and from Trout Mills.

43. Doug Pickering noted in his third logbook on July 17, 1941: "North Bay – Movies." Private collection.

44. This and the next two quotes are from Rudy Mauro, "Captains of the Clouds: A Postscript," *Journal of the CAHS* (Spring 1995): 22-3. All the bush flying scenes in *Captains of the Clouds* were performed by Frank Clarke, Howard Batt, Garland Lincoln, Jerry Phillips, and Herb White, members of the legendary Associated Motion Picture Pilots (AMPP). Clarke had been flying for films since 1918, according to Orriss, *When Hollywood Ruled the Skies*, 44.

45. Mauro, "The Making of Captains of the Clouds," 90.

46. Orriss, When Hollywood Ruled the Skies, 43.

47. Mauro, "The Making of Captains of the Clouds," 48, and Mauro, "A Postscript," 23.

48. The quoted material in the previous paragraph taken from: Mauro, "A Postscript," 23.

49. "Captains of the Clouids," International Movie Database, <http://www.imdb.com>. In 2007 the film was re-released on DVD with additional features.

50. Orriss, *When Hollywood Ruled the Skies*, 43. Billy Bishop lent his support to the film in other ways as well; he was featured in the movie speaking at an actual RCAF graduation ceremony at Uplands, bestowing wings on students.

51. Doug Mackey, "North Bay's Big Movie – Captains of the Clouds 1941," *Community Voices*, August 29, 2003.

52. Bosley Crowther, "'Captains of the Clouds,' Heroic Film About Royal Canadian Air Force and Starring James Cagney, Arrives at the Strand," *The New York Times*, February 13, 1942.

Chapter 3: A Growing Fleet and a Going Concern

1. J.P. McIntyre had been Walter Deisher's office manager when he helped found Laurentian in 1936. McIntyre stayed on with Laurentian after Deisher's departure.

2. A.D. McLean, Controller of Civil Aviation to Secretary of the Air Transport Board, June 9, 1945. RG 12 vol. 2249, LAC.

3. W.B. Burchall, "Canada Needs an Air Policy," *Canadian Aviation*, July 1946, 50.

4. Brochure in private collection. Domaine d'Estérel was built by Baron Louis Empain of Belgium in the 1930s and included a luxury hotel, commercial complex, sports club, and theatre. Information taken from the following websites: Multicultural Canada's website, <http://www.multiculturalcanada.ca/ecp/content/belgians.html> and l'Estérel's website, <http://www.esterel.com/contenu/galerieDImages_historiqueDeLEsterel_ang.cfm>.

5. Air Transport Board decision, November 2, 1945, RG 12 vol. 2249, LAC. According to an article in the *Montreal Gazette*, "Laurentian Air Service Authorized by Board," published November 15, 1945, C.D. Howe – who was now Reconstruction Minister for the federal government – rubber-stamped Laurentian's licences for both its Ottawa and Lac-Masson operations. It was only one of five non-scheduled air carriers to receive official approval at this time.

6. Gray Rocks Inn, which was owned by the Wheeler family, was the first year-round resort in the Laurentians and one of the best-known downhill skiing destinations in the region in the 1930s. Ray and Diana Baillie, "Gray Rocks Inn, Mont Tremblant," <http://laurentian.quebecheritageweb.com/article_details.aspx?articleId=37> and Sandra Stock, "The Laurentians: A Very Concise History, Part 2," <http://laurentian.quebecheritageweb.com/article_details.aspx?articleId=76>.

7. Barnet Maclaren to the Secretary of the Air Transport Board, December 18, 1945. Private Collection. The proposed charge was $10 per person one way or $18 return (plus taxes).

8. R.A.C. Henry, chairman of Air Transport Board, March 8, 1946. Private collection.

9. H.R. Foottit to Mr. Wallingford, Department of Transport. March 29, 1945, RG 12 vol. 2249, LAC, and "War Surplus Aircraft," *Canadian Aviation,* May 1945, 51.

10. Dick Pickering, "The Life of a Bush Pilot," 102.

11. "Twenty-five years in aviation" *Canadian Flight*, and Ross, "Laurentian Air Services."

12. "Bush and Charter Air Routes Sought by Many Operators," *Canadian Aviation*, December 1946, 50-1, and "Converting Military Aircraft Profitable to Many Firms," *Canadian Aviation,* December 1946, 54.

13. A.D. McLean, Controller of Civil Aviation to Barnet Maclaren, January 10, 1946, RG 12 vol. 2249, LAC. Laurentian also bought an Airspeed Oxford V (serial no. 2582, RCAF no. EB515) from the War Assets Corporation for parts, and a Wasp Jr. engine. H. Chase, Aircraft Division of the War Assets Corporation to Department of Transport, Civil Aviation Branch in Montreal, February 4, 1946 RG 12 vol. 2249, LAC.

14. The quoted material in this paragraph is taken from R.F. Corless, Jr., "Suggested Economical Northern Work Horse described in detail," *Canadian Aviation,* March 1945, 82.

15. Fred W. Hotson, *De Havilland in Canada* (Toronto: CANAV Books, 1999), 126.

16. "'Beaver' Bush Aircraft to Fly This Summer," *Canadian Aviation,* April 1947, 34-5.

17. Hotson, *De Havilland in Canada*, 131.

18. Dirk Septer, "Beaver Turns 50: The Great Birthday Bash," *Aviation Quarterly* (1997), 9.

19. Hotson, *De Havilland in Canada*, 130.

20. John Bogie to Jack Schofield, 1997. Private Collection and "Beaver production begins," *Canadian Aviation,* January 1948, 57.

21. There appears to be some debate over whether it was Beaver c/n 3 or 6. The consensus appears to be that it was no. 6: XdH Aviation Services Inc. <www.xdh.ca/DHC_Aircraft/DHC-7/DHC-2_Production/dhc-2_production.

html>; Hotson, 132; and Doug Pickering in his unofficial 1975 history of Laurentian, all confirm this.

22. Dick Hiscocks, "The Beaver and STOL," *West Coast Aviator Magazine,* July/August 1997, 29. Hiscocks was part of the design team at DHC that worked on the Beaver.

23. Ronald A. Keith, "Impressive Three-Point Take-Off Most Vivid Beaver Flight Feature," *Canadian Aviation,* April 1948, 26-7.

24. Doug Pickering to Secretary of Air Transport Board, May 17, 1950, RG 12 vol. 2249, LAC.

25. A de Havilland Canada ad in *Canadian Aviation,* April 1949.

26. The information in this paragraph was taken from "Twenty-five years in aviation," *Canadian Flight,* July/August 1961.

27. Sylvain Gingras, *A Century of Sport: Hunting and Fishing in Quebec,* trans. R. Clive Meredith (St-Raymond, Que.: Éditions Rapides blancs, [1994?]), 114. As Gingras notes, it was actually the strong presence of private clubs that hired guardians and stocked the rivers that saved Eastern Canada's major salmon rivers. Since the Atlantic salmon had been eradicated in most of New England's rivers by this time, many Americans came north to Quebec's private clubs.

28. "Air Tourist Prospects," *Canadian Aviation,* August 1945, 84.

29. Gingras, 305-311.

30. Gingras, 314.

31. The club had an office at the Waldorf Astoria Hotel in New York City for its American members according to John Bogie.

32. According to the Echo Beach Club logbooks from the 1940s, Robert Laidlaw had been a member since 1938 and Henry Borden since 1936. Borden's uncle and Prime Minister of Canada, Sir Robert Borden, had also been a member of long standing and introduced his nephew to the fishing club in the 1920s. Echo Beach Club fonds, LAC.

33. Gingras, *A Century of Sport,* 319.

34. Frank Manning Covert, *Fifty Years in the Practice of Law* (Montreal: McGill-Queen's University Press, 2005), 62.

35. Gingras, *A Century of Sport,* 293.

36. Echo Beach Club Log Book #3. Echo Beach Club fonds, LAC.

37. Gingras, *A Century of Sport,* 87.

38. "The Governor's Visit," *Moccasin Telegraph,* n.d.

39. Based on correspondence found in RG 12 vol. 2249, LAC.

40. The information and quoted material in the following paragraph come from David Gordon Frosst's written statement, September 22, 1949. Private collection. I would like to thank Jack "Thumper" Thorpe for bringing this incident to my attention and providing me with valuable records.

41. M.M. Fleming, Inspector for Air Regulations, Department of Transport intra-departmental correspondence, September 10, 1949. Private collection.

42. M.M. Fleming, Inspector for Air Regulations, Department of Transport intra-departmental correspondence, September 10, 1949. Private collection.

43. *Ottawa Citizen,* September 10, 1949. Private Collection.

44. M.M. Fleming, Inspector for Air Regulations, Department of Transport intra-departmental correspondence, September 10, 1949. Private collection.

44. David Gordon Frosst to Department of Transport, October 2, 1949. Private collection.

46. Dick Pickering, e-mail message to author, June 13, 2008.

Chapter 4: A Favourable Time for Flying

1. John Bogie, e-mail message to author, February, 12, 2009.

2. Application to Air Transport Board, May 7, 1952. Private collection.

3. Correspondence from Air Transport Board, September 11, 1952. Private collection.

4. Doug Pickering to Mr. S. T. Grant, September 26, 1952. RG 12 vol. 2249, LAC.

5. John Bogie, interview with author, October 7, 2007.

6. Instructions from the DOT, July 26, 1951. RG 12 vol. 2249, LAC. They also made a refuelling stop at Rouse's Point in New York State, on their way out and back.

7. According to Library and Archives Canada online information about the H.F. McLean fonds, he worked on the following projects: Grand Falls Hydroelectric dam in New Brunswick, the Flin Flon Railway, the Gusboro Railway, Wolfe's Cove Terminal Tunnel, Temiskaming and Northern Ontario Railway, among others.

8. "Candidates for Canadian Hall of Fame," *Liberty,* April 30, 1988, H.F. McLean fonds, LAC.

9. "Generous Mr. X is Identified as H.F. McLean." *Globe.* November 9, 1943, H.F. McLean fonds, LAC.

10. "Police Protect McLean After He Distributes $50,000 to Windsorites," *Globe,* March 30, 1944, H.F. McLean fonds, LAC.

11. Dick Beddoes, "Nice Going, Old Girl," *Globe and Mail,* October 26, 1976. H.F. McLean fonds, LAC.

12. Harry had a Waco and later bought Beaver serial no. 42 for his personal use according to Fred W. Hotson, *De Havilland in Canada* (Toronto: CANAV Books, 1999), 132. One writer noted Harry felt safer in the air even though he had once crashed. April 30, 1988, *Liberty* "Candidates for Canadian Hall of Fame," H.F. McLean fonds, LAC.

13. Doug Pickering to the Secretary of Air Transport Board, May 17, 1950, RG 12 vol. 2249, LAC.

14. According to John Bogie, they also went down to Chicago in 1954 to pick up a body.

15. Bill Peppler, e-mail to author, May 4, 2008.

16. Bill did not come away from the experience completely empty-handed either. When the surveyors went about naming landmarks, he had a lake named after him: Peppler Lake.

17. "Twenty-five years in aviation," *Canadian Flight.*

18. Philip Smith, *Brinco: the Story of Churchill Falls* (Toronto:

McClelland and Stewart Ltd., 1975), 14.

19. Smith, *Brinco*, 3.

20. Smith, *Brinco*, 9.

21. Smith, *Brinco*, 28.

22. Smith, *Brinco*, 29.

23. Gerald Morisset, Secretary of Air Transport Board, to Doug Pickering, July 4, 1952, RG 12 vol. 2249, LAC.

24. George Beveridge to D. Jackson, superintendent of air regulations for the DOT, June 23, 1950. Private collection.

25. Of course, John Bogie and Bill Peppler also knew each other from working in Northern Quebec and from the newly-founded Canadian Owners and Pilots Association. Jack Fleming, who had flown summers for Laurentian while at university, now worked for Spartan, along with his wife, Betty.

26. Smith, *Brinco*, 29.

27. Smith, *Brinco*, 56-7.

28. Smith, Brinco, 57. John Bogie also recalls that Labradorite was discovered in this region, and Paul Saunders would make beautiful jewelry out of it for family and friends.

Chapter 5: Losing Altitude

1. F.H. Wheeler, "Outlook for '56: Industry Leaders Show the Way Ahead," *Canadian Aviation*, January 1956, 31.

2. John Roberts, "Outlook for '57: Industry Leaders Forecast," *Canadian Aviation*, January 1957, 35.

3. "Capacity Surplus Dictates Caution," *Canadian Aviation*, May 1959, 21-22.

4. According to John Gill, his godmother, Jean Brinckman, and her sister, as well as his Aunt Betty were three of the first pilots in Ottawa. His Aunt Betty knew Beryl Markham, the first woman to fly across the Atlantic. The RCAF director, Squadron Leader Cathcart-Jones, was a friend of his parents and got him and his brother onto the set at Uplands when they were filming *Captains of the Clouds*. During his childhood he also met Billy Bishop, who was an occasional guest of his parents. J.A.D. McCurdy, who piloted the Silver Dart in 1909, had been an old boyfriend of his mother's.

5. Ross, "Laurentian Air Services."

6. In 1953 Laurentian applied to increase the number of passengers it could carry for fire prevention services in its Beavers and the Goose for precisely this reason – the aircraft were often packed! Beavers CF-FHR, 'EYT, 'GIB, 'EYU, 'GCN, 'EYN and Grumman Goose 'BXR were the aircraft most often used for fire prevention work at this time. C.T. Travers to Doug Pickering, July 20, 1953. Private collection.

7. Betty Campbell, interview with the author, June 10, 2008. She found the specific dates in Jack Fleming's logbooks. This particular incident occurred July 15, 1955, and the flights were made between June 2 and Sept. 26, 1955.

8. The information and quoted material in this and the following four paragraphs are from: Barnet Maclaren to the Air Transport Board, November 13, 1958, RG 12 vol. 5325, LAC.

9. It is unclear what the outcome of Joseph Bertrand's application was, although I would like to thank Tim Dubé, Terry Judge, Neil Aird, Bill Peppler and Ian Macdonald, who all tried to help figure it out. In 1963, the tables were turned when Laurentian was among those blocking Bertrand's application for a secure base at Rapides-des-Joachims. In the end, a former Laurentian employee, Bob Burns, bought Bertrand Airways in 1973 and renamed it Calumet Air Service, using two former Laurentian aircraft: a Cessna 180, CF-HLY, and a DHC-2 Beaver, CF-GIB.

10. Barnet Maclaren to the Air Transport Board, November 13, 1958, RG 12 vol. 5325, LAC.

11. Barnet Maclaren to S. Graham, Superintendent Air Regulations Branch of the Civil Aviation Division of the DOT, October 2, 1945, RG 12 vol. 2249. LAC.

12. S. Graham to Barnet, October 10, 1945, RG 12 vol. 2249, LAC.

13. George Beveridge to Director of Air Services for the DOT, January 17, 1950, RG 12 2249, LAC and George Beveridge to Mr. D Jackson, DOT, September 7, 1951, RG 12 vol. 2249, LAC.

14. *Canadian Aviation*, April 1949, 62.

15. Sunderland to Superintendent of Air Regulations for the DOT, December 14, 1945, RG 12 vol. 2249, LAC.

16. Chief Aeronautical Engineer to District Controller of Air Services, August 16, 1950, and George Beveridge to D. Jackson, Superintendent of Air Regulations for the DOT, June 23, 1950. Private collection.

17. D.T. Jackson, Chief Aircraft Inspector to C.A.E., July 15 1953. Private collection.

18. D. Saunders, District Superintendent Air Regulations to Director of Air Services, June 19, 1953. Private collection.

19. Memo to Inspector P.S. Walker from Inspector W.M. Johnson, July 8, 1953. Private collection.

Chapter 6: New Blood and Nouveau Québec

1. "Announcing … Laurentian Air Services Ltd.," *Canadian Flight*, Feb/March 1960.

2. Laurentian's application for a protected air base at Schefferville, November 14, 1962. Private collection.

3. Keith Baker, interview with the author, July 21, 2008.

4. Gord McNulty, "February 14th, 2002 Meeting. Speaker: Reg Phillips," *Flypast*, March 2002.

5. By the summer of 1963, however, John Bogie wrote Gordon Hamilton, president of Hamilton Aircraft Company, that Laurentian had had to sell the aircraft "as we did not have enough work for it." In July 1963, though, he was asking Hamilton for estimates on another Beech C18S, "with the cargo door and high density folding seats" but without any engines, since they had plenty of those sitting around already. A short while later he received a response from Hamilton that there just happened to be an aircraft with a cargo door (and no engines) that he

would be willing to sell for $23,000. George B. Hamilton to John Bogie, August 2, 1963. Private collection.

6. M.E. Louch to Barnet Maclaren, May 5, 1960, and telegram sent to Laurentian September 24, 1965. Private collection.

7. Langevin Coté, *Heritage of Power: the Churchill Falls Development from Concept to Reality* (St. John's, Nfld: Churchill Falls [Labrador] Corporation Ltd., 1972).

8. Doug Pickering, "Resume: Laurentian Air Services"; Ross, "Laurentian Air Services"; and Coté, *Heritage of Power*, vi-vii.

9. Keith Baker, interview with the author, July 21, 2008.

10. Barrie Martland, "Hunting, fishing fly-in business booming, " Canadian Aviation, May 1963, 14-15, 25. In the early 1960s Laurentian bought a fishing camp on Lac Kamachigama not far from Ottawa. As John Bogie told me, he purchased it from "a big Quebec contractor who used to entertain Maurice Duplessis," one of Quebec's most powerful (and infamous) premiers.

11. "Fly in for Fishing and Hunting: Air Transportation for Easy Holidays," *Ottawa Journal*, May 25, 1965.

12. While Laurentian flew in and out of Rapide-des-Joachims from 1945 onwards, it was never able to secure a base there. In 1963 it applied for one, but was opposed by Bertrand Airways and other competitors. In the end, the Air Transport Board decided it was better for the region if the point were left open to all aviation companies.

13. Marc Terziev, "New Landlock Salmon Water," *Outdoor Life*, July 1964, 21.

14. Pickering, "Resume: Laurentian Air Services."

15. Marc Terziev, "Northern Quebec's Unfished Regions Luring Sportsmen," *Syracuse Herald-American*, September 20, 1964.

16. Marc Terziev, "Looking for 'Big Ones'? Labrador Fishing Grounds Within Air Miles of Your Own Syracuse Hearth," *Syracuse Herald-American*, September 6, 1964.

17. Terziev, "New Landlock Salmon Water"; Marc Terziev, "Silvery Brook Trout Abound in Labrador," *Syracuse Herald-American*, September 13, 1964; Marc Terziev, "Hooking, Landing Arctic Char Real Thrill for Local Sportsman," *Syracuse Herald-Journal*, September 10, 1964; Terziev, "Northern Quebec's Unfished Regions."

18. Marc G. Terziev, "We Blazed Wild New Trails," *Outdoor Life*, May 1965, 32.

19. Terziev, "We Blazed," 32.

20. Nicholas Karas, "The River Where Fishing Dreams Come True," *Sports Afield Fishing Annual*, 1966.

21. M.J. Boylen continued to turn to John Bogie and other Laurentian pilots to fly CF-IFN on charter from time to time. For two weeks during the summer of 1963 Laurentian flew Boylen in IFN around northern Manitoba, Ontario and the Northwest Territories. In August 1964, Laurentian flew Boylen and three other passengers to northern Labrador on a prospecting trip.

22. Guy Beauregard, "Lost for Nine Days: Ordeal and Death," *Outdoor Life*, July 1968, 29-31 and 84-5.

23. Marc G. Terziev, "Not by the Book," *Field and Stream*, February 1968, 61: "Ted had left a 2-way radio set with us so we could keep in touch during our stay. This equipment is a must in case of emergencies and it's handy for arranging pickup details. We had set a cutoff date for him to come after us if we lost contact, and we were carrying extra food against weather contingencies. Daily check-in time is usually after breakfast and when we called next morning, Ted immediately inquired about the fishing."

Chapter 7: Tales from the Boardroom and the Bush

1. Ross, "Laurentian Air Services."

2. In 1968, Flamand had several aircraft at his disposal for teaching students how to fly: a Cessna 172H, CF-VBQ; a Cessna 172I, CF-OSJ; and a Cessna 150F, CF-UQI.

3. Canadian Transport Commission, Air Transport Committee Decision, August 26, 1968 RG 12 vol. 5325, LAC.

4. DOT Report, January 8, 1969, RG 12 vol. 5325, LAC.

5. C.E. Blair to CAR Ottawa and QCAR Montreal, February 27, 1969, RG 12 vol. 5325, LAC.

6. According to the DOT records, Laurentian was authorized for Class 4 Groups B and C charter and Class 7 specialty commercial air services, as well as Class 3 irregular specific point commercial air service and class 9-4 international non-scheduled charter commercial air service.

7. All the staff information and names are taken from reports and applications submitted by Laurentian to the DOT in 1967 and 1968, RG 12 vol. 2249, LAC.

8. John Bogie, email to author, February 23, 2009.

9. Deane E. Bostick, "Bush Pilot." From the available information, it appears Paul Saunders worked for Laurentian until 1968.

10. Paddy Gardiner, "It's a long hot summer for flying bushmen," *Canadian Aviation*, October 1969.

11. Paddy, "It's a long hot summer."

12. That summer, Laurentian had the following aircraft registered to it: Piper PA-18 150s CF-PUZ and CF-LHQ; Beavers CF-FHR, CF-FHP, CF-HOE and CF-GCW; Cessna 172G CF-SZJ, Cessna 172H CF-VBQ; Grumman G-21A Goose CF-BXR; Cessna 180H CF-VXB; and Otter CF-VQD. Pilots Jules Pilon and Tim Cole also recall flying a second Piper Apache, CF-MUA, out of Maniwaki on fire patrol as well as on executive charters

13. Laurentian application to the DOT, November 28, 1966 , RG 12 vol. 2249, LAC.

14. Memo, January 24, 1968 , RG 12 vol. 2249, LAC.

15. "'Business as usual' in air service fire," [newspaper unknown – likely *Ottawa Citizen* or *Ottawa Journal*], February 19, 1972. Private collection

16. John Bogie's notes "Course of events: Fire – Alliance Aviation Engine Shop Friday Evening," February 18, 1972." Private collection.

Chapter 8: Great Canadian Bushplanes

1. All the information in this paragraph comes from Jack Leggatt, "The de Havilland Beaver," *Plane & Pilot*, August 1969, 44-46 and 51-53.
2. Fred W. Hotson, *De Havilland in Canada*, 146; Neil Aird, phone conversation with author, July 14, 2008; and Phil Hanson, "Happy 30th Birthday Beaver! You're Not Getting Older, You're Getting Better," *Canadian Aircraft Operator*, August 16, 1977, 3.
3. Jack Schofield, "Variations on a Theme," *West Coast Aviator*, July/August 1997, 25
4. All the information and quoted material in the rest of this section is from Leggatt, "The de Havilland Beaver," 45-52.
5. Fred W. Hotson, "North of the Polarsirkelen," *Air BP*, 1951.
6. John Bogie to T. Hovda, September 10, 1971. Private collection.
7. T. Hovda to John Bogie, September 22, 1971. Private collection.
8. Invoice from Wideroe to Laurentian, December 1, 1971. Private collection.
9. John Bogie to Jerry Smith, December 9, 1971. Private collection.
10. John Bogie to G. Smith, January 18, 1972. Private collection.
11. Dirk Septer, "Beaver Turns 50," 13.
12. John Bogie to Torfinn Hovda, July 21, 1972. Private collection.
13. Karl E. Hayes, "Otter 201," *De Havilland Canada DHC-3 Otter: A History* (Dublin: Self-published CD, 2005) and and Eddy Lord, phone interview with author, August 25, 2008 .
14. Peter Marshall, "De Havilland Beaver: Plain is Perfection," *Canadian Aviation,* October 1976, 21; and "64 Beavers Purchased by Ottawa Firm," *The General Aviation News*, May 1, 1973.
15. Aerial Agriculture to John Bogie, September 22, 1971. Private collection.
16. Aerial Agriculture to John Bogie, September 22, 1971; John Bogie to Jack Schofield, date unknown. Private collection.
17. Neil Aird, "c/n 1612," <http://www.dhc-2.com/id622.htm>.
18. Aird, "c/n 646," <http://www.dhc-2.com/id859.htm>.
19. Marshall, "De Havilland Beaver," 21-22.
20. Hanson, "Happy 30th Birthday," 3.
21. "64 Beavers," *The General Aviation News.*
22. Carl Mills, "A Tech Rep in Korea: Maintaining and Adapting the de Havilland DHC-2 Beaver as a Technical Representative," *Journal of the CAHS* (Fall 2000): 84-93, 116-117.
23. Mills, "A Tech Rep."
24. Information taken from letters and documents in private collections.
25. Ross, "Laurentian Air Services" and "64 Beavers," *General Aviation News.*
26. All the information and quoted material in the previous paragraph was taken from Ross, "Laurentian Air Services."
27. James Duff, "Aircraft deal set for takeoff," *Montreal Gazette*, [n.d].
28. "Aircraft Industry lands in Lachute," *The Watchman* (Lachute, QC), April 18, 1973.
29. Pierre Vennat, "Lachute deviendra centre aéronautique," *La Presse* (Montreal) April 18, 1972.
30. "B.M. Aviation a acheté 64 Beaver," *Le Pilote*, May 1973, 5.
31. Ross, "Laurentian Air Services,"
32. Ross, "Laurentian Air Services." John Bogie recalls that after B.M. Aviation purchased the 64 Beavers, it brought Laurentian's total to 96 Beavers in inventory and operation in 1973.
33. Duff, "Aircraft deal."
34. Information in this paragraph taken from Aird, "c/n 1098," <http://www.dhc-2.com/id323.htm> and "c/n 1233," <http://www.dhc-2.com/id188.htm>. John Bogie has a different interpretation of events. He recalls that the aircraft were ferried by a pilot for Braniff International Airways, one on floats and one on wheels. According to John, VP-FAT was damaged before the war and VP-FAV was anchored at Port Stanley in the Falkland Islands, where 'FAV's pilot became connected to several British Special Forces men who had parachuted on to the island and blended into the local population. For approximately ten nights, Bogie says, these agents would sneak onto 'FAV and contact the British Navy fleet with the aircraft's high-frequency radio, advising them where the Argentinian forces were located. The next morning, the carrier aircraft could use the coordinates to bomb them. According to John, the Argentinians became suspicious and sank 'FAV but "this broke the back of the Argentine invasion and the war ended shortly after."
35. Marshall, "De Havilland Beaver."
36. Tim Dubé, "DHC-2 Beavers in Our Backyard: Laurentian Air Services," *Observair*, November 2007.
37. "Twenty-five years in aviation," *Canadian Flight.*
38. *Sport Flying*, October 1973.
39. This quotation as well as the next are from Septer, "Beaver Turns 50," 8.
40. Neil Aird, interview by Terry MacLeod, August 13, 1997, <http://www.dhc-2.com/CBC%20Summerside%201997.html>.

Chapter 9: Change in the Air

1. Doug Pickering, "Resume: Laurentian Air Services Limited," November 25, 1975. Private collection
2. John Bogiek interview with author, October 7, 2007.
3. Paddy Gardiner, "James Bay scheme may give us a lift here," *Ottawa Citizen*, February 5, 1972.
4. M. L. (Mac) McIntyre, "The James Bay Hydro Project: Flying Out of Matagami," *Journal of the CAHS*, Winter 1999.

5. Jules Pilon, interview with author, May 16, 2008.
6. Henry Holden, "The DC-3 Genesis of the Legend," *The Legacy of the DC-3*, excerpted on the DC-3/Dakota Historical Society's site <http://www.dc3history.org/douglasdc3.html>.
7. Larry Milberry, *Austin Airways: Canada's Oldest Airline* (Toronto: CANAV Books, 1985), 120-121.
8. DOT Records, RG 12 vol. 5325, LAC.
9. Jules Pilon, who by 1973 was flying several of Laurentian's Beavers in northern Quebec, also remembers the Lalancette brothers would come up during the winter to fly the DC-3s. Other known pilots of Laurentian's DC-3s in the early 1970s include Jules Proulx, Gordon Norel, Claude Rousselle and Walter Ferguson, who all flew on the Canadian International Paper contract in 1974.
10. John Bogie, interview with author, October 7, 2007, and Iain Bogie, interview with author, May 12, 2008.
11. John Bogie, interview with author, October 7, 2007 and Pickering, "Resume: Laurentian Air Services Limited."
12. McIntyre, "The James Bay Hydro Project."
13. Deane E. Bostick, "Bush Pilot," *Cavalier*, August 1974, also wrote: "Laurentian Air Services has averaged fifteen charters a day since 1936 without recording a fatality or serious crack up."
14. Andre Côté, "Les bucherons voyagent en avion," *Mauricie Journal*, March 24, 1974
15. "I've had it with planes," *Ottawa Citizen,* August 7, 1974; "Un DC-3 s'écrase dans le parc des Laurentides et fait quatre morts," *La Presse* (Montreal),. August 7, 1974.;This is my translation of the French-language article.
16. <http://www.crash-aerien.com/www/database/liste.php?id=1974> and <http://www.planecrashinfo.com/1974/1974-41.htm>.
17. The author and a research assistant at the University of Ottawa, Aaron Boyes, attempted to track down the names of the two passengers who were killed in this crash. Surprisingly, there was very limited coverage of the accident in the major Montreal and Ottawa papers after the initial reports and we could not find mentions of the names.
18. Neil Aird, <http://www.dhc-2.com/id622.htm>.
19. Jules Pilon, interview with author, May 16, 2008; the Air Crashes Record Office in Geneva, Switzerland, has the crash listed as having occurred on August 7, 1975 <http://www.baaa-acro.com/archives/1975-JUL-DEC.htm> but all other records indicate it occurred on August 5th. I have not been able to positively identify the second Laurentian employee that was on board CF-BPA that day.
20. <http://www.policeandpeaceofficers.ca/dedication_info.html>.
21. <http://www.releases.gov.nl.ca/releases/2002/forest/1104n05.htm> and <http://www.releases.gov.nl.ca/releases/2001/forest/1024n02.htm>. The two men were added to the Canadian Police and Peace Officers Memorial Honour Roll early in the 21st century, joining over 650 other officers who died in the line of duty.
22. Bostick, "Bush Pilot."
23. Neil McArthur, "In Memoriam," *Journal of the CAHS*, winter 1992/93 and Dick Pickering, "The Life of a Bush Pilot: Douglas S. (Doug) Pickering," *Journal of CAHS,*, Fall 2001,
24. Doug Argue and Keith Maxsom were listed as the personnel.
25. Laurentian had applied for a base at Fort Chimo in 1972, bringing on a fierce response from St. Félicien Air Service Ltée. Laurentian had already been flying people and goods back and forth between Fort Chimo and Schefferville and wanted to create a base there with one Beaver, one Otter and one Cessna "to meet the requests of existing lodge operators and others who may wish to move into the area." Its application was denied after St. Félicien intervened.
26. DOT Records, June 1970, RG 12 vol. 2249, LAC.
27. Laurentian records and notes. Private collection.

Chapter 10: Outfitting Dreams

1. James C. Jones and Len Barnes, "To Quebec for Atlantic Salmon: Previewing Michigan's Newest Fish," *Motor News*, May 1975.
2. Lee Wulf, "A Great Unspoiled River to Explore, " *Sports Afield*, May 1976.
3. Aaron B. Stevens, "Ungava Means Far Away," *The Atlantic Salmon Journal*, November 2, 1975 and Gaetan Hayeur and Gilles Shooner, "The Unique Koksoak Salmon."
4. John Power, "Bagging Bulls Above the Treeline," *Legion*, September 1978. Power wrote that according to the Canadian Wildlife Service the Labrador herd alone numbered 80,000. Laurentian had an allotment of 75 caribou for the 1978 season.
5. Craig Boddington, "Go East for Caribou," *Petersen's Hunting*, July 1984. Boddinton and three other California hunters chose to go with Laurentian Ungava Outfitters and they were joined by several others: Ken Carson, who worked for *Outdoor Life* magazine; two Remington representatives, Tom Rawson and Dick Dietz; and Kim Adamson from Salt Lake City, Utah, who bagged "a truly magnificent bull" during the trip.
6. Gordon Christiansen, "Ungava Caribou Hunt," *The Vermont Sportsman*, July 1984.
7. John Wootters, "Quebec-Labrador Caribou: The Real Test," *Petersen's Hunting*, March 1983. According to Craig Boddington, Boone and Crockett created this category in 1968, Boddington, "Go East for Caribou." As H. Lea Lawrence noted in his article, "Quebec is for Caribou," *Archery World – Bowhunting Guide 1985*, the caribou are relatively small compared to the racks they produce. The bulls generally do not get over 350 pounds.
8. Wootters, "Quebec-Labrador Caribou," and Boddington, "Go East for Caribou."
9. H. Lea Lawrence, "Payoff at Dihourse Lake," *American Hunter*, August 1983.
10. Lawrence, "Quebec is for Caribou."

11. Christiansen, "Ungava Caribou Hunt."
12. Lawrence, "Payoff at Dihourse Lake."Other guides in the late 1970s and early 1980s included: Tom Jones and Raymond Desjardins from Arundel; Moise Dominique from Mashteuiatsh reserve; and Barnaby Raphael.
13. H. Lea Lawrence, "Right Time Caribou: When Bulls Come Down," *Backcountry Hunting*, Fall 1983.
14. Boddington, "Go East for Caribou" and Lawrence, "Quebec is for Caribou" also noted these amenities.
15. H. Lea Lawrence, "Double Play on the Delay," *Golden Eagle Bow Hunting Guide 1986*; Tom Martin, "Quebec: Cross-Country," *Safari*, Nov/Dec 1986; and the Delay River Outfitters brochure stated that Maricourt salmon camp "can lodge up to 10 guests. Equipped with showers, indoor toilets, oil-heated separate rooms. You will also enjoy home-cooked meals and experienced guides." Private collection.
16. Information and quoted material in this paragraph from author interview with Jack Hume. During the decades he spent in northern Quebec and Labrador, Jack Hume named over 20 lakes and built more camps than anyone else, 49 in total. A few years later, after Quebec's licensing laws had changed, Jack received an outfitting licence for a new company, Jack Hume Adventures. While Jack ran both companies for a few years, in the late 1980s he decided to sell Laurentian Ungava Outfitters. Jack Hume Adventures continues to be a successful outfitting company run by Jack's son, Richard, and daughter-in-law, Amanda.
17. Lawrence, "Double Play on the Delay."
18. As H. Lea Lawrence wrote in "North to Trophies," *The Complete Book of Bowhunting 1986*;, "native Indian hunters and visiting hunters harvest only about 7000 animals maximum per season, while the herd is growing at a rate of something like 20,000 per year, it could be feasible for hunters to bag three animals each season. The indian hunters have no limit imposed on them."
19. H. Lea Lawrence, "Arctic Caribou," Petersen's 1987 *Hunting Annual* and "Four-of-a-Kind-Caribou," *Outdoor Life*, March 1987.
20. H. Lea Lawrence, "Tundra Trickster," *Game Country: The Journal of Big Game Hunting*, July/August 1989.
21. H. Lea Lawrence, "The Quebec Combination: Caribou and Bear," *Petersen's Hunting*, November 1988. According to Lawrence, Bob Foulkrod also operated an archery deer camp in his native Pennsylvania and an archery bear camp in Ontario at the time with a partner.
22. Don Kirk, "Caribou: The Fun Way," *Blackpowder Guns and Hunting 1987*.

Chapter 11: Laurentian's Last Flight
1. Delay River Outfitters' Application to the DOT, July 1984. Private collection.
2. "Quebecair," Wikipedia, <http://en.wikipedia.org/wiki/ Quebecair>. According to the DRO application, the three cities of Wabush/Labrador City and Fermont had a combined population of about 18,000 in 1984.
3. Michel T. Barbeau, "Schefferville: relations inter-ethniques et dynamique du développement en milieu nordique" (master's thesis, Université du Québec à Chicoutimi, February 1987), 32.
4. Hotson, *De Havilland in Canada,* 234. Hotson was DHC's representative in Afghanistan at this time and the fascinating story as well as a fantastic photo of YA-GAS, which became C-GDQY, can be found on pages 242-4.
5. Other maintenance workers included: Claude Hanson, Bob Pickering, and Mike Irvin, son of Jim Irvin.
6. Quebecair was later renamed Inter-Canadien.
7. H. Lea Lawrence, "Tundra Trickster," *Game Country: The Journal of Big Game Hunting*, July/August 1989.
8. Leonard Lee Rue, III, "Caribou Paradise," *Archery World*, February 1989.
9. Dan Brockman, "Delay River Caribou," *Great Lakes International Bowhunter*, November/December 1989.
10. G. Fred Asbell, "On Turning 50 … an Old Man's Hunt," *Bowhunter*, October/November 1991.
11. Brockman, "Delay River Caribou."
12. Monty Browning, "Mountain Caribou in Quebec," *Traditional Bowhunter*, Fall 1991.
13. Don Kirk, "Migration Bulls," *American Hunter*, February 1990.
14. Browning, "Mountain Caribou in Quebec."
15. Monty Browning, "Caribou Camp," *Traditional Bowhunter*, Fall 1992.
16. Asbell, "On Turning 50."
17. "NAHC Life Member – Road Tour (Quebec)," *North American Hunter*, April/May 1994.
18. Mike Roberts, "Hang In to the Last Minute Caribou Hunt," *Bowhunting News*, August 1994.
19. According to <www.delayriver.com>, Delay River Outfitters is now co-owned by Denis Lachapelle, and the company still specializes in Atlantic salmon fishing and caribou hunting.
20. The information in the preceding paragraph was taken from a variety of sources including: Air Canada, *En Route*, April 1995; Peter Pigott, *Flying Colours: a History of Commercial Aviation in Canada* (Vancouver: Douglas & McIntyre Ltd., 1997), 218 and 197; and documents in a private collection
21. Before the company began shutting down operations, it had created a website, <www.airschefferville.com>. This information came from a printout of that website from 1998. Private collection.
22. The information in this next section comes from: Notice issue by H.R. Wheeler, president of Placements Preservation, June 12, 1997. Private collection; Iain M. Bogie to Roger McCarthy, VP and GM of Tremblant, June 13, 1997. Private collection.

SOURCES

A note on sources

In an attempt to do the history of Laurentian Air Services justice, I undertook substantial primary and secondary research. What follows is a list of the sources I consulted in the preparation of this book. Please note that I have omitted specific references to the periodical, *Canadian Aviation*, as I did a survey of that publication from 1930 to 1980. For specific references to those articles, please see the chapter notes.

I have also heavily relied on private collections of papers as well as interviews with the following individuals: John Bogie, Iain Bogie, Dick Pickering, Keith Baker, Bill Peppler, Tim Cole, Jean-Guy Whiteduck, Betty Campbell, Jules Pilon, Carmen VanDette, Brad Mackie, Eddy Lord, Jack Hume, Wendell Hume, Richard Hume, Neil Aird, Peter (Lou) Goodwin, John Kenny, Dave Saunders and Rudy Mauro.

Archival collections

Canadian Civil Aircraft Register, 1955-1982. Library and Archives Canada (LAC).

Department of Defence Production fonds. LAC.

Department of Transport fonds. LAC.

Echo Beach Fishing Club fonds. LAC.

Harry Falconer McLean fonds. LAC.

The Churchill Falls (Labrador) Corporation Limited fonds. LAC.

Published materials

"64 Beavers Purchased by Ottawa Firm." *General Aviation News* (May 1, 1973).

"A History of Coast Guard Aviation." U.S. Coast Guard Aviation Society. <http://uscgaviationhistory.aoptero.org/history02.html>.

"Accident Details." Plane Crash Info. <http://www.planecrashinfo.com/1974/1974-41.htm>.

Asbell, G. Fred. "On Turning 50 ... an Old Man's Hunt." *Bowhunter* (October/November 1991).

"Aircraft Industry lands in Lachute." *Watchman* (April 18, 1973).

"Airdrome notes." *Aviation and Aircraft Journal* (September 1921).

Air Crashes Record Office in Geneva Switzerland Online. <http://www.baaa-acro.com/archives/1975-JUL-DEC.htm>.

Aird, Neil. *de Havilland DHC-2 Beaver.* <www.dhc-2.com
___. Interview by Terry MacLeod (August 13, 1997). <http://www.dhc-2.com/CBC%20Summerside%201997.html>.

"Announcing ... Laurentian Air Services Ltd." *Canadian Flight* (February/March 1960).

Ashley, Charles A. *A Study of Trans-Canada Airlines: The First Twenty-Five Years.* Toronto: Macmillan, 1963.

Baillie, Ray and Diana. "Gray Rocks Inn, Mont Tremblant," <http://laurentian.quebecheritageweb.com/article_details.aspx?articleId=37>.

Barbeau, Michel T. "Schefferville: relations inter-ethniques et dynamique du développement en milieu nordique." Master's thesis, Université du Québec à Chicoutimi, 1987.

Beauregard, Guy. "Lost for Nine Days: Ordeal and Death." *Outdoor Life* (July 1968).

"B.M. Aviation a acheté 64 Beaver." *Le Pilote* (May 1973).

Boddington, Craig. "Go East for Caribou." *Petersen's Hunting* (July 1984).

Bostick, Deane E. "Bush Pilot." *Cavalier* (August 1974).

Bothwell, Robert and William Kilbourn. *C.D. Howe: A Biography.* Toronto: McClelland and Stewart, 1979.

Brockman, Dan. "Delay River Caribou." *Great Lakes International Bowhunter* (November/December 1989).

Browning, Monty. "Caribou Camp." *Traditional Bowhunter* (Fall 1992).

___. "Mountain Caribou in Quebec." *Traditional Bowhunter* (Fall 1991).

"Business as usual' in air service fire." [*Ottawa Journal?*] (Feb 19, 1972).

Canada Aviation Museum. <www.aviation.technomuses.ca>.

Canadian Civil Aircraft Register Online. <http://www.tc.gc.ca/aviation/activepages/ccarcs/aspscripts/en/history-search.asp>.

"Captains of the Clouds." International Movie Database. <http://www.imdb.com/title/tt0034578/>.

"Cessna T-50 Crane." Aviation Enthusiast Corner. <http://aeroweb.brooklyn.cuny.edu/specs/cessna/csn-50.htm>.

Charleson, Jack C., "Rambles of a Pioneer Pilot: A Half Century of Hangar Flying By One Who Was There, Part II." *Journal of the CAHS* (Spring 1985).

"Civil Aircraft Register – Canada." Golden Years of Aviation. <http://www.goldenyears.ukf.net/reg_CF-1.htm> and <http://www.goldenyears.ukf.net/reg_CF-2.htm>.

Crash Aérien. "Les accidents aériens de 1974." <http://www.crash-aerien.com/www/database/liste.php?id=1974>.

Christiansen, Gordon. "Ungava Caribou Hunt." *Vermont Sportsman* (July 1984).

Covert, Frank Manning. *Fifty Years in the Practice of Law.* Montreal: McGill-Queen's University Press, 2005.

Coté, André. "Les bucherons voyagent en avion." *Mauricie Journal* (March 24, 1974).

Coté, Langevin. *Heritage of Power: the Churchill Falls Development from Concept to Reality.* St. John's, Nfld: Churchill Falls (Labrador) Corporation Ltd., 1972.

Crowther, Bosley. "'Captains of the Clouds,' Heroic Film About Royal Canadian Air Force and Starring James

Cagney, Arrives at the Strand." *New York Times* (February 13, 1942).

"de Havilland DHC-2 Beaver." XdH Aviation Services Inc. <www.xdh.ca/DHC_Aircraft/DHC-7/DHC-2_Production/dhc-2_production.html>.

Dotto, Lydia. "Canada's Aviation Medicine Pioneers." Canadian Space Agency. <http://www.asc-csa.gc.ca/pdf/osm_aviation.pdf>.

Dubé, Tim. "DHC-2 Beavers in Our Backyard: Laurentian Air Services." *Observair* (November 2007).

Duff, James. "Aircraft deal set for takeoff." *Montreal Gazette* [n.d.].

"Economic Life." Excerpted from Cornelius J. Jaenen's entry on the Belgians in *The Encyclopedia of Canada's People*. Multicultural Canada. <http://multiculturalcanada.ca/Encyclopedia/A-Z/b4/4>.

Ellis, John R. *Canadian Civil Aircraft Register, 1929-45.* [Weston, Ont.?] Canadian Aviation Historical Society [n.d.]

"Estérel's History." *L'Estérel: Resort and Convention Centre.* <http://www.esterel.com/contenu/historique_ang.cfm>.

"Fly in for Fishing and Hunting: Air Transportation for Easy Holidays." *Ottawa Journal* (May 25, 1965).

Gardiner, Paddy. "It's a long hot summer for flying bushmen," *Canadian Aviation* (October 1969).

___. "James Bay scheme may give us a lift here." *Ottawa Citizen* (February 5, 1972).

Gingras, Sylvain. *A century of sport: hunting and fishing in Quebec.* Translated from French by R. Clive Meredith. St-Raymond, Que.: Éditions Rapides blancs, [1994?].

Goldenberg, Susan. *Troubled Skies: Crisis, Competition and Control in Canada's Airline Industry.* Whitby, Ont.: McGraw-Hill Ryerson, 1994.

Government of Newfoundland and Labrador. "Department represented at national memorial day ceremony (October 24, 2001). <http://www.releases.gov.nl.ca/releases/2001/forest/1024n02.htm>.

___. "Forest ranger added to Canadian Police and Peace Officers Memorial Honour Roll." (November 4, 2002). <http://www.releases.gov.nl.ca/releases/2002/forest/1104n05.htm>.

Gradidge, J.M. *The Douglas DC-1/DC-2/DC-3: The First Seventy Years, Vols. 1 and 2.* Tonbridge, UK: Air-Britain (Historians) Ltd., 2006.

Hanson, Phil. "Happy 30th Birthday Beaver! You're Not Getting Older, You're Getting Better." *Canadian Aircraft Operator* (August 16, 1977).

Hayes, Karl E. *De Havilland Canada DHC-3 Otter: A History.* Dublin: Self-published CD, 2005.

Haynes, Eddy. Goose Central. <http://www.geocities.com/alaskangoose/>.

Hiscocks, Dick. "The Beaver and STOL." *West Coast Aviator Magazine* (July/August 1997).

Holden, Henry. "The DC-3 Genesis of the Legend." Excerpt from *The Legacy of the DC-3* on the DC-3/Dakota Historical Society website. <http://www.dc3history.org/douglasdc3.html>.

Hotson, Fred W. *De Havilland in Canada.* Toronto: CANAV Books, 1999.

___. "North of the Polarsirkelen." *Air BP* (1951).

"I've had it with planes." *Ottawa Citizen* (August 7, 1974).

"Jean-Paul Fournier." Fondation Aérovision Québec, Inc. <http://www.aerovision.org/doku.php?id=en:jean_paul_fournier>.

Jones, James C. and Len Barnes. "To Quebec for Atlantic Salmon: Previewing Michigan's Newest Fish." *Motor News* (May 1975).

Karas, Nicolas. "The River Where Fishing Dreams Come Drue." *Sports Afield Fishing Annual* (1966).

Keith, Ronald A. "Impressive Three-Point Take-Off Most Vivid Beaver Flight Feature." *Canadian Aviation* (April 1948).

Kirk, Don. "Caribou: The Fun Way." *Blackpowder Guns and Hunting* (1987).

___. "Migration Bulls." *American Hunter* (Feb 1990).

Lapointe, Pierre-Louis. *La Vallée assiégée: Buckingham et la Basse-Lièvre sous les MacLaren, 1895-1945.* Boisbriand, Que.: Diffusion Prologue, 2006.

"Laurentian Air Service Authorized by Board." *Montreal Gazette* (November 15, 1945).

"Laurentian Air Services Help Speed the Victory." *The Salesmotor* [n.d].

"L'aviation à la portée de tous." *La Presse* (July 22, 1919).

Lawrence, H. Lea. "Arctic Caribou." *Petersen's Hunting Annual* (1987).

___. "Quebec is for Caribou." *Archery World Bowhunting Guide* (1985).

___. "Payoff at Dihourse Lake." *American Hunter* (August 1983).

___. "Right Time Caribou: When Bulls Come Down." *Backcountry Hunting* (Fall 1983).

___. "Double Play on the Delay." *Golden Eagle Bow Hunting Guide* (1986).

___. "Quebec: Cross-Country." *Safari* (November/December 1986).

___. "North to Trophies." *The Complete Book of Bowhunting* (1986).

___. "Four-of-a-Kind-Caribou." *Outdoor Life* (March 1987).

___. "Tundra Trickster." *Game Country: The Journal of Big Game Hunting* (July/August 1989).

___. "Caribou Bulls and Black Bear." *Petersen's Annual Hunting* (1988).

___. "The Quebec Combination: Caribou and Bear." *Petersen's Hunting* (November 1988).

Leggatt, Jack. "The de Havilland Beaver." *Plane & Pilot* (August 1969).

Mackey, Doug. "North Bay's Big Movie – Captains of the Clouds 1941." *Community Voices* (August 29, 2003).

MacLaren, Duncan. *From Bush to Boardroom: a Personal View of Five Decades of Aviation History.* Toronto: J. Gordon Shillingford Pub Inc., 1996.

Mauro, Rudy. "Captains of the Clouds: A Postscript." *Journal of the CAHS* (Spring 1995).

___. "The Making of Captains of the Clouds: A Half-Century's Perspective on the First Canadian Air Epic." *Journal of the CAHS* (Summer 1991).

___. "The Making of Captains of the Clouds: Filming the Bush Flying Sequences of Canada's First Air Epic." *Journal of the CAHS* (Fall 1991).

McArthur, Neil. "In Memoriam." *Journal of the CAHS* (Winter 1992/93).

McGrath, T.M. *History of Canadian Airports.* Canada: Lugus Publishing, 1992.

McIntyre, M.L. (Mac). "The James Bay Hydro Project: Flying Out of Matagami." *Journal of the CAHS* (Winter 1999).

McNeal, Wayne C. "General Aviation in Canada." Master's thesis, University of British Columbia, 1969.

McNulty, Gord. "February 14th, 2002 Meeting. Speaker: Reg Phillips." *Flypast* (March 2002).

Milberry, Larry. *Air Transport in Canada.* Toronto: CANAV Books, 1997.

___. *Austin Airways: Canada's Oldest Airline.* Toronto: CANAV Books, 1985.

Mills, Carl. "A Tech Rep in Korea: Maintaining and Adapting the de Havilland DHC-2 Beaver as a Technical Representative." *Journal of the CAHS* (Fall 2000).

Molson, Kenneth M. *Canada's National Aviation Museum: its History and Collections.* Ottawa: National Aviation Museum, 1988.

___. *Pioneering in Canadian Air Transport.* Winnipeg: J. Richardson, 1974.

Orriss, Bruce, W. *When Hollywood Ruled the Skies: The Aviation film classics of World War II.* n.p. Aero Assoc., 1985.

"Ottawa has Air Service all its own." *Ottawa Evening Journal* (July 21, 1919).

"Ottawans See Big Searchlight 'Cover' Aircraft." *Ottawa Citizen* (March 31, 1941).

"NAHC Life Member – Road Tour (Quebec)." *North American Hunter* (April/May 1994).

Nanton Lancaster Society Air Museum. <www.lancastermuseum.ca>.

Newfoundland & Labrador Police and Peace Officers' Memorial Website. <http://www.policeandpeaceofficers.ca>.

Parke, Robert B. "Wallace." *Flying: 50th Anniversary Issue* (September 1977).

Parmerter, Robert K. *Beech 18: A Civil and Military History.* Tullahoma, TN: Twin Beech 18 Society, 2004.

Pickering, Dick. "The Life of a Bush Pilot: Douglas S. (Doug) Pickering." *Journal of the CAHS* (Fall 2001).

Pickering, Doug. "Flying the Delta," *SKY-ADS* [n.d].

Pigott, Peter. *Flying Colours: A History of Commercial Aviation in Canada.* Vancouver: Douglas & McIntyre Ltd., 1997.

Power, John. "Bagging Bulls Above the Treeline." *Legion* (September 1978).

Rennert, Robert. *A City Takes Flight: the Story of Ottawa International Airport.* Montreal : R. Rennert, 2000.

Reynolds-Alberta Museum. <http://machinemuseum.net/>.

Roberts, Mike. "Hang In to the Last Minute Caribou Hunt." *Bowhunting News* (August 1994).

Ross, Bob. "Laurentian Air Services: In 35 years, 500 million charter miles." *Ottawa Journal* (October 2 1971).

___. "Laurentian Air Services involved in $1 million deal: Sixty-four Beavers to be refurbished for resale." *Ottawa Journal* (April 14, 1973).

Rossiter, Sean. *The Immortal Beaver: The World's Greatest Bush Plane.* Vancouver: Douglas & McIntyre, 1999.

Rue, III, Leonard Lee. "Caribou Paradise." *Archery World* (February 1989).

Schofield, Jack. "Variations on a Theme." *West Coast Aviator* (July/August 1997).

Septer, Dirk. "Beaver Turns 50: The Great Birthday Bash." *Aviation Quarterly* (1997).

Smith, Philip. *Brinco: the Story of Churchill Falls.* Toronto: McClelland and Stewart Ltd., 1975.

Sport Flying (Oct. 1973).

Stevens, Aaron B. "Ungava Means Far Away." *Atlantic Salmon Journal* (November 2, 1975).

Stock, Sandra. "The Laurentians: A Very Concise History, Part 2." *Laurentian Heritage WebMagazine.* <http://laurentian.quebecheritageweb.com/ article_details.aspx?articleId=76>.

Terziev, Marc. "Hooking, Landing Arctic Char Real Thrill for Local Sportsman." *Syracuse Herald-Journal* (September 10, 1964).

___. "Looking for 'Big Ones'? Labrador Fishing Grounds Within Air Miles of Your Own Syracuse Hearth." *Syracuse Herald-American* (September 6, 1964).

___. "New Landlock Salmon Water." *Outdoor Life* (July 1964).

___. "Northern Quebec's Unfished Regions Luring Sportsmen." *Syracuse Herald-American* (September 20, 1964).

___. "Not by the Book." *Field and Stream* (February 1968).

___. "Silvery Brook Trout Abound in Labrador." *Syracuse Herald-American* (September 13, 1964).

___. "We Blazed Wild New Trails." *Outdoor Life* (May 1965).

"The Governor's Visit." *Moccasin Telegraph* [n.d].

Thomson, James W. *Lumbering on the Riviere du Lievre: a saga of Maclaren's [sic] and Buckingham* [Ottawa?, 1973?].

"Three dead, six injured in wreck on C.P.R. Line at Inkerman, Ont." *Ottawa Citizen* (April 1, 1941).

"Twenty-five years in aviation: the Success Story of Laurentian Air Services Limited." *Canadian Flight: the Pilot's Magazine* (June/July 1961).

"Un DC-3 s'écrase dans le parc des Laurentides et fait quatre morts." *La Presse* (August 7, 1974).

Vennat, Pierre. "Lachute deviendra centre aéronautique." *La Presse* (April 18, 1972).

Waco Air Museum. <http://www.wacoairmuseum.org/history/history.htm>.

"Waco Cabin Biplanes – Part 2, the Development of the 'Custom Cabin' and 'Standard Cabin' Series, 1936-1940." *American Aviation Society Journal* (Summer 2005).

Wootters, John. "Quebec-Labrador Caribou: The Real Test." *Petersen's Hunting* (March 1983).

Wulff, Lee. "A Great Unspoiled River to Explore. " *Sports Afield* (May 1976).

INDEX